The Long W

Nakhon Nowhere

The Long Winding Road to

Nakhon Nowhere

When Thailand truly was the Land of Smiles

By Roger Crutchley

DCO

The Long Winding Road to Nakhon Nowhere:
When Thailand truly was the Land of Smiles
Copyright © Roger Crutchley, 2018
First Published 2018

First edition published by
DCO Books, 2018
Proglen Trading Co., Ltd.
Bangkok Thailand
http://www.dco.co.th

Book ISBN 978-1983766251

All Rights Reserved

Front cover designed by Colin Cotterill

These are purely personal observations of my early days in Thailand and are not intended to be a comprehensive historical account of events in the kingdom or at the Bangkok Post. - Roger Crutchley.

DEDICATIONS

To my dear late brother Eric, his wife Cindy and family, and my long departed mum and dad who gave me their blessings to embark on an unknown journey.

Also my lovely wife Aon, who has put up with me for the last 18 years with unremitting cheerfulness.

Not forgetting my late maid Tong (Ms Yasothon) and her husband Noi, who still looks after me, the house and the garden.

And Toby the dog, who has faithfully sat at my side through every chapter, accompanied by the music of Miles Davis, which does wonders for the soul.

Special thanks to friend and editor John Leicester for gallantly wading through my efforts and making sense of it all, well most of the time.

My appreciation to good friends and long-time colleagues Peter Finucane and Tony Waltham for their invaluable input and jogging the memory when mine fell far short. The same goes for Alan Dawson who has given me great encouragement over the years.

Also to former Bangkok Post editor Pichai Chuensuksawadi for his support and Kateprapa Buranakanonda for her help with the photographs.

Particular thanks to Danny Speight, who spurred me on when all looked lost.

Greetings to Clarence Shettlesworth with whom I shared so many experiences on the overland trip and those early days in Bangkok. Also to Brett Bartos, who was particularly helpful when I first arrived.

Special thanks to long-time friend and colleague Kusuma Bekenn, who has been very supportive over the years.

Finally, thanks to all my colleagues at the *Bangkok Post* over the past four decades, who are too numerous to name but have all in their own way contributed to this book.

It has been a memorable journey.

TABLE OF CONTENTS

1. Far Away Places	1
2. Saved by the Beatles	8
3. The Land That Time Forgot	16
4. Porridge, Passengers and Luggage Racks	23
5. Welcome to Thailand	31
6. An Apple for the Teacher	39
7. The Ratchadamnoen Days	50
8. Eventful Times at U-Chuliang	65
9. The Day 100,000 Students Marched	81
10. The Awkward English Patient	90
11. On (And Off) the Rails	97
12. Cambodge - The War Next Door	106
13. From Nakhon Nowhere to Tambon Too Far	115
14. Dancing in the Dark	126
15. Good Vibes on the Strip	136
16. Sukhumvit Sojourn	142
17. Bases Loaded	152
18. Southern Comfort	161
19. The Legend of the Mighty Mitr	171
20. The Perils of Postscript	181
21. A Man Needs a Maid	190
22. Soi 8 Greens	200
23. The Hardest-Working Legs in Show Business	211
24. Terror of the Tones	218
25. This Sporting Life	227
26. The More Things Change…	241
Epilogue	250

1. FAR AWAY PLACES

Getting itchy feet in not-so-sunny England

After more than four decades I still find it hard to explain how I ended up in Thailand in early 1969. There is no rational answer because fate played such a strong hand. I had no real plans concerning my destination after leaving England. A few different turnings *en route* and I could just have easily ended up in Timbuktu, Ulan Bator or Woy Woy in Australia. Or even back in my home town of Reading in Berkshire.

As a young lad in the mid-1950s, I remember thumbing through an atlas to find the location of a mysterious place called Thailand. What prompted this research by an eight-year-old were a couple of postage stamps from the kingdom in my collection. I couldn't even pronounce the place properly, using a soft "TH" sound for the first two letters and only knew it was somewhere far, far away. When I did eventually locate it in the atlas, I admit to being intrigued by the unusual shape of the country, with the long isthmus extending down into what was then called Malaya.

Matters became more confusing in 1956 when my mother purchased the vinyl album from the hit film *The King and I*, the fanciful Hollywood musical featuring an exotic place called Siam. Mum loved the music and would perform her daily chores singing *Getting To Know You* and *I Whistle A Happy Tune*, although her whistling wasn't so hot. Then in 1957 came the blockbuster film, *The Bridge on the River Kwai*, although it didn't tell you much about Thailand and was shot in Sri Lanka anyway.

For years its exact location baffled most Westerners. At that time, many people in Britain - with the possible exception of philatelists - thought Siam and Thailand were two different places, wherever they might be. There weren't many Thais living in England in those days, apart from a few students, and I doubt there was even a Thai restaurant in the country. How did we Brits survive without Thai food?

Thailand was definitely an enigma. When I first returned to England in the early 1970s and said I had been living in Thailand,

1

I was often met with a blank look. On one of my first trips back, I ran into an old friend who greeted me with: "You're in Bangkok now? I've always wanted to go to Taiwan." (The confusion is still happening. Reporting on the 2014 coup in Thailand, *Metro*, a Canadian newspaper in Vancouver, carried the headline "Government overthrown in Taiwan").

Home Sweet Home: With my parents in Reading while on a visit to England in the 1970s.

Others thought Bangkok was the capital of Burma. A colleague told me he once received a letter, posted about three months earlier, addressed to "Bangkok, India". Well, it's only an inch or so away on a world map. Many had seen *The King And I,* and I had to explain that life in Thailand was not exactly how it was portrayed in that film.

A lady later told me that when she was leaving England for Thailand in the early 1970s, a man from the Electricity Board asked for a forwarding address. She gave him her husband's address in Thailand, which the fellow dutifully wrote down. He didn't seem the brightest of people and even struggled over Bangkok, which she had to spell out for him. She took a precautionary look at what he had written down to make sure that at least the country's name was written correctly. And there it was in black and white… TOYLAND.

For a lot of us, our knowledge of Thailand was limited to Siamese Cats, Siamese Twins and Yul Brynner dancing with Deborah Kerr. On occasions, when BBC TV sports news needed a filler, there would be a flickering 30-second black and white newsreel of Thai-style boxing, with legs flying all over the place. For those of us brought up on the Queensbury Rules, it looked totally off the wall - an early introduction to Amazing Thailand.

I did get a slight taste of Asia from my elder brother Eric, who was stationed in Singapore in the late 1950s in the final year of compulsory National Service. It was just before Lee Kuan Yew took over and Singapore was still a pretty wild place. I used to wait eagerly for my brother's letters which were full of exotic tales about triad gangs and Chinese millionaires being kidnapped, along with standard fare about elephants blocking the railway line to Penang, strange sounding fruit and noisy games of *mah jong* that went on deep into the night. Admittedly, even a palm tree seemed exotic to me in those days.

Little did I know that armed with this scanty information about Thailand, I would go on to spend more than four decades in the country, most of that time working on the popular daily newspaper, the *Bangkok Post*.

My knowledge of newspapers was not much better than it was of Thailand and the possibility of a job in journalism had never crossed my mind. It was never brought up by our school careers officer, who only seemed interested in recommending "going into insurance". There but for the grace of God…

I did have some tenuous links with the newspaper industry, though. From the age of 14, for about three years I worked on a newspaper delivery round early in the morning before I went off to school, earning 14 shillings a week. It required getting up at 6 a.m., which was tough enough in the summer months, but absolute torture in the winter. Our house had no central heating and the first 10 minutes of every morning saw me shivering by the gas stove, preparing the life-saving cup of tea that was to keep me going for the next hour. Looking back, I'm amazed at my willpower getting out of bed on those freezing mornings... all for a mere pittance.

The daily round took little more than 45 minutes 6 days a week, but on Sundays it became a two-hour job. As soon as I set off from the newsagents, the *News of the World* would come out of my bag and my nose would be buried into wonderful court cases featuring vicars and choirboys, actresses and bishops, pimps, poodles and politicians. I certainly developed a thorough grounding in the less savoury side of the news.

My mum actually asked me why it took so long on the Sunday morning round; I explained it was because I was reading all the weekend football match reports. No, she didn't believe that either.

My only other contact with newspapers, apart from being an avid reader since I was a kid, came some years later, shortly after I had graduated in Economics from what is now Kingston University in Surrey. Jobless, I was wandering along Reading's Friar Street one sunny morning in the first week of October 1967, when I was cornered on the pavement by two young men. If that happened these days, it would probably mean a mugging or some sort of shakedown, but this was in more civilized times. The two fellows, one a photographer, were from the *Reading Evening Post* newspaper and were collecting reactions from "the man in the street" to the new BBC Radio One service, which had been launched a couple of days earlier amid much fanfare.

I didn't give the most lucid response, but the journalists seemed happy enough and wandered off. I hadn't thought much more about it until the following afternoon; there it was - a front page mug shot of a spotty, longish-haired Crutch with the awe-inspiring quote in the headline: "It's a hit with me".

I still claim I never uttered those actual words, although it probably made more sense than whatever it was I had burbled at the reporter. Gazing at the page, I was torn between being excited at the novelty of appearing in a newspaper and the uncomfortable feeling that I probably sounded, and looked, like a total twit.

The defining response came that evening upon entering the Bull's Head pub in town, when my mates looked over from their table and chanted at me in derisory fashion: "It's a hit with me." I was definitely a certified twit and condemned to buying rounds of beer for the rest of the night.

In a way, I suppose that was my first headline. Little did I know that within two years I would be sitting at the newsdesk in the *Bangkok Post* office on Ratchadamnoen Avenue, writing my own headlines for the next day's paper. Sadly, I never did get the opportunity to use "It's a hit with me" in a headline.

It was November 1967, winter was approaching and following assorted temporary jobs after leaving college, including an eventful period in an East End wine cellar, I managed to acquire a permanent position with the Cable and Wireless (C&W) communications company in Holborn, in central London. Our particular section of about a dozen people included several colourful characters who were normally based abroad, but had to serve a compulsory year at head office. Most of them were British, but they couldn't wait to get overseas again. Their tales of life in far-away places with strange-sounding names certainly sparked my wanderlust and undoubtedly contributed to my departure from Britain at the end of the following year.

One colleague was an Egyptian named Mr. Trigaci and we called him 'Trig'. He was the first Egyptian I had ever met and was a most interesting gentleman. He was about 50, bald, smartly dressed, wore black horn-rimmed spectacles, spoke perfect English and was a jolly fellow, always making jokes. Trig was delightful company and had a favourite saying: "Don't be sorry, life's too short," which he would come out with several times a day, followed by a hearty laugh. Trig had worked all over the world and had many tales to tell. To this day, when I'm feeling a bit down, his "life's too short" homily always strikes a chord.

The company had a strong presence in the Caribbean and part of my job was to write to companies in such places as British Virgin Islands, Turks and Caicos, Cayman Islands, St Kitts and Nevis. They all sounded exotic to me, especially when I looked out of the office window and saw the miserable grey buildings and the London rain piddling down.

Even better, the amiable bronzed fellow called Dick Boot sitting at the next desk had actually worked in these places and so I heard the colourful tales befitting ex-pats on the loose in some very remote locations. He readily admitted that he would have much rather been on Ascension island, little more than a dot in the middle of the South Atlantic, than Holborn in the middle of the City of London. I thought at the time that he might have been a little mad, but now I can see it in a different perspective. It must have been so dull for him in our office.

We also dealt with the "Far East" as we called it then, and there was considerable excitement when the big boss "Mitch" was heading off to Phnom Penh and nobody even knew how to pronounce the place or exactly where it was, for that matter.

Then there was Bangkok, a city I knew absolutely nothing about, and some might say, still know nothing about. It may seem strange now, but in the 1960s Bangkok simply never made the news in England. But the seeds for travel had been sown in that distinctly unexotic office in Holborn.

At C&W, whenever the boss wanted to talk to one of us in his office, he didn't ask his secretary to phone us, but instead buzzed our initials in Morse Code. All day we worked to the sounds of dots and dashes whizzing through the air. I answered to "dot dash dot" (R) "dash dot dash dot" (C). It might sound quirky, but undoubtedly made work a bit more fun, especially when the buzzer jammed and nobody had a clue who he wanted to see.

This was many years before computer terminals, but we did have a large telex machine, which I found quite exciting. It used to clatter into life with messages from company men in remote-sounding places like the Falklands, Diego Garcia and the Solomon Islands. Just the racket from the machine itself, when it danced into action, sounded like important information was coming through, although sometimes it was simply a homesick operative enquiring about the latest football results. I marveled at this "cutting edge" of technology, little knowing that in a few years it would be a museum exhibit.

But I was getting weary of dots, dashes and telex messages… and the English weather.

It must have been about October 1968 that in the classified section of the *Evening Standard* I spotted a small advertisement for 'Overland trips to India or Africa'. There was a weekly gathering in a south London pub where the organizers discussed the different routes over a few pints with potential travelers. After a couple of nights at the Dog and Duck listening to tales of previous expeditions, I was completely hooked. I'd had enough of Holborn - next stop, New Delhi and hopefully, on to Australia. There was no planning as such. All I had to do was choose between the Asian and African routes - and Asia won. After that, it was simply a case of pointing East and seeing what happened.

I had no intention of including Thailand on my travels, so what transpired in the following months is nothing but old fashioned fate and fortune, with more than a sprinkling of good luck.

2. SAVED BY THE BEATLES

Overland to Asia on an ancient bus, with musical accompaniment

It didn't exactly look promising.

There were about 25 of us, of assorted nationalities, huddled on a street corner near Victoria Station in London, fighting off the biting wind on a miserable January evening in 1969. We had all signed up at a cost of 50 pounds for an overland trip to New Delhi aboard two sorry-looking single deck buses, or what we then called "coaches", which appeared to be survivors of the Second World War. The vehicles looked like they would struggle to make it to the English Channel, let alone the distant lands of Asia. Unfortunately, that turned out to be an entirely correct assessment.

Not the best of starts: The author and the ancient buses after the vehicles had broken down in an Alpine village in southern Austria in January 1969.

My plan, if you could call it that, was to head on to Australia after India and perhaps make my fortune, or at least tackle some

SAVED BY THE BEATLES

Aussie meat pies, sink a few "tinnies" and maybe watch a bit of cricket. But things didn't quite work out that way.

I didn't know any of the other travelers and we arbitrarily split into two groups of a dozen or so on each bus. I guess we were all intent on escaping the English winter. Little did we know what we had let ourselves in for as we set forth on what was to become known as the Hippie Trail. Not that any of our contingent were "hippies", more a mixture of former students, bored professionals and perhaps a few oddballs.

It was a real "budget trip" and we were to spend most nights sleeping on the bus or occasionally in seedy hotels - and I do mean seedy. The buses wheezed their way out of London's southern suburbs on a journey that was to take us through more than a dozen countries, although neither vehicle was to make it further than the Afghan desert.

Of that first night I have vague memories of sheltering from the howling wind aboard the car ferry as it approached the Belgian port of Ostende from Ramsgate. The choppy waters of the English Channel seemed quite menacing and had me wondering if I had made a big mistake. My cosy family home in Reading suddenly seemed very inviting. But it would have been a bit embarrassing to have shown up on the doorstep in Berkshire a couple of days' later, saying I was homesick.

While on the boat my thoughts turned to my parents, Kath and Eric, who had given me their blessing to embark on this foolish adventure. My older brother, also called Eric, was already working overseas for Barclays Bank in the Caribbean, and now I was off in the opposite direction. That was my mum and dad's reward after two decades of raising us with plenty of love, but little money. I already began to have pangs of guilt before even reaching the Continent and all its funny smells.

My only previous adventures abroad had been some rather tatty package holidays with my mates to Spain and Italy. This was going to be a very different experience. I was half excited and half scared - it was, corny though it may sound, a journey into the unknown.

The early days took us relatively swiftly through Belgium, Germany and Austria. Being on a tight budget, it wasn't until Munich that I enjoyed my first tipple of the trip in a beer cellar. We found ourselves at a long table with some German football supporters, who were surprisingly friendly considering some of our party launched into an ill-advised chant of "In-ger-land", recalling that memorable sunny day at Wembley less than three years earlier. Those joyful days of 1966 seem so long ago now.

From the time we left Frankfurt we experienced what the BBC politely term "changeable weather", but sporadic sunny spells made it quite bearable for a few hundred kilometres as we crossed into Austria. That was when the buses broke down for the first time, a sign of things to come. But to be fair, the vehicles couldn't have chosen a more pleasant spot at which to splutter to a halt than an Alpine village in Austria, mid-way between Salzburg and Graz. In the winter sun the Alps looked so inviting I was tempted to abandon the bus there and then and settle for a skiing holiday with wine and wiener schnitzels. But we had to move on.

The final evening in Austria I have vague memories of dancing in a restaurant with a large local lady to the accompaniment of an accordion. I think I must have imbibed in too much local plonk as the accordion is one of my least favourite instruments.

This was in the days when the map of Eastern Europe was much simpler, before the breakup of the Soviet Union and also Yugoslavia. From Austria we trundled our way through what is now Slovenia, Croatia and Serbia, but in those days was simply Yugoslavia, with Marshal Tito at the helm.

Belgrade was rather depressing, although the filthy weather probably had something to do with it. In the Serbian city of Nish I recall being pursued down the street and spat at after apparently upsetting some locals who, it turned out, simply didn't like foreigners. Can't say I blamed them - we did look a bit scruffy.

Horses and carts became the norm as we approached the Bulgarian border and at this stage the weather had deteriorated. But the bus somehow slid its way to the capital, Sofia, in a raging blizzard. I felt a bit melancholy, attempting not entirely successfully to cut out thoughts of sitting on the comfortable carpet in front of a log fire at home. It seemed a million miles away.

The streets of Sofia were as dismal as one could imagine. All the locals wore thick, dark clothes as protection from the biting cold and everyone looking quite depressed, which was understandable. As an advertisement for life in a Communist state it could not have been worse, although they couldn't do anything about the weather. Everything was a dark shade of grey. The city seemed bereft of life, but we were fortunate enough to find a cheap restaurant in a somewhat unappealing cellar.

This was the time when the Cold War - a most appropriate description on that particular evening - was still going strong and we were a bit concerned how we would be received by the average Bulgarian citizen, no doubt a little wary of jumped-up liberals fresh from 'Swinging London'. We needn't have worried. They either totally ignored us or were cautiously friendly while we communicated through basic sign language.

Some of the locals were also quite drunk, arguing loudly with one another. Almost inevitably an altercation broke out, almost worthy of a western movie saloon punch-up, so it seemed a timely moment to beat a discreet retreat. But it was almost comforting in a way to witness Communists getting plastered and misbehaving just like everyone else.

My one bright memory of the next 24 hours was consuming some of the finest yoghurt I have ever tasted in a bleak snow-bound Bulgarian mountain village not far from Plovdiv, the country's second city.

It wasn't until we arrived at the Turkish border near Edirne that it felt like we were getting somewhere. Again it was a country I knew little about, although I was quite partial to Turkish Delight confectionery. Asia was beckoning, as mosques replaced churches, smells became increasingly exotic and the people, well they actually looked a bit different. We must have looked a bit different too - for the first time since we had left England, we were followed by local kids fascinated by these weird characters stepping off a clapped-out bus.

It wasn't just the kids that followed us. In Istanbul I was walking down the street with a New Zealand girl from our group, when she suddenly let out a scream. A local fellow had walked up behind us and grabbed her bottom. He stood there grinning, but quickly ran off when we displayed a united front of displeasure. I was quite relieved he left because he was much bigger than me. I was just thankful he chose her backside and not mine.

Istanbul was an exciting, bustling, ancient city befitting a waterfront metropolis marking the gateway from Europe to Asia. We spent several days there getting visas, while our buses also needed to recuperate from the Bulgarian snow.

A visit to the magnificent Topkapi Palace gave a brief taste of the might of the Ottoman Empire and the days when the city was called Constantinople. It also offered stunning views of the Bosphorous, which the city straddles.

Much of our time in Istanbul was spent in the Grand Bazaar, which has been there since the 15th century and was certainly a bit different to shopping at Reading market. Not that I had any money to spend, but I found it fascinating just wandering around and getting totally lost in the labyrinth of alleyways.

One amiable Turkish stall owner gave up trying to sell me a carpet when he discovered, first that I had no money, but more importantly that I shared his love of English football. He turned out to be a devoted Arsenal fan and we became involved in an ardent discussion, which included some less than complimentary views on 1968 English champions Leeds United. He then trotted out the back and returned with an old Arsenal programme, which he insisted I keep. It had never crossed my mind that in 1969 you would come across a passionate Gooner in an Istanbul souk. This was in the days long before they showed English games on TV around the world.

We made one expedition to a red-light area across the Bosphorus. It was as seedy as it comes, featuring plump, semi-naked ladies covered in hideous make-up, sitting in shop windows trying to lure in passers-by. It was all a bit scary and enough to put you off sex for life. Well, a few months anyway.

After Istanbul, the capital Ankara was by contrast quite modern and did not capture the imagination, so we were soon on the road again heading east towards the Turkish city of Erzerum and the Iran border.

We had originally intended to travel through Iraq. However, the public execution in Baghdad the week before of 14 Iraqis for "spying" put an abrupt end to that idea. Because we had been on the road, we were blissfully unaware of what had become a big news story, internationally known as the "Baghdad Hangings". A certain General Saddam Hussein happened to be vice president and in charge of security at the time. The net result was that no visas were being issued by the Iraq embassy in Istanbul - none of us complained. So Iran it was to be.

The further east we ventured in Turkey, the bleaker it got in the wintry conditions and the people were less hospitable than in the cities. In one isolated area we had to sprint back to the bus when villagers started throwing rocks at us. I don't think it was anything personal - just like the earlier incident in Yugoslavia, they simply didn't like strangers. It was particularly difficult for the females in our group, who frequently found themselves the unwanted centre of attention in the more remote villages.

Crossing into Iran we were greeted by more snow at the border. Tabriz looked like it would be a nice place to explore... in the summer. But conditions were so bleak that after one night we moved on and a few days and several blizzards later we reached Tehran. The Iran capital was much bigger than I had anticipated and seemed to go on forever. I think "sprawling" might be the correct word. We even lashed out on a trip to a cheap nightclub, one of the few evenings of entertainment on the entire trip, but we could only afford one drink.

One day outside the British embassy in Tehran we met a gentleman calling himself "Captain Walli", who claimed to be a fighter pilot with the Iran Air Force. Later in the day we began to get a bit suspicious when he said he wanted to fly us in his jet to the ancient city of Isfahan, 330 kms to the south. He appeared to be a bit drunk and there was no way I was getting in any vehicle this fellow was in charge of, let alone a jet fighter. Eventually it became evident he was just after the females in our party and Capt Walli ended up spending the whole night banging on the door of our room at a cheap guest house, screaming at us to let him in. We were beginning to learn in painful fashion that not everyone who befriends you while travelling is good news.

It took us several weeks to traverse Turkey and Iran and conditions deteriorated the further we nosed our way East. It was a bit late to think of it by that time, but travelling through the winter had not exactly been a brilliant idea. We frequently had to light fires under the bus in the mornings to melt the frozen diesel oil. With such treatment there was no wonder that the vehicles would eventually expire.

Several times the buses lurched into snowdrifts and had to be dug out. On the outskirts of Iran's holy city of Mashhad, a few hours from the Afghan border, our bus slid off the road late at night ending up precariously close to a ravine. There were plenty of wolves about so we spent the night holed up in the freezing bus with wolves howling outside. It took the whole of the next morning to dig the bus out of the snowdrift.

Making those long hours on the road through Turkey and Iran a bit more bearable were the sounds of the Beatles, for whom I have ever since been eternally grateful. One of our fellow travelers had a tape cassette of what was then the new Beatles record, simply called *The Beatles,* but better known as "The White Album". It was one of the few tapes in our possession, so after a few thousand kilometres we had become very familiar with all the songs, right from the opening sounds of jet engines on *Back in the USSR.* I grew fond of many tracks on the album, some of which I associate with certain places *en route.* I always remember in eastern Turkey going past Mount Ararat of biblical fame, to the strains of *Dear Prudence,* one of my favourite tracks. Covered in snow, the mountain was a breathtaking sight, especially with the musical backing.

To this day, whenever I hear any track from the album it is an instant reminder of that journey. Those songs kept us sane through the freezing deserts, hostile mountains and occasional yearnings for home life. Even *Ob-La-Di, Ob-La-Da* sounded good. It was so silly that it became the bus theme song, partly because it was easy for everyone to sing along to. Thank goodness it was a Beatles tape and not a rap album.

Late in February 1969, after an exhausting stretch from Mashhad, we approached the border with Afghanistan. We had been on the road for more than a month and to have got this far was not bad going, considering the inclement weather and the deteriorating state of our elderly vehicles. We spent the night sleeping on the bus near the border in an extremely bleak spot in a kind of no man's land.

Shortly after dawn the bus reluctantly trundled towards the Afghanistan checkpoint. A whole new experience awaited across the border.

3. THE LAND THAT TIME FORGOT

Carrying on up the Khyber after the buses expire in the Afghan desert

It is a trifle embarrassing to admit it now, but four decades ago Afghanistan was little more than another country on the map for me - a purple colour as I recall. It just happened to be on our route East. I was ill-prepared for the place known as the "graveyard of empires", in just about every way.

In 1969, armies from foreign lands weren't shooting at one another or blowing one another up in Afghanistan and there was no Taliban. It was another 10 years before the Russians were to invade the kingdom in the latest episode of the "Great Game", which has been played since the 19th century. The Russian move in 1979 was to spark more than three decades of war that has spawned the horrors we have been witnessing up to the present day.

But in the 1960s, Afghanistan was not in the news and most people in the UK, and elsewhere in the world for that matter, would have been hard-pushed to point it out on a map. It wasn't totally peaceful with numerous tribal conflicts going on and places you were advised to avoid if you valued your life. And to say the terrain was "inhospitable" was an understatement in every sense of the word.

But of the dozen or so countries we passed through on that journey, Afghanistan was definitely the most memorable. There was a certain magical feeling about the place. It was so different to anywhere else I had experienced before or since. It felt like entering a time warp.

Breakfast was the main item on our minds when we crossed the border from Iran shortly after dawn and were taken to what seemed to be little more than a cave. It didn't look too promising. After some comical sign language, an Afghan man disappeared into the cave and I didn't hold out much hope for breakfast. My stomach was rumbling loudly when, about 15 minutes later, the fellow returned with a wonderful spicy omelette for each of us. As far as I was concerned, it was the best omelette I have ever tasted, although my hunger may have influenced this judgement a little. At least it was a promising introduction to Afghanistan. However, a meal a week later was to prompt a very different reaction.

It was still snowing heavily. I had always pictured Afghanistan as hot and dusty - which is the case much of the time - but never envisaged it covered in the white stuff. The westernmost city of Herat was under a complete blanket of snow as we arrived and actually looked quite picturesque. Horse-drawn carts were in abundance with their quaint bells. But I didn't see any kids throwing snowballs.

The following morning we ventured out into the foothills overlooking Herat. Ostensibly we were members of a not very serious hunting party, the prey being the packs of wolves that roamed the hills. We had rented some ancient rifles for a small sum, but after a couple of erratic pop-shots at some rocks which resulted in nearly blowing our hands off, quickly realized we were more likely to become casualties of the rifles than our prey.

The wolves must have sensed our ineptitude too, as the occasional creature felt brave enough to put in an appearance and inspect these weird people trespassing on their patch. There was also a smattering of Afghan tribesmen sitting on a rock some way off. If they were amused by our ill-disguised incompetence, they didn't show it. They simply stared at us as if we were some alien beings that had mysteriously emerged from the desert, which in a way we were.

We wisely abandoned the hunting and instead savoured the astonishing view, which was much more rewarding. In every direction there was nothing but the rugged, inhospitable mountains that the whole world has witnessed on CNN and BBC for the past two decades. In the distance, far below us, a lengthy camel train snaked its way eastwards along a narrow valley, just as they had done for centuries. I had to pinch myself - it was fairy-tale time.

I quite enjoyed Herat. Every little street seemed to offer a specific function. On one stretch there was nothing but shoemakers, but the shoes were all the same - sandals which had been carved out of discarded rubber tyres from the colourful trucks which raced along the highway to Kandahar and Kabul. Then there was a lane we named "Tin Pan Alley" - not for musical reasons, but because everything on sale appeared to be made of tin. Despite the snow, Herat was reasonably mild, with glimpses of sun making it the warmest weather we had experienced since Austria.

A few days later we headed southeast towards Kandahar, the country's second-largest city. We had been intending to take the shorter, but more hazardous, mountainous northern route to Kabul, but were advised that some of the tribes in that area did not take kindly to strangers. A previous bus had been ambushed and robbed on that route, so prudence prevailed. A decision I thoroughly agreed with, by the way.

While the road remained in the mountains, snow and ice was still the norm, but when we began the descent into the fringes of the desert, the conditions rapidly changed. Instead of snow we now had heat and dust to contend with. And it was the heat and dust which won a clear victory, as far as the buses were concerned anyway.

The buses had already broken down in nearly every country we had passed through, so it came as no great surprise when they expired rather unhelpfully in the middle of the Afghan desert. In fact it was almost like a conspiracy between the vehicles, as they gave up the ghost within a kilometre of one another. This time it was for good. The buses had found their final resting place a long way from home. Their skeletal remains might still be sitting there in the desert, for all I know.

While the drivers attempted the futile task of trying to fix the engines, the rest of us played an improvised game of football in the desert, a rather surreal experience considering none of us knew where we were going or even exactly where we were (it turned out to be Helmand province, later to become a Taliban stronghold). As I recall, in our football match England beat the Rest of the World something like 6-5, a rare victory for the British in Afghanistan.

THE LAND THAT TIME FORGOT

We spent that night sleeping under the stars, or trying to. I couldn't nod off, partly because of the spectacular display of shooting stars hurtling across the clear desert sky and partly due to the sunburn picked up during the football madness earlier in the day.

After a wasted day, during which the drivers basically told us we were stuffed and on our own, we left our transport to rot in the desert. Splitting up into small groups, we continued towards Kandahar on colourful buses whose passengers included goats, chickens and assorted locals. Regrettably we no longer had the Beatles tape to smooth the way, its owner heading off in another direction on his own magical mystery tour.

By that time I had become good friends with another Englishman in our group, Clarence Shettlesworth and three of the girls - Katie, Maria and Lennie (two Aussies and an American). We decided to undertake the rest of the journey together, wherever it would take us. You didn't want to be wandering about Asia on your own, especially when you hadn't a clue where you were going. Clarence had a good sense of humour, which is most important when you are travelling, especially in our frugal circumstances.

Accommodation in Afghanistan was "basic", to put it politely. One night at a small town on the Helmand River, six of us paid 2 afs each to sleep on the stone floor of a place masquerading as a hotel, or "olet" as the sign in English quaintly read. It was just one cavernous room, which was no problem, except it was already occupied by a dozen fearsome-looking, bearded tribesmen, all bearing rifles.

Having been on the road for a couple of months we were not exactly a pretty sight either, so maybe we scared them as much as they scared us, although somehow I doubted it. For what seemed a lifetime there was a peculiar silence as we settled in, broken only by some nervous observations about our fellow guests. There were no reassuring murmurs of approval from the tribesmen. They simply stared at us, which was quite unsettling in itself... beards, eyes and rifles.

A few western cigarettes turned out to be a satisfactory peace offering, although one old boy who looked like the chief, spent the rest of the night suffering a coughing fit after taking a hefty drag of what must have been his first-ever taste of Benson and Hedges. Fortunately he eventually recovered, but his aides kept a close watch on these aliens across the room. None of us got much sleep that night.

It was just as well that I had yet to read George MacDonald Fraser's first *Flashman* novel set primarily in Afghanistan a century before. Flashman's albeit fictitious experiences at the hands of Akbar Khan and his associates are enough to make the knees of the bravest men tremble.

We eventually made it to Kandahar, which was uneventful, apart from witnessing some poor fellow being run over and seriously injured at an intersection by a speeding horse and cart. I made the mistake of venturing down a small lane to experience some local "colour" only to stumble on a sheep being slaughtered at an improvised abattoir, the unfortunate creature's guts spilling forth at my feet.

From Kandahar we headed north on a local bus for the 450-kilometre journey to Kabul, which considering the road conditions, surprisingly took us just one day. We even had time to stop-off at a village in mid-journey for a tasty roadside barbecue. That proved to be a mistake.

In Kabul I was sick as a dog.

There is no need to go into the sordid details, but from the moment my head started spinning while walking down a street in Kabul I knew I was in trouble. I went on to experience 48 hours of absolute misery, suffering from chronic food poisoning. Everything was coming out of both ends and I was confined to a stinking "bathroom" with just a hole in the floor and a few cockroaches for company. On reflection, I should never have eaten those barbecued goat balls or whatever they were from that roadside stall.

The lone entry in my diary for the next two days simply read: "Feeling very ill". But that did not tell half the story. I had never before or since, felt so sick and for a period seriously wondered if

I would survive, my ribs aching from constantly throwing up. All my strength and willpower was being drained out of me. After all, I wouldn't have been the first Brit not to make it out of Kabul.

I tried to cheer myself up by recalling scenes from the silly *Carry On Up The Khyber* comedy film I had seen only a few months earlier in London, featuring the kilted "3rd Foot and Mouth Regiment", who scare away the attacking tribesmen by lifting up their kilts.

A sight to behold: Travelling through the magnificent Khyber Pass was one highlight of the overland trip, despite the author still recovering from a nasty sickness experienced in Kabul. -
Bangkok Post photo

Maybe this desperate therapy worked, because by some miracle, after one more day simply lying on the very basic bed feeling sorry for myself, the illness showed signs of abating. I was still quite tottery, painfully weak and at least five kilos lighter, but the Khyber Pass and the Pakistan frontier town of Peshawar beckoned. My friends had also experienced enough of Kabul and just wanted to get out of the place. I didn't want to hold them up, although I could have done with another couple of days' rest. It was time to push on.

Just like the British forces a century before, I left Afghanistan in a state of complete disarray. But I was more fortunate than that wretched force which retreated from Kabul back in 1842. A total of 16,000 souls took part in that ill-fated trek, including 4,500 British soldiers - one survived.

My fragile state did not stop me being left in awe of the mighty Hindu Kush as the Afghan bus gasped its way up and down the Khyber Pass, a route described by Rudyard Kipling as "a sword cut through the mountains". It was a truly humbling experience. Those towering mountains could tell some tales over the centuries, most of them quite bloody featuring the likes of Alexander the Great and Genghis Khan. It was definitely not a place to mess with.

As we stretched our legs upon arrival at the Pakistan border, high up in the mountains near the summit of the pass, I looked back at Afghanistan, trying to imagine what it had been like for those wretched soldiers a century before. It must have been absolute hell… and worse. Almost inevitably came to mind those chilling words from Kipling in his poem *The Young British Soldier:*

"When you're wounded and left on Afghanistan's plains,
"And the women come out to cut up what remains,
"Just roll to your rifle and blow out your brains,
"And go to your Gawd like a soldier."

4. PORRIDGE, PASSENGERS AND LUGGAGE RACKS

Full steam ahead through Pakistan and India, with an excursion to Nepal

At the bustling Pakistan frontier city of Peshawar I experienced an early reminder of the legacy of the colonial days - hot English-style porridge at the railway station restaurant. And it went down a treat too, especially as I was still feeling fragile from my nightmare in Kabul and was struggling to hold down any solids. For the next few weeks, porridge at assorted Pakistan and Indian railway stations played an essential role in my recovery. So my humble thanks to the days of the British Raj.

The experience in Peshawar, a real melting pot of people, was also an introduction to how the railways on the sub-continent had a distinctive way of operating. After buying the tickets for Lahore, we were led along the tracks by a local fixer and boarded the train in the sidings about a kilometre down the line, more than two hours before it was scheduled to depart Peshawar.

We would have looked pretty silly sitting there if that hadn't been the right train, but it turned out okay. The express was jam-packed with passengers before it even left the sidings. As it backed into the station for the official start of its journey, it became clear that we would never have got on if we had waited on the platform in the traditional manner.

To pinch the words of Paul Theroux from his classic travelogue, *The Great Railway Bazaar,* "I sought trains, I found passengers."

We found millions of them... passengers, that is.

In the coming weeks I was to experience assorted extraordinary railway journeys through Pakistan and northern India. To get any chance of a seat you had to dive through the open windows of the carriages as the train chugged into the station. It was total mayhem and also quite dangerous. More often than not we had to sleep, or at least try, in the packed and frequently filthy train corridors.

The trains were all pulled by magnificent steam engines, although there were frequent breakdowns. This often led to long conversations with the locals, who were always keen to know your life history. One Indian gentleman refused to believe I was an Englishman because I was "too scruffy". Perhaps he thought I should have been wearing a bowler hat and pinstripe suit. He was certainly right about the scruffiness. I was also probably pretty smelly too in all that heat and only having sporadic access to anything resembling a shower. But by this time I had reached the stage where I didn't really care about sartorial splendour.

There were some days when things were bit of a blur owing to weariness from rail travel and sleep deprivation, but I can recall five of us sharing a large bed in a dilapidated colonial-style Lahore hotel. Fortified by yet another excellent bowl of porridge, I even had the strength to play a brief game of tennis on the hotel's neglected court. The net was full of holes, which just about matched the standard of tennis. The next morning there was a massive street demonstration in Lahore, which appeared to be getting out of hand, so it seemed a good idea to get out of the place as soon as possible. We quickly took a bus to Ferozepur, 100 kms south of Amritsar, at the Indian frontier.

We had to walk across the border and I found myself unwittingly involved in a quirky ritual involving the guards. A Pakistan guard gave me some dying flowers and made me promise to give them to the Indian guard just down the road. I realized it must be some kind of insult, but dutifully handed over the flowers at the border point. To my relief, the Indian guard gave a hearty laugh and threw the flowers away, adding a few insults of his own.

There followed a punishing 3rd-class train journey to Delhi. The carriages were so crowded it was a bit like the London Underground at rush hour, except it was a 390-km journey, a sleepless one at that, sitting on ancient wooden seats that guaranteed a "numb bum" experience. We eventually rolled into the Indian capital the following morning around dawn, well and truly frazzled.

After a couple of months on the road, Delhi was quite a welcome respite and we all kind of "regrouped". I was feeling much better, thanks to my daily input of porridge - usually consumed at railway stations - and some tasty cheap Indian food. More significantly, we had at least reached our original destination, albeit minus our original transport. It was a triumph of some sorts, although it didn't really feel like it. It was also time to take stock, as our meagre funds were running out.

The fact that we had made it to Delhi in one piece was remarkable in itself. These days, low-budget travelers have a wealth of information at their fingertips, thanks primarily to the Internet and *Lonely Planet* guides. But in 1969 we had to rely on messages pinned on notice boards in assorted dodgy hotels as we made our way across Asia. There would be scraps of paper with handwritten information along the lines of: "Don't eat at Mr. Singh's café in Calcutta unless you have health insurance", or "Beware of the friendly one-armed man in Kabul. He's after your traveller's cheques."

In Delhi someone had written a warning about ladyboys in Thailand. I didn't even know what a ladyboy was. It read simply: "Beware! Not all ladies in Bangkok are ladies." It turned out to be quite useful information really, although I wasn't aware of it at the time.

Communicating with home was another matter. It generally featured the traditional hand-written letter and ensuring that you mailed it at a reliable post office, something I was to discover to my cost later. To receive correspondence from home required a tedious trip to the nearest *"poste restante"* where, if you were lucky, there might be a letter awaiting written a month before, usually wanting to know when you were going to return home.

In the bigger cities, you could try placing international phone calls, but for budget travellers low on funds that was an unwelcome expense and the odds were that you would only be greeted by Chinese opera at the other end of the line.

It was through the bush telegraph that in Delhi we ended up staying in a guest house near Connaught Square run by a Mrs. Colaco, who was quite a colourful character. She took a kind of fancy to me in a maternal sort of way, partly because she liked my first name, which was similar to Rajah, regarded as an auspicious moniker in India. Unfortunately her ceiling fans were anything but auspicious, rotating so slowly they might just as well have been switched off and in the middle of March, temperatures were rising into sauna-type figures. A series of sweaty, sleepless nights meant that once again, it was time to move on.

Marble marvel: A trip to Agra to visit the Taj Mahal was a truly memorable experience, despite being pursued by a snake charmer. - Bangkok Post photo

I did manage a solo diversion to Agra, 210 kms south of Delhi, to experience the delights of that amazing shrine to love, the Taj Mahal. It was one of the more pleasant railway journeys I experienced in India, primarily because it only took about three hours each way. It was a blisteringly hot day and I felt compelled to give the skinny rickshaw driver a decent tip after he had pedaled me the five kms from the railway station to the temple with sweat pouring off him - but nowhere near the amount of sweat that poured off me. On first viewing the Taj was certainly quite a stunning sight, although after taking my shoes off at the temple, I burnt my feet on the searing hot marble steps and had to sprint for the shade. There were not many people around at that time and no other western tourists, so I felt quite privileged taking in that extraordinary white marble mausoleum.

Unfortunately, in India moments of peace and solitude rarely lasted very long. In Agra, I was pursued by a snake charmer who wanted to tell my fortune and an assortment of characters who wouldn't leave me alone. They were only trying to do a bit of business, but in the end I was relieved to get back on the train to Delhi.

From the moment I had set foot in India, the locals had shown great interest in my shabby denim jeans. With funds running low, I ventured into the Delhi market and sold one pair in a flash. I was also happy and surprised that I was able to unload my college scarf, which had kept me from going numb with cold through the frozen landscapes of Turkey and Iran, but was of no use in steaming hot Delhi. The merchant who bought the scarf told me he could sell it at a considerable profit in the colder climes of Kashmir. So there may still be a red, white and blue Kingston scarf roaming around the Himalayan foothills, although it would be a bit moth-eaten by now.

Nepal, or more specifically, Kathmandu, beckoned. We embarked on another series of grueling train journeys in northeastern India and at times it felt like we were going around in circles. I am convinced we passed through Lucknow and Muzaffarpur several times on the same journey. Eventually, after one ridiculous night trying to sleep perched in a luggage rack, we arrived at the Nepalese border town of Birganj. We stayed in a stifling small room that appeared to be hosting the annual mosquito convention. "A place to avoid", was the lone entry in the diary.

But the 206-km journey through the mountains to Kathmandu on the back of an open truck made it all worthwhile. It took nine hours and the diary suddenly became enthusiastic again as I recorded "the most fantastic scenery" as the truck wound its way around the mountains. I still have this image of pink, purple and deep red rhododendrons everywhere, a plant I hadn't seen since the country lanes of Surrey and Berkshire. It was only later that I discovered to my surprise it was the national flower of Nepal.

The only damper on that particular journey came at one daunting hairpin bend, where a small crowd of farmers had gathered, looking down into the valley. But they weren't there to admire the view, stunning though it was. A hundred metres below them was a truck just like ours, smashed to pieces after skidding off the road.

Our week or so in Kathmandu was most agreeable, considering that we were almost broke. Having the Himalayas as a backdrop helped, I suppose. Even from the Nepal capital the truly majestic mountains made you feel you were somewhere special. After all, we were almost on top of the world.

Recollections of Kathmandu are somewhat hazy, although I can remember devouring plenty of delicious banana pancakes. It was the time of "Flower Power", which had gripped the US and a few outposts around the world. There weren't many foreigners in Kathmandu, but most were classic hippies, looking like they had recently escaped from San Francisco, living in their own permanent marijuana haze. Evenings were spent in cheap cafes listening to Dylan, Hendrix, Cream and the Beatles. There are definitely worse ways to pass the time.

One day we hired bicycles to explore villages about 20 kms away that somebody had recommended. The road quickly disappeared and we were soon cycling through paddy fields, wading across streams, and staggering up what I would like to call mountains, but what were in reality just foothills. But pushing the bike, they felt like mountains. I think we had half hoped to discover that "green-eyed yellow idol to the north of Kathmandu" J. Milton Hayes was on about in *The Green Eye of the Yellow God*. Instead we had a reminder of the frightening power of Mother Nature.

A menacing black storm was ominously brewing in the distance and we somewhat belatedly decided to head for home. All of the bikes had punctures by this time, so even when we found a road back to Kathmandu, we couldn't ride the wretched things. The road had just reached the summit of a steep hill when the heavens opened, unleashing a startling volley of hailstones the size of marbles. The ensuing storm was of such intensity with terrifying lightning crashing all around us, all we could do was huddle by an embankment and hope for the best. We were totally exposed to the elements, and I was scared stiff, convinced I was going to be struck by lightning. I don't think I have ever experienced a storm of such ferocity at close quarters. It was almost my personal Armageddon.

After what seemed an eternity, much to our relief the storm eased a little. We were now so cold, soaked and miserable that we hopped on our punctured bikes and wobbled down the hill back into Kathmandu, lucky not to fall off on one slippery bend covered in mud. We arrived back at the guest house looking a sorry sight. A few pancakes later we were all feeling much better and quite relieved to be in one piece after our close encounter with the elements. At least it taught me never to underestimate a tropical storm, which has proved equally useful living in Thailand. I could have happily spent much longer in Nepal as there was so much out there waiting to be explored. But rapidly diminishing funds meant that Australia beckoned even more urgently.

Ten days later, after an educational excursion on the Ganges at Benares (Varanasi), we found ourselves in a Sikh temple in Calcutta (now Kolkata), where the hosts were generous and friendly. It was free food and lodging, sleeping on the floor and all we were asked to do was clean our plates. Alas, some idiot, whom we did not know, abused the hospitality and we all had to leave. So the last two days on the Sub-continent we stayed at the Salvation Army hostel on Sudder Street in Calcutta.

Earlier in the week I had attended the 9.30 a.m. service at Sudder Street Methodist Church. This wasn't prompted by any spiritual emergency, but primarily to please my mum, who was a Methodist. I'm sure that within a few weeks everyone at her local church in Reading had been informed about my Sudder Street experience.

The church visit was also partly to escape the crowds in Calcutta - a hugely fascinating city, but quite overwhelming at times. I spent one afternoon in a cheap café, gazing at the impressive Howrah Bridge spanning the Hooghly River. The owner told me it was the busiest bridge in the world and watching the continuous stream of traffic and pedestrians, it was an assertion I would not dispute.

I made one big mistake in Calcutta. Someone had told me the postal system wasn't reliable in Thailand, which for the first time was looking likely to be our next port of call. So foolishly I collected all the reels of colour slides I had taken on the journey and mailed them back to England from Calcutta. They never arrived. (Hence, the absence of photographs of our journey in this book.)

Sitting in the packed departure lounge at Calcutta's Dum Dum airport on April 9, I actually felt a bit guilty about getting on a plane - it was the end of the "overland" part of the journey. It hadn't been in the plans, but it was impossible to travel overland through Burma. So Thailand awaited, a country I knew very little about as I had never planned on going there.

Having been living rough for a couple of months, even an economy ticket on an aging Thai International Airways Caravelle jet seemed like absolute luxury, especially after the collective chaos of Calcutta. It got even better when, early on the flight from Dum Dum, a lovely Thai air hostess came down the aisle and asked me if I would like another glass of wine. That was music to the ears. It won't come as any surprise that she received a positive reply. She was probably the first Thai I had ever spoken to and was quite stunning. The wine wasn't bad either.

From that moment I had a sneaking suspicion I was going to enjoy my "brief stay" in the Land of Smiles.

5. WELCOME TO THAILAND

Hitchhiking from Bangkok to Malaysia

My first night in Thailand, on April 9, 1969, can hardly be described as exotic. It was spent primarily on the roof at Bangkok's Don Mueang Airport after our flight from Calcutta had landed about 11 p.m..

The entry in my diary noted that it was "the most superb flight I have ever been on", although after three months of roughing it, even the smallest luxury would have been greeted with similar enthusiasm.

There were five of us - Clarence, myself and three of the girls from the overland trip. The combination of not having much idea where to go, fatigue and being broke, prompted our decision to try and grab some sleep at the airport overnight and head into the city in the morning.

It was not a busy airport at that time and security did not appear to be a major concern. We went up some stairs and found ourselves on the flat roof, naively thinking we might be able to get some sleep with a bit of welcome breeze on a stiflingly hot night. Of course, squadrons of mosquitoes quickly put paid to that daft idea and we ended up retreating downstairs, half asleep in the airport's modest restaurant.

It was in the restaurant that we were befriended by a Thai Airways crew from another flight. They must have felt sorry for us because, as dawn was breaking, they gave us a lift in their company van to the Victory Monument. I was impressed by the crew's cheerful disposition and genuine friendliness towards us total strangers, scruffy ones at that - a first taste of the legendary Thai hospitality.

Desperate for sleep, our immediate task was to find somewhere to stay for a while. Khao San Road was just an ordinary street in those days, not known for guest houses. But during our travels the name Thai Son Greet had been touted as the place for budget travelers to hang out. So we headed for this noisy little shophouse hostelry on Rama IV Road, just around the corner from Hua Lamphong railway station. The morning traffic hadn't yet built up and the diary refers to "a lunatic bus driver" as we hurtled across town towards the station. There was also a reference to "pretty girls", so it seems not a lot has changed in the ensuing four decades.

Three wheels, nine lives: You could come across some strange sights on Bangkok's roads in those early days.

The Thai Son Greet was full-up, but they allowed us to dump our rucksacks while we searched for alternative accommodation. We were all dog-tired and nobody really fancied the idea of traipsing around Bangkok's streets in the April heat. Unfortunately I drew the short straw and along with the American girl, Lennie, we set off.

We headed into Chinatown not having a clue what we were going to find and there were virtually no signs in English, hardly a surprise in 1969. Eventually we spotted a likely looking place and clambered up some steep stairs to find an ancient gentleman who

WELCOME TO THAILAND

looked a bit like Ho Chi Minh, sitting at an equally ancient desk in front of a wall full of keys. It looked promising... sort of.

We couldn't speak a word of Thai and he didn't know any English; he peered at us quizzically from behind his abacus. We made sleeping gestures with our hands and he seemed to understand, responding with a toothless grin. But he kept asking a question that sounded something like "showtime?" It was at this stage I heard a lot of giggling and noticed several doors down the adjacent corridor had opened. The gigglers all appeared to be young Thai ladies in a state of undress. They seemed fascinated by our presence, which was sparking animated conversation.

It was then I realized that perhaps we were not in the sort of hotel of which my mum would approve and the "showtime" I had been hearing was actually "short time". The old boy had presumably thought the two of us had nipped in for a quickie. We nipped out pretty smartish, amidst much laughter from the assembled gathering.

Despite the heat, traffic chaos and choking pollution in that part of town, in those first few hours I had already taken a liking to Bangkok. There were wonderful exchanges with smiling vendors at the assorted stalls and I had never seen such magnificent-looking tropical fruit, which was thankfully also cheap enough for my limited budget. I survived the next few days consuming juicy pineapple slices and mouth-watering mangoes and melons.

Most of all, it was the atmosphere generated by the people. There seemed to be so much less pressure on us than in the other countries we had passed through. I immediately felt comfortable. And then there were the smiles. By some incredible piece of luck and good fortune, without any planning, I had ended up in the Land of Smiles. It might be a tired cliché these days, but those smiles went down a treat. Everybody at least *looked* happy, even if they weren't.

We eventually found a dingy 20 baht a night hotel opposite the railway station, the Jeep Singh as I recall. Our female companions hated it and I can't say I blamed them - it wasn't exactly the 5-star Oriental Hotel. They had probably experienced enough of us too and it was no surprise when they announced they were flying off to Australia in the next couple of days. At least it made our travel plans easier, as Clarence and I tried to figure out how we could get to Malaysia, more specifically the town of Alor Star (now Setar), in the cheapest possible way. Hopefully awaiting Clarence in a bank there would be the precious money transfer from London, which would resolve our financial woes, albeit temporarily.

The only answer was to hitchhike.

A couple of days later, on April 14, we found ourselves standing by the Petchkasem Highway on the outskirts of Thonburi. The heat was overwhelming and at a roadside stall we purchased ridiculous sombrero-type straw hats in what turned out to be, for me at least, a futile attempt to ward off the sun.

After a long wait, to our relief a Shell petrol tanker stopped and a wizened old driver beckoned us aboard. The tanker never seemed to get above 40 kph, which was probably just as well considering the way he drove and it took us all day to reach Hua Hin. In those days the Thonburi-Pak Tho highway didn't exist and the only road to the South took a time-consuming route via Nakhon Pathom.

We were not aware of it at the time, but it was the middle of the Songkran festival and Hua Hin beach was jam-packed with Thai holiday makers - not a *farang* (foreigner) in sight. The crowded beach didn't stop us taking a dip in the sea, which was absolute heaven after three months of backpacking. It was also my first-ever experience of tropical waters and I couldn't believe how warm the water was. It was certainly an improvement on Brighton. Even the bed in the 20-baht-a-night wooden hotel felt comfortable.

Hua Hin has remained one of my favourite resorts and I have returned many times over the years, paying a bit more than 20 baht for a room, I might add.

From Hua Hin we hitched to Chumphon, by which stage I was suffering what turned out to be heat-stroke and felt almost as dreadful as in Kabul - well not quite that bad. However, a splitting headache meant that upon arrival in Chumphon, I staggered to the hospital where I was duly fussed over and generally pampered by several nurses, who performed various tests and administered assorted pills.

Remarkably, after a few hours, I began to feel considerably better, confirming that a pretty Thai nurse beats anything modern medicine can provide. Feeling rejuvenated, I somewhat reluctantly announced I was fit enough to leave.

Then came the awkward bit - the bill. Stupidly, it had never entered my mind that I would have to pay for the treatment, ludicrous though that may sound. But I only had about 60 baht left for the rest of the journey, which I offered them, explaining that was all I had. It was politely declined. I was embarrassed and felt like I had cheated them. But as often happened in Thailand in those early days, the problem swiftly became no problem - *"mai mee panha"*. The nurses said they hadn't treated a *farang* for ages and had enjoyed practicing their English, so I could regard the medical fee having been paid for by their unexpected English lesson.

And I had enjoyed a Thai lesson too, learning my second Thai phrase, *"mai mee panha"*, which was to come in very useful over the years. For the curious, the first Thai phrase I picked up was, not surprisingly, *"mai pen rai"* - never mind.

From Chumphon we hitched westwards across the isthmus to Ranong as the more direct route to the South via Surat Thani had no functioning highway. It was thick jungle on either side of the tortuously bending road to Ranong. Spotting some wild elephants just off the road, it felt for the first time I was in the steamy tropical Asia I had read about as a child.

In Ranong, the pleasant Thai gentleman who had given us a lift from Chumphon unfortunately knocked someone off a motorcycle on the main street and so we had to find new transport. Thankfully the motorcyclist was not seriously injured, but I shudder to think how many motorcycle accidents I have witnessed in Thailand since that early mishap. We were lucky to be picked up in Ranong by a family who owned a tin mine in Phuket. As we snaked down the west coast of the isthmus, they invited us to stay with them on the island. It was hugely tempting, as in those days Phuket was undeveloped with pristine beaches and had a reputation as a place where you didn't have to lock the doors at night as break-ins were almost unheard of. But we had to get to Malaysia as quickly as possible.

They dropped us off just outside Phang-nga. As dusk approached we were quite exhausted and decided to sleep in a bus shelter. But once the mosquitoes moved in, it didn't seem such a good idea. Also, I hadn't entirely shaken off the heatstroke and was feeling a bit run-down. We were saved by Thai hospitality once again. A passing student found us flaked out in the shelter and offered to put us up in his father's garage for the night. It was not exactly five-star accommodation, but an improvement on the bus-stop.

The next morning we hitched an exhilarating ride in the back of a brand new Toyota pick-up being delivered to Hat Yai. The scenery was absolutely magnificent as we climbed through the mountains in Phatthalung and Krabi. Indeed, all the way from Chumphon, everything was so lush and unspoilt. In Krabi we attracted a number of onlookers as I don't think they had ever heard of tourists, let alone seen any. How times have changed.

It was so blisteringly hot that the tarmac on the highway had melted. It wasn't until we climbed out of the Toyota that we realized we had left tarmac footprints all over the back of the sparkling new van. Understandably the driver was not too amused. All we could do was apologise, feeling guilty about unintentionally abusing the hospitality.

Up to this point the hitchhiking had been a rich experience, especially with all the helpful people we had met. However, not everything was to go according to plan.

The last stage required a shared taxi from Hat Yai to the Malaysian border at Sadao. The taxi was a clapped-out Chevrolet that should never have been allowed out on the road and was about to prove so in spectacular fashion.

Eight people had crammed into the rattletrap in Hat Yai and about 20 minutes later eight of us crawled out from a muddy roadside ditch after the taxi had "turned turtle" when a rear tyre burst during a fierce rainstorm. Shaken, mud-splattered and in a mild state of shock, but not seriously hurt, the two of us had to

WELCOME TO THAILAND

resort to hitching again. We made the last stretch to the Malaysian border in the back of a smelly fish truck full of gasping red snapper, giant squid, menacing-looking crabs and assorted unidentified denizens of the deep.

Not surprisingly, the Malaysian immigration authorities were less than enthusiastic about allowing into their country two dishevelled, penniless Englishmen, who had climbed down from the back of a truck, soaking wet, covered in mud and stinking of fish.

"We get too many of your sort," sniffed one officer, but following considerable haranguing, we eventually persuaded them to let us through after Clarence sold his watch so that we had enough for the bus fare to Alor Star.

We had hoped to stay with an English friend of Clarence, who was teaching in Alor Star, but unfortunately she was out of town (probably heard we were coming). Not having enough money for a hotel, in desperation we went to the local police station - maybe we could get a cell for the night. Well, you never know. There we got into conversation with a charming policeman, who escorted us to an old Chinese hostelry and told them we could stay there the night and not to charge us.

There seemed to be a disproportionate number of "painted ladies" in the establishment and it turned out to be as much a brothel as a hotel. But by this time nothing surprised us and we were simply thankful for a room each. I remember as a bonus that night in the small restaurant downstairs sitting under a large ceiling fan and enjoying a sumptuous sweet and sour dish, washed down with a Tiger beer.

To our relief, the money eventually found its way to the bank in Alor Star. Although it was not a huge sum, it meant we could continue our travels again, this time paying our own way. We even celebrated with a visit to the local cinema, where we watched Robert Mitchum starring in the *Battle For Anzio*, the first movie I had seen since England. After a week in Malaysia, which included a few days in Penang and Kuala Lumpur, we decided to put Australia on hold for a few months and return to Bangkok.

Apart from the taxi accident, we had really enjoyed our brief time in Thailand.

We had experienced our fill of road travel, however, and returned to the Thai capital by sea, aboard a Thai Maritime Navigation Company vessel from Songkhla. I've still got the ticket somewhere, dated April 26, 2512 (1969). The vessel was called the *Bangmara* and the fare 75 baht deck class, which basically meant sleeping anywhere on the deck, just like the crew. That trip up the Gulf of Thailand turned out to be one of the most relaxing journeys I have ever experienced, despite a lively storm which severely tested my somewhat fragile sea legs.

We ate with the Thai crew, who were mainly young lads delighted to have a couple of *farang* on board. They had a transistor radio and spent much of the time hunting down western pop music for us. I remember watching the splendid schools of flying fish performing alongside the ship to the strains of Petula Clark singing *Wish Me Goodbye*. Another song which kept surfacing and was a big hit in Thailand was *Crimson and Clover* by Tommy James and the Shondells.

In the evening the crew pulled out their guitars and played their own music with assorted pots and pans used as percussion instruments, providing a raucous backing. I was beginning to learn the true meaning of *sanuk* (having fun). It was fish for breakfast, lunch and supper, but we didn't mind as we knew it was very fresh, having witnessed it being caught minutes earlier. The voyage included a brief stopover at Koh Samui, which was nothing but coconut trees and pristine beaches - not a tourist to be seen.

As the *Bangmara* eased its way up the Chao Phraya River the next day towards the Bangkok port at Klong Toey, Clarence and I sat on the deck pondering our next move. We agreed that maybe we could spend a little more time in Thailand. It turned out to be somewhat longer than we could ever have imagined. Just like the fish we had consumed earlier, we had both been truly hooked.

6. AN APPLE FOR THE TEACHER

A songbook proves more useful than a textbook

On the flight from Calcutta to Bangkok a couple of weeks earlier, we had found ourselves sitting next to a chatty Thai gentleman, Mr. Prayoon, who owned a commercial college in Bangkok. Upon learning that Clarence and I were graduates from England, he promptly offered us a job teaching at his establishment. It was the shortest job interview I had ever experienced and definitely the first at 30,000 feet.

Sir and friends: With Pattana college students on Chulalongkorn Day, October 1969, outside Parliament House.

We had expressed reservations to him about our effectiveness. Apart from the minor point of never having taught before, we only had a smattering of the Thai language and wondered how we could possibly explain things to the students. However, we were assured that the pupils had a good command of English. Ha ha!

The college was in the Makkasan area on Soi Rajaphand. On our meagre pay we were lucky to find a small house with two bedrooms nearby for a total rent of 800 baht a month.

I was initially assigned to teach economics and geography. After the first geography lesson it became clear it was going to be harder than I thought - a lot harder. I invested in a large map of the world and pinned it up on the board. To ease the students into it I thought it might be more interesting if I retraced my overland journey, to see what they knew of the world. The answer was, not a lot.

I began proceedings by pointing at London and asking which country it was in. No one seemed to know, although one suggestion of the United States was bit of a worry. Not the greatest start. Undeterred, I then progressed through Europe, asking the pupils to name the countries as we came to them. Belgium drew a complete blank, which was understandable, not being the best of known countries in this part of the world. My hopes briefly rose when one student got Germany right, but that proved something of a false dawn. By the time we got to Bulgaria, I had just about given up.

It called for desperate measures, so I abandoned the rest of the journey. Instead, I pointed at Thailand and asked what country it was. Everyone just sat there in total silence, broken by a few embarrassed giggles. Eventually a brave girl in the front row said "Thailand", which came as a mighty relief. At the time I put it down to shyness and language problems rather than lack of geographical knowledge, although I wasn't totally convinced. I got the distinct feeling that many of them had never looked at a world map before.

Surprisingly, I made more progress with the economics, once the laws of supply and demand were sorted out. The students seemed to understand my wretched diagrams on the blackboard quite well, even if I didn't.

Generally speaking the students were hugely polite and a pleasure to teach considering the language limitations. Of course, there were a few who were not interested in learning anything. They usually had a laugh at my expense when I attempted to

AN APPLE FOR THE TEACHER

speak Thai and got all the tones wrong. One attentive female student in the front row - the girls always sat at the front - even used to give me the occasional apple, which was a nice touch, especially considering apples were bit of a luxury in Thailand in those days.

However, when end-of-term exams arrived, things became a little more complicated. The students kept pestering me about what the questions would be. And I was inundated with apples. I explained that if they listened closely to the lessons in the coming fortnight, they ought to have no worries. So without telling them as such, we covered all the questions they would face in the exams. They didn't know it, but I wanted them to pass as much as they did.

When it came to marking the papers, it was the anticipated mixture of good, bad and ugly, probably an accurate reflection of the teacher. I tried to be as generous as possible with the marking and duly sent the papers off to the principal.

The next morning I was summoned to the principal's office. "Mr. Loger," he said sternly, waving the papers at me, "marks too low. Please do again." He went on to explain quite openly that I had failed too many students and parents would not send their children to the college if they thought they might not pass. I briefly pondered an impassioned speech concerning "integrity", but thought better of it. In hindsight it all made sense. The owner was running a business as much as an educational establishment. He could not afford to lose students, but teachers were expendable.

A trifle disillusioned, I duly bumped up all the marks in generous fashion, but even so could not rescue the no-hopers. I suspect that in the end even those who were a lost cause duly received pass marks from the boss. Just as long as the one who gave me the apples got through, I didn't mind.

It was at this time we were invited by a student to his house where we met his parents. They were friendly, perhaps a bit too friendly. It soon became clear that all they wanted was for us to give their son good marks. I always remember the mother asking "are you boring?". Those English tenses are a real pain.

Early days: With Clarence Shettlesworth (left) and a student on "freshy day" at Pattana in 1969.

Once a week we were assigned to a school in Bang Khen, adjacent to the superhighway on the way to Don Mueang airport. The students were in their early teens, much younger than at the college. The kids were lovely and well behaved, but there was a massive language problem. I was supposed to be teaching them English, but they couldn't understand a word I was saying. Conventional teaching had to go out of the window.

I had a songbook and the big hit amongst youngsters in Thailand at the time was the bubblegum song, *Simon Says*, by the

AN APPLE FOR THE TEACHER

1910 Fruitgum Company. I wrote the lyrics on the blackboard and got the kids to repeat them after me. They really got into this, especially when I started performing the actions "put your hands in the air... shake them all about" and they quickly followed suit. There was plenty of laughter, so at least there was some sort of communication going on.

Towards the end of the lesson, as a treat, I let the class sing the song and perform the actions. It was total mayhem, but great fun. The whole class was going full throttle when I noticed someone standing in the doorway. It was the Thai head teacher, who had come to find out what all the racket was about. I grinned rather sheepishly at her and she shook her head in a mildly disapproving manner as I waved my arms about, but to her credit she didn't stop the fun.

The problem was that I had only achieved a short-term fix. Every week the only thing the kids wanted to do was "sing song" as they nicely put it as soon as I had walked into the classroom. So we waded through the Bee Gees and the Beatles in the following weeks. I don't think the pupils picked up much English, but seeing them happily singing away to songs they didn't understand was a reward in itself. Maybe some of them even went on to be musicians. Looking back, those were probably the most successful lessons during my year of teaching.

Like most new arrivals in the kingdom, I experienced a variety of emotions adapting to the culture and the new environment, sometimes thinking I had landed in paradise, but occasionally wondering what on earth was going on. It was primarily positive, but there were times when I was very confused, to put it mildly. Over the years nothing has changed in that respect. The old adage still rings true - the longer you live in Thailand, the more you realize how little you know about the place.

At our modest abode we left the doors and windows open to let the breeze in - it also let in the neighbours. There was little privacy. People were always dropping by to say hello, understandably intrigued by these two foreigners suddenly surfacing in their patch of the woods. It was an excellent introduction to the Thai community spirit, something we would have to get used to in the coming weeks, months and years.

Some mornings I would get up to find neighbours sitting on the floor downstairs, making themselves at home. But there were no security issues. No one was going to pinch anything - we didn't have anything to pinch for a start. A tiny 200 baht fan from Pratunam market was about our sole asset. Sometimes I awoke to the sounds of a pestel hammering away and knew that downstairs were a few ladies tucking into a mid-morning *somtam* (spicy papaya salad).

I can safely say that every day I learnt something new, most of which was a definite reminder that I was no longer in England. One of our regular visitors was a young tall woman from a few doors down. She was pleasant and eager to learn English, but there was something about her that seemed a bit odd and I couldn't quite nail it down. A helpful neighbour later explained to me that she might well be attractive, but unfortunately she was a he. I never had that problem in Reading. Still it's good to learn these things early on.

Then there was the matter of learning to *wai* - the graceful Thai mode of greeting - in the appropriate manner. I remember being mildly reprimanded for offering a *wai* to a much younger person. For Thai citizens this comes naturally from their childhood days. But for a newly-arrived foreigner, when to *wai* and when not to *wai* can at first seem quite complicated. There is probably not a foreign resident in Thailand who hasn't experienced a situation of giving a *wai* to a Thai person, who at the same time is trying to shake your hand - a classic case of East meeting West.

Robert and Nanthana Cooper summed it up best in their excellent book *Culture Shock Thailand*: "If you have never suffered from culture shock, Thailand is a good place to start."

There was also the minor matter of the first manned moon landing on July 20. I watched Neil Armstrong's historic walk at a Makkasan noodle shop near our house. Over the previous three months it had become our regular eating establishment, partly because just about everything cost three baht, not including the beer, unfortunately.

We didn't have a television at home, so on the big day the noodle shop owner kindly invited us upstairs to his inner sanctum where we sat on the floor in front of a flickering TV to watch the event. He even gave us a free coke and fried rice to celebrate. Watching Armstrong make his "one small step for man" was an unforgettable moment. I was forever grateful to that humble noodle shop owner, who hardly knew us, for making it possible to witness such an historic event.

It sounds stupid, but later that night I couldn't resist looking up at the moon, half-expecting to see Armstrong striding about clutching the star-spangled banner and munching on a Big Mac. Incidentally, the Bangkok restaurants called Neil's Tavern, now at Ruam Rudee and Asoke, were named in honour of Armstrong.

I remember President Richard Nixon congratulating the astronauts with the message: "For years politicians have promised the Moon. I'm the first one to be able to deliver it." That wasn't a bad line for Nixon, not particularly known for his wit.

Nixon happened to visit Bangkok just a week after the Moon landing and he was greeted by enthusiastic crowds. He appeared to thoroughly enjoy the experience, despite his name being spelt "Nixson" on some official posters. He called Bangkok his favourite city, having visited on three previous occasions. He once wrote: "If there was a perfect place, I would nominate Bangkok."

But it was the people of Thailand that charmed Nixon, not a man to be easily charmed. He said at that time: "The Thai people have a verve and mystique not to be found anywhere on Earth." That was something I was discovering at first-hand after just three months in the kingdom.

Clarence and I still hadn't entirely shaken off the travel bug and would make periodic visits to the Thai Son Greet to see what was going on. Apart from the usual travellers, there always seemed to be a motley collection of shady Thai businessmen trying to cash in on the backpackers in some way.

Some of the Thai gentlemen had also heard about the curious western practice of "free love" and one suspects were hoping for a bit of practical experience.

One of the more dubious operations was run by someone we dubbed the Medicine Man. The idea was that he would hire a foreigner to be the front man to sell fake medicine to gullible Thai villagers in the provinces. Some months later I came across a *farang* doing just that in front of an audience of curious spectators on the main street in the southern town of Chumphon. He was holding up what looked like a bottle of ordinary cough mixture, but it was being presented as a miracle cure for just about everything.

I later spoke to this fellow, who turned out to be English. He admitted that he couldn't speak a word of Thai, so when he stood there on the street he just recited the lyrics of Beatles songs as if delivering a lecture. I think he was doing *Hey Jude* when I was there, sensibly refraining from the "la, la, la-la-la" bits. This was then translated by the Thai entrepreneur into tales of how wonderful the medicine was. The Englishman had been promised 3,000 baht a month for his services, but whether he survived a month was highly unlikely.

Another common ploy was to hire foreign travellers as boxers to take on Thai fighters upcountry. Once again it was the rural folks who were taken for a ride. I met a Welshman who said he was introduced to the crowd in Roi-Et as a leading contender for the British featherweight title. In fact, he had never put on a pair of boxing gloves in his life.

The tough Thai boxers could have knocked this guy out with one punch. But to string people along, and more importantly encourage rash betting, he was allowed to look good in the first round or so. The Thai boxer would then rally to knock him out in the third or fourth, depending on how the betting was going. The Welshman retired from his brief career in the ring after being floored by an overzealous opponent and spending the next few days in hospital, trying to get his head together.

So, I decided to stick with teaching for the time being.

AN APPLE FOR THE TEACHER

The college held a big end-of-term party with a band on stage and hundreds of students in attendance. I was quite enjoying proceedings until I saw Clarence whispering mischievously to the principal, who then got on stage and announced: "Now Mr. Loger will sing song". My immediate reaction was "Oh no, he bloody well won't, " but I was stuffed. Clarence had the smirk of someone who knew he had just ruined my night.

Despite my protestations that I couldn't sing a note, I was dragged up on stage and an electric guitar was thrust in my hand. I could only play a few basic chords, but more to the point what could I sing? I knew the opening line to hundreds of songs, but after that it was "dooh da da, mumble mumble". The old Rolling Stones song *The Spider and the Fly* then came into my head, primarily because it only required about three chords and I roughly knew the words. Unfortunately, from the first discordant notes it was obvious the band had never heard of the song.

For three excruciating verses I stumbled on before we finally stuttered to a halt, not all together of course. There was a ripple of applause, primarily prompted by the relief of seeing me stepping off the stage. I wasn't asked to sing again.

During those early days I was fortunate enough to meet Brett Bartos, a New Zealander who was working in the sports section of the *Bangkok Post* and lived just around the corner from us. Brett was to become a good friend, giving very useful "old hand" advice to us green newcomers. He was also in possession of an invaluable *Sgt Pepper's* vinyl album, which on his old record player helped us while away many an evening.

I initially saw Brett sitting at a mango and sticky rice stall on the *soi* near our college. It was the first time I had eaten the dish and it was absolutely delicious. Equally mouth-watering was the young lady in charge of the stall, which of course had nothing to do with Brett's eating habits.

It was about this time I also taught English sporadically at Thammasat University's Faculty of Law. The pay was a grand 50 baht for an hour's lesson. For obvious financial reasons I used to get there by bus, which was 50 satang in those days. The dear old blue No 1 took me from Makkasan to Sanam Luang, from where I would walk to the nearby campus.

On one occasion I got off the bus at Sanam Luang in a heavy thunderstorm. Not having an umbrella, I sheltered in a shop doorway for 10 minutes, but the rain refused to ease up. The university was quite strict on teachers being punctual, so in the end I had little choice but to sprint to the campus in the driving rain.

I finally reached the classroom and walked in looking like a drowned cat, understandably to an assortment of giggles from the assembled students. I apologized for my wretched appearance, but they were very understanding and one of them kindly appeared with a towel to help me dry out. Somehow I got through the lesson, by which time there was a puddle of water at my feet. Then I started sneezing. That was when I experienced one of those "what am I doing here?" feelings that sporadically surfaced in that first year.

One benefit of going to Thammasat was that just around the corner there was a noodle shop run by a Chinese fellow, who was the spitting image of Genghis Khan. He did good business too and not without reason - a tasty steak and chips for the massive sum of 12 baht. Even in those days it was a good deal - and no extra charge for the flies.

It will probably come as no surprise that after a few months I was getting a little weary of teaching. I decided to try my luck at the *Bangkok World* newspaper, which in those days was a morning daily on Phrasumane Road, near Ratchadamnoen Avenue. I think I arrived at a bad time. The editor, Denis Horgan, appeared to be somewhat harassed as he marched across the newsroom. When I approached him about possible employment, he displayed commendable judgement by informing me that my services would not be required. I think I would have reacted in much the same way if I was him. Denis has incidentally written an intriguing book, simply called *Bangkok World*, about his time at the paper.

I had given up any ideas of a newspaper career when a few months later Brett suggested I give it a try at the *Bangkok Post*. I somehow passed a proofreading test and to my delight heard the Australian editor Nick Nagle say something like "I'll suppose he'll do." Not exactly a ringing endorsement, but at last the opportunity to escape from being an *acharn* (teacher).

Teaching in Thailand had been a rich experience, but it is definitely not easy to hold the attention of 40-60 students for an hour at a time, especially if they don't understand a word you are saying. It was also an unexpected role reversal - only two years before I was the student, not the teacher. Fortunately, the Thai students were very respectful. I wouldn't have lasted five minutes in England.

On November 12, 1969, I officially joined the *Bangkok Post*, hoping to earn enough to finance my journey on to Australia. It took a little longer than I anticipated. Suffice to say, I finally arrived in the Land of Oz approximately 27 years later - possibly a candidate for the *Guinness Book of Records* as the slowest-ever journey from London to Sydney.

Little did I know that for the next four decades I would be working for the *Post*.

7. THE RATCHADAMNOEN DAYS

Learning the ropes at the Bangkok Post, 1969-73

When I joined the *Bangkok Post*, the office was located on Ratchadamnoen Avenue very close to the Democracy Monument. It was, and still is, one of the most pleasant parts of the city, which had hardly changed over the previous half-century. The newspaper had been in that location since 1962, having moved from across the road, its home since 1956. The rent for the office was minimal as it was owned by the Crown Property Bureau, which hadn't changed its rates since the end of the Second World War.

By some quirk I happen to be the same age as the *Post*, a few weeks older in fact - we were both "Established in 1946", the newspaper on August 1. So when I joined the paper in 1969 we - the paper and me - were both mere striplings of 23. It has been quite an experience to watch the newspaper - if not the author - mature over the years.

To put things into perspective, it was the year of the first manned Moon landing, the Beatles had just released *Abbey Road*, Harold Wilson was at No. 10 Downing Street, Richard Nixon was firmly established in the White House, the Vietnam War was at its height and not looking good for the Americans. Also making the news was the Chappaquiddick incident, the Manson Family murder of Sharon Tate and the death of Judy Garland from a drug overdose. The Rolling Stones' Brian Jones also died, drowning in a swimming pool. To put it mildly, 1969 was quite a year.

The *Post* cost two baht, and the hot local topics then were three mega projects - the Skytrain (BTS), the second international airport at Nong Ngu Hao (now Suvarnabhumi) and the Kra Canal. We finally got the Skytrain 30 years later and the airport opened in 2006, so that's two out of the three, even though it's taken a bit of time. The Kra Canal still gets talked about, but one suspects that's how it will remain. There were also regular stories about imminent crackdowns on corruption, dark influences,

THE RATCHADAMNOEN DAYS

gambling dens, illegal vendors and traffic jams, so the news hasn't changed that much in the past four decades.

One important difference was that there was no satellite television or Internet in Thailand in those days. With local TV being frankly pretty much of a write-off, people actually relied on the newspaper for an accurate source of news.

Day off: Bangkok Post staff visit Ayutthaya on Reporter's Day in the early 1970s. At left is the late reporter Yuwadee Thanyasiri. The author is in a check shirt standing next to Oran Chongkulstidchai, Keysanee Chumgvanich, and Sayant Pornnantharat.

The newspaper was a much smaller operation then and you knew just about everybody, from the editor-in-chief, to the paste-up men, from the social editor to the printers and packing ladies. The editorial department was particularly cramped, which actually made it great fun. Whenever there were any personal conflicts, everyone immediately knew about it. However, considering the cosmopolitan nature of the staff, we all got along pretty well. It felt almost like a family business. We even went on excursions together on Reporter's Day, one of the few days of the year we didn't publish the *Post*. It resembled a large family outing. Sadly that tradition has long gone.

I began with a brief stint as a proofreader, which proved to be a very insightful and necessary introduction to both the newspaper and Thailand. Some of the finest Thai journalists began their careers in the *Post* proofreading room. I remember being very proud after reading my first page and there not being any complaints about mistakes the next day. That didn't last long though. Proofreaders tended to be scapegoats on any newspaper and were usually blamed for any errors that appeared in print, even if it was often the sub-editor's original error. I made mistakes too, plenty of them. When you are reading thousands of words in a few hours to a strict deadline, something will inevitably slip through.

Thai names are a minefield for newcomers at the paper, especially when people who share a common first name in Thai, choose to spell it in different ways in English. One reporter's copy might spell a name Vichit, while a different journalist might write it, Vijitr. One politician might like his name spelt Tavatchai, while another prefers Dhawatchai. Then you have MR, which in Thailand doesn't stand for "mister", but *mom rachawong*.

After a couple of months I graduated to sub-editor, which was good news, primarily because it involved a 1,000-baht-a-month pay increase. We sat at a traditional horseshoe-shaped desk and there was plenty of banter, especially when the Aussies, Poms and Kiwis were winding one another up.

We used typewriters, with not a computer in sight - oh, happy days. The office was certainly much noisier in those pre-computer times. Copy boys were on hand to take the edited stories to be typed and they were alerted by shouts of "copy!" from the chief sub-editor and senior copy editors when a story was deemed ready to go. One Thai reporter told me that when he was first at the paper, he was under the impression that the sub-editors were an unusually thirsty lot because he thought they kept shouting "coffee!".

Speaking of sustenance, we mainly ate at the newsdesk with noodles or basic rice dishes costing just a few baht being brought up from a stall out on the street. Occasionally, if I had time (and money), I would slip out to the *Sorn Daeng* (Red Arrow) restaurant, uniquely located facing the Democracy Monument. It was a lovely spot and the food was excellent, although somewhat pricey for my salary. The only danger was that you might run into colleagues who had finished work for the day and were settling in for an extended evening session. It could be hard to get away, especially once the beer started flowing. It was usually "safer" and much cheaper to eat at the newsdesk.

Amongst my early tasks at the newspaper as "late sub" was to give the paper a final check as it came off the press, just to ensure there was nothing upside down or inside out. The thrill of watching the press - a modern (for 1969) Goss Community offset - crank into action was tinged by a slight nervousness of possibly missing some ghastly error. It would be about 2 a.m. and with a fresh copy of the paper in hand I would dash across Ratchadamnoen Avenue to catch the white No. 2 bus home, which in those days was on Sukhumvit Soi 1, adjacent to Khlong Saen Saeb.

There was a certain excitement in knowing you held the latest news in your hand. Unfortunately, the ink on those newly printed papers came off rather too easily and I often arrived home looking like someone out of the Black and White Minstrels show. Occasionally I would drop in at the late-night Thai Yonok coffee shop on Ploenchit Road and hand out free copies of the next day's paper to anyone who was still sober enough to read it.

A big plus in being late sub was that while waiting for the paper to print, I got to chat with the ladies who collected the papers as they came off the press and prepared them for the motorcycle boys to deliver. The ladies, some of them mums, daughters and grannies from the same family, were always great fun and loved chatting to this strange *farang*, as they did to my colleagues. There were lots of jokes about marrying somebody's daughter and there was plenty of laughter every night, quite often at my expense, but it was *sanuk*.

The *Bangkok Post* had just been taken over by the Canadian press baron, Lord Thomson of Fleet. It was his first acquisition of a publication in Asia and a big boost for the paper, giving it financial security. Not long after, Michael Gorman arrived from

England and was to run the company successfully until 1983, by which time the *Post* had expanded considerably.

Lord Thomson himself came out to Thailand and I remember him giving a stirring speech while standing on a chair in the newsroom, even though he was in his late seventies at the time and looking a bit frail. Apart from the reporters, most of the Thai staff wouldn't have understood much of what he was saying, but they could see the passion and gave him a hearty reception. It was certainly quite a sight observing a man of Lord Thomson's international stature addressing the "motley crew" in our modest office.

Lord Thomson's granddaughter, Sherry Brydson and her partner, came out to work with us in the editorial department and were a very pleasant couple, mixing in with everyone. Sherry was also noted amongst *Post* staff for making an excellent eggnog. She loved Thai food and upon returning to Canada opened the highly acclaimed Bangkok Garden restaurant in Toronto. An active philanthropist, Sherry was in 2013 named the richest woman in Canada, her net worth estimated at US$6.5 billion.

I had only been working at the newspaper for six weeks when I experienced my inaugural Christmas in Thailand. It was the first time in my life that I had not celebrated the festive season at home with my parents. I didn't really know what to expect as December 25 is just another working day in Thailand. On my way to the office on Christmas Eve, there was no hint of any festivities. It was the usual traffic jams, perspiring policemen, samlors stalling at traffic lights and weary-looking passengers sweating it out, crammed into clapped-out buses - hardly conducive to the Christmas spirit. I suspected it was going to be just another working day.

However, one step inside the office told a different story. With the strains of *Santa Claus is Coming to Town* echoing through the building, a young Thai man from the advertising department, with a distinct glow about him and wearing a rumpled paper hat, greeted me with "Melly Chrissamass Mister Loger." Now this looked more promising.

THE RATCHADAMNOEN DAYS

I proceeded upstairs to the editorial department. In hindsight it might have been prudent to promptly turn around. The paste-up men, never ones to miss out on a party, were already in full swing, aided by a generous supply of Mekhong whiskey and other lethal-looking concoctions.

Unfortunately, and probably just as well, I couldn't join in the drinking as I was recovering from a bout of hepatitis (see The Awkward English Patient). However, I could still enjoy the atmosphere, with vague recollections of someone dancing with a typewriter.

The four festive seasons I spent at Ratchadamnoen were all quite lively. On one memorable occasion in 1972, with editor Graeme Stanton and his wife Heather, we all ended up performing the *ramwong* around the newsdesk, blowing noisemakers and singing *Jingle Bells*, or rather *Jinger Ben*. Just another day at the office.

When it came to New Year, the paste-up guys really knew how to party, as long as there were adequate supplies of Mekhong, or even better, the odd bottle of Scotch. Christmas was treated like a training session to ensure they were in good drinking shape for the New Year celebrations. Amidst all the distractions, somehow we managed to put out a newspaper.

Those early days at the *Post* were most enjoyable for me - I actually looked forward to going to work. For a couple of years I was a general dogsbody, working on nearly every section of the editorial department - news, features, business, sport and supplements. I enjoyed working on the news section most of all, partly because there was always something happening.

Admittedly there was the occasional dark side to the job. It took me a while to get used to public executions, which were still being carried out in some provinces. There were grotesque scenes of the condemned, sometimes three or four convicts, being given a last meal in a big field watched by thousands of people, including schoolchildren who had bizarrely been given the day off. The culprits, usually convicted of murder or rape, were then placed behind a makeshift screen and shot. Thankfully this practice was discontinued in the early 1970s, although it briefly resurfaced in the late 70s.

Another grim case was the Cathay Pacific Airways plane on a flight from Bangkok to Hong Kong, which blew up over Vietnam in June 1972, killing all 81 souls on board. It was a complex case, but during the next six months a mountain of evidence implicated a Thai police lieutenant called Somchai Chaiyasut, who it was claimed blew up his girlfriend and seven year-old daughter in an almost unbelievable insurance scam. The judge apparently also found it unbelievable and delivered a 'not guilty' verdict, amidst gasps of disbelief from onlookers. The acquitted policeman picked up several million baht in insurance claims, but died of cancer not long after.

Playing a key role in the production of the newspaper were the aforementioned Thai paste-up men, with whom we worked closely on page layouts. At the Ratchadamnoen office they were also physically close, operating adjacent to the newsdesk.

The paste-up men were all characters in their own way and I became good friends with most of them. But there were two in particular I will always remember - Louie and Chalie. Louie was a lovely fellow who came from the South. He had a beautiful voice and would serenade the newsdesk all night with Thai ballads. Now, that's something you wouldn't experience at the *Washington Post*. He was also very polite and didn't complain when I messed up a layout, creating more work for him. On one occasion, when I was getting flustered near deadline, he asked me what to do with my layout, which resembled a dog's dinner. I responded in exasperated fashion *"arai gor dai"* (roughly "do what you want"). He was quite amused by this unexpected delegation of duty, and in the following years, whenever there was a problem with the layout he would look at me with a big grin and ask *"arai gor dai?"* and sort it out himself.

Chalie came from Borabue, a district of Maha Sarakham, and had a strong northeastern accent. Every now and again he would suddenly burst forth into song in his rich *Isan* lilt with wistful refrains about how much he missed his home - something like "I left my heart in Borabue". He also performed a great *Isan* version of the big hit *Kung Fu Fighting*, although he didn't know the English lyrics and sang whatever came into his head. His version of *Guantanamera* came out as "want an American".

One day there was a sudden commotion amongst the paste-up men - Chalie had won the 20,000 baht prize in the national lottery. On a meagre wage, he had never seen such a grand sum of money before. But what was he to do with it? Ultimately he came to the only possible solution - spend the whole lot, quickly.

So off he went with a few friends for a lively weekend in Pattaya. For the first time in his life Chalie found himself wandering around a first-class hotel, although he was not staying there. He had often dreamed of dining in a sumptuous hotel and this was his big opportunity. Mind you, he was already learning that 20,000 baht didn't travel very far, so he decided to be careful about how much he spent on his meal.

He walked into the hotel restaurant and was very impressed by the long table with never-ending plates of meat, vegetable and fancy desserts. He would have loved to have a taste of all the exotic dishes, but knowing that funds were low decided to play it safe and stick to the cheapest-looking food. So he piled his plate high with rice and crowned it with a sorry-looking fried egg. Not exactly a gourmet meal, but at least it wouldn't cost too much.

As you will have guessed, Chalie had never experienced a hotel buffet before and was not aware that the tariff was the same whether you had one plate of rice or 20 plates of the finest meat or desserts. By the time one of his mates told him about this, Chalie was full up with rice and egg and couldn't face any of the fancy stuff. So he ended up paying the same as everyone else and all he had was a measly fried egg on rice.

While the *Post* was at Ratchadamnoen there was a considerable turnover of foreign sub-editors, some very competent, others less so. There was one Australian veteran who was a really nice guy and possessed a wealth of information about Asia. Unfortunately he hit the amber liquid a little too often and it affected his work. One afternoon he came into the office considerably the worse for wear. To be more accurate, he was plastered. It was clear that he wasn't going to be of any use to us that day but, as a joke, the chief sub-editor gave him the Yokohama Raw Silk Market daily report to edit. Any other sub would have thrown it straight into the waste bin, as it was something we never ran in the paper and was just a mass of incomprehensible figures. But the inebriated Aussie gamely battled away at the copy for 20 minutes before saying in all seriousness: "Sorry mate, I'm having a bit of a problem writing the headline for this."

Then there was an Egyptian who liked to call himself "The Colonel". He was in his thirties, intelligent, eccentric, full of bluster and could be quite intimidating if you didn't know him. His desk was near the door of the office and he had a habit of bellowing at any newcomer or visitor passing through, "Who are you? What! Speak up! Don't you know who I am?" They often assumed he was the editor or at least someone very important. As a colleague commented years later: "John Cleese could have done a perfect imitation."

Work was never boring when "The Colonel" was around. He had a short fuse and this was ignited one day in spectacular fashion. He had just started work on the afternoon shift when something really upset him. He proceeded to furiously grab all the hard news agency stories the copy taster had carefully compiled for him from the teleprinters and marched around the newsdesk throwing the copy all over the place until there was nothing left. It took us 20 minutes scrambling about on the floor to rescue the next day's news. Five minutes later he was back working, barking orders as if nothing had happened.

Someone who was very helpful to me in the early days was chief sub-editor Bob Boys, from Adelaide. He quite regularly - and rightly - rejected the headlines I wrote and along with fellow chief-sub Peter Finucane from Bath in England, maintained a high standard of journalism. It was through Bob that I first became aware of the Thai tradition of a different colour for each day of the week. One day I commented on his bright orange shirt and he informed me it was his "Thursday shirt" and that he always tried to wear the colour to match the day. So it was a red shirt on Sunday, yellow on Monday, green on Wednesday. However, he drew the line at pink on Tuesday. While this might seem a little eccentric, it meant that he never had a problem on deciding which shirt to wear, and all his shirts got an equal airing. Sadly, in recent times we have experienced the virtual hijacking of colours by certain political groups.

I loved watching the teleprinters clattering into action when big news was breaking, although admittedly I was often looking for football results from England. I was working that extraordinary day in September 1970, when Palestinians hijacked four international jetliners in the space of a few hours. On the newsdesk we couldn't believe it as bulletin after bulletin came in reporting the hijackings, three of which were successful. The front page was constantly being updated.

Two years later the Palestinian conflict came much closer to home in dramatic fashion.

It was arguably the biggest story while we were still at Ratchadamnoen. In December 1972, four Black September guerrillas took over the Israel embassy on Soi Langsuan and threatened to kill all the hostages. It was a very tense situation, which ended amazingly without any bloodshed thanks to some classic Thai-style diplomacy by Deputy Foreign Minister Chatichai Choonhavan (later to become prime minister) and Air Chief Marshal Dawee Chullasapya. It was diplomacy at its most pragmatic and later became known as "curry and whisky diplomacy".

No one took much notice when four men stepped out of a taxi near the embassy on December 28. But suddenly everything transformed as the quartet of guerrillas, armed with assault rifles, seized six staffers and trussed them up. Their demands were simple, but chilling - free 36 Palestinian prisoners in the Middle East, or the hostages would be executed.

Despite the tension, the two ministers rose to the occasion. Langsuan was just a narrow tree-lined *soi* in those days and the ministers shuttled between the embassy and the emergency police headquarters set up on the *soi*. They explained to the guerrillas that the Thai people were celebrating the investiture of Crown Prince Maha Vajiralongkorn and it was most upsetting to have an incident like this on such an important day.

They followed it up by feeding the guerrillas plates of chicken curry, washed down by a few glasses of wine and whisky - anything to relax the four armed men. Showing a lot of patience, ACM Dawee and Major-General Chatichai successfully defused the situation and persuaded the Palestinians to abandon the raid and fly to Egypt with them the following morning. A few days later the ministers were photographed perched on camels in front of the Pyramids, mission accomplished. Most importantly, no one got hurt.

It happened to be my day off, but curiosity got the better of me. I found myself squashed against the railings opposite the Israeli Embassy all night with scores of other journalists and armed soldiers watching the drama unfold. I was hoping to contribute an element of colour to the *Post* coverage, but that was rather wishful thinking. It was such a crush that, apart from seeing ACM Dawee and Maj-Gen Chatichai entering the besieged embassy and observing Colonel Narong Kittikachorn pacing about looking very important, I didn't really know what was going on. There were no mobile phones in those days, so I battled my way into a nearby Japanese restaurant to call the newsdesk. All I could tell them was that I didn't really know what was happening and I was getting hungry - hardly a Pulitzer Prize performance.

In fact, there was far more drama at the *Bangkok Post* newsdesk later that night, which staffers Peter Finucane and John McBeth will not forget.

At the height of the stand-off at about 4 a.m., Peter casually telephoned the Israeli Embassy "just to see what would happen". It was a long shot, but you never know. For 10 seconds, as he expected, there was no answer. Then, much to his surprise, someone picked up the receiver. Peter handed the phone to John.

"Hello, is this the Israeli Embassy?" John asked, a little sceptically.

"No, this is the Palestinian Embassy," came the response.

"Who am I speaking to?" he asked.

"This is Black September," came the reply.

It later transpired that before their assault on the embassy, the guerrillas had spent a few days tasting the delights of Pattaya, which may have softened them up just a little.

John relates in detail his conversation with what he called a "calm, quietly-spoken Arab" in his excellent book, *Reporter*.

Mission Accomplished: ACM Dawee Chullasapya and Maj-Gen Chatichai Choonhavan aboard camels in Egypt after resolving a Black September attack on the Israeli embassy in Bangkok in 1972. - Bangkok Post photo

Unlike myself, John was a trained reporter and a very good one at that, but there was one story he got that I was glad I didn't. After we finished our regular shift around midnight, sometimes John and I headed for the Thermae coffee shop on the corner of Sukhumvit Soi 13 for a few late night beers. One night in April 1971, we left the Thermae in the early hours after a good session. John turned right to head for his hotel on Soi 2, while I went straight across the road to my home on Soi 8. I was the lucky one.

While undressing in his room, John heard screams and then saw flames coming from the Imperial Hotel on the adjacent Soi Ruam Rudee just across the railway tracks. John dashed around to the hotel and his harrowing eyewitness reports of the tragic fire, which claimed at least 24 lives, filled up half the *Bangkok Post* news pages for the next few days. It was an amazing effort and a superb piece of journalism, especially considering he hadn't had a wink of sleep and must have been absolutely exhausted. Just a few *sois* away, I had slept through the whole thing. No wonder John went on to enjoy a successful career with *Asiaweek* and then the *Far Eastern Economic Review*.

A quite bizarre incident, involving the misuse of a helicopter, occurred in April 1973, in what became known as the Thung Yai Affair. A military helicopter on its way back to Bangkok from a "secret mission" in the Kanchanaburi area, crashed in Nakhon Pathom, killing six high-ranking officials on board. It transpired that the cause of the accident was that the aircraft was overloaded - stuffed full of carcasses of deer and other wild animals. I remember subbing the lead story written by one of the talented young Thai reporters, Anuraj Manibhandu, who had recently joined the *Post*. In her well compiled report she described the copter as having been "smashed to smithereens", a wonderfully evocative description and an expression I had not heard for some years.

Despite attempts at a cover-up, the "secret mission" began to bear a suspicious resemblance to a hunting party to Thung Yai, a supposedly protected forest reserve. The party included businessmen, military officers and an actress, who, fortunately for her, had decided to return by road.

THE RATCHADAMNOEN DAYS

The story was splashed all over the front pages of the *Bangkok Post* and the Thai-language press. It turned out the secret mission was so secret that none of those taking part could remember its objective. Coincidentally, the survivors seemed to be suffering from collective amnesia. The actress, however, *did* remember she had been sent there to scout a location for her next movie, an account which raised a few eyebrows. The case even went to court with 10 people, mostly uniformed types, facing charges of misusing military transport and illegal hunting. At least justice would be done. Well, not quite.

It will probably come as no surprise that only one defendant was found guilty and he happened to be the village headman who acted as a guide for the visitors from Bangkok - not exactly a big fish. The remaining members of the hunting party were all acquitted due to "lack of evidence", a verdict which I recall prompted much mirth in the *Bangkok Post* newsroom. Not even an inactive post was dished out.

Later that year, however, the military government fell following the mass student protests in October (see The Day 100,000 Students Marched). Some believe the blatant injustice of the Thung Yai Affair may have played a small part in getting the ball rolling.

It was while we were at the Ratchadamnoen office, on November 17, 1971, that I experienced my first Thai coup. But it wasn't at all how I imagined this sort of event would unfold; in fact, it was quite disappointing in a strange sort of way. Prime Minister Field Marshal Thanom Kittikachorn effectively staged a coup against himself.

That's when I realized I would never understand Thai politics. There were no tanks on the streets - well, there might have been, but I didn't see any. There wasn't even any fighting, not that I wished for that.

What prompted this unusual manoeuvre is too complex to go into. The prime minister was under pressure from all sides, as the people pushed for a more open style of democracy. Thanom's answer was to overthrow his own government, dissolve

63

parliament, ban political parties and reject the Constitution. Not exactly a democratic move.

But he couldn't keep the lid on forever and within two years he was to pay for his stubbornness in no uncertain manner.

8. EVENTFUL TIMES AT U-CHULIANG

Coups, strikes and a gifted character called Uncle Ayu

As the *Bangkok Post* expanded, new premises became an urgent need. The necessary move came in mid 1973 when we relocated from Ratchadamnoen to the U-Chuliang Building on Rama IV Road, a pleasant location overlooking Lumpini Park. When I had joined in 1969 the circulation was under 14,000; by the time we moved it had reached 20,000 and was steadily increasing. These figures might seem ludicrously small, but at that time they were quite substantial for a country with few English speakers.

During the next 19 years at this location, the *Post* experienced two mini-revolutions (1973, 1992), three successful coups (1976, 1977, 1991) and three unsuccessful coups (1977, 1981, 1985), so life was not exactly boring in the newspaper business. The news content was certainly a bit different to that of my local newspaper in Reading.

We had only been at the U-Chuliang for a few months before the big upheaval of October 14, 1973. Ironically, if we had remained at our old office, we would have been in the thick of it, as Ratchadamnoen Avenue was where much of the action took place. Mind you, we probably could not have produced a paper from that location, so maybe it was just as well we had moved. (I have written about October 14 and the subsequent October 6 bloodbath in the following chapter "The Day 100,000 Students Marched".)

Life at the U-Chuliang Building had its lively moments. One morning I arrived to find a fleet of fire engines parked outside the building and water cascading down the stairs. There had been a fire on the ninth floor, but because of low water pressure most of the water from the fire engines only reached the third floor, where the *Post* was located. The office was awash and it felt quite bizarre to slosh my way through mini-waterfalls in the empty workplace to my desk in order to retrieve some soggy pencils and pens. The editorial department had to put the newspaper out from a small non-air-conditioned room out the back, attached to the car park. It wasn't much fun because of the heat. Still, the paper got printed, which was the important thing.

Another unexpected situation we experienced right on our doorstep came in 1975, when the girls at the textile firm Standard Garments, on the ground floor, went on strike - or to use the official Thai term *"sa-trike"*. Between 1974 and 76 hardly a week went by without some sort of labour unrest in Bangkok. Workers were testing out the new-found "freedom" that is supposed to accompany democracy and discovering it didn't come easily.

Too close for comfort: The strike by workers at neighbouring Standard Garments in 1975 also proved quite hazardous for Bangkok Post staff. - Bangkok Post photo

Initially the Standard Garments strike was something of a novelty and it proved quite entertaining watching the girls marching around with their banners and singing songs. But after a few days things began to get a bit nasty, with gun-toting thugs running around the car park at night attempting to disrupt the strikers with petrol bombs and scare tactics.

EVENTFUL TIMES AT U-CHULIANG

It was quite uncomfortable for those of us on night duty at the newsdesk, as through the windows we could see the gunmen running around in the adjacent car park on the same third-floor level. Even more scary, with no curtains or blinds on the windows, the gunmen had a clear view of us. It was not exactly ideal working conditions, putting out the paper with sporadic explosions and the sounds of bullets ricocheting off the building.

One evening as the situation deteriorated, chief sub-editor Peter Finucane sat at the horseshoe-shaped desk with his back to where the gunmen were running around. He admitted to feeling "a bit of a target", but manfully stuck to his task. His confidence was not helped when Mantana, one of the Thai lady compositors, announced with disarming frankness: "I hope they don't shoot Peter because it will make us late going home."

Fortunately they didn't shoot Peter and the strike ended the next day following a big scrap with the police. When I looked out of the window, the street below was littered with numerous abandoned sandals and flip-flops left by the fleeing workers.

There was widespread lawlessness at the time and students from rival technical colleges regularly took to the streets in armed battle. It turned into tragedy when popular *Post* photographer Kuang was shot dead while covering a street battle, caught in the crossfire between two idiotic school gangs. Paisal Sricharatchanya was news editor at the time and was extremely distressed when he took the call about Kuang. It was a very emotional moment and the whole office went silent - we were all in a state of shock. Kuang was a much-loved photographer from the Ratchadamnoen days and his senseless death stunned everyone at the newspaper.

Paisal himself had been hospitalized after being badly beaten by policemen in the bloody Plabachai riots in Chinatown in 1974. The police claimed they had mistaken Paisal for a rioter, but he didn't exactly look like a hoodlum. He was simply risking his neck trying to get an accurate story for the newspaper. Later that night, John McBeth and I visited Paisal at the Bangkok Nursing Home just to check how he was, but he was fast asleep under heavy sedation as he had taken quite a beating. If he had woken up, he would have wanted to know why we were not at the office working.

There was another shocking incident in March 1974 when Claudia Ross, an American investigative reporter for the *Bangkok Post*, was stabbed to death in the bedroom of her Bangkok house. Claudia was an effervescent character and quite fearless, writing about several sensitive subjects. Her murder prompted all sorts of theories, especially as she had just published a long article about a controversial American religious sect which had begun operating in Thailand. Conspiracy theories were rife, especially as her typewriter was found on the house lawn, which some viewed as symbolic. She was also said to be close to Thai student activists who were agitating for reform. The case was never resolved; it may even have been a simple house robbery that went horribly wrong.

Another sad time was the death of Australian NBC newsman Neil Davis and his American soundman Bill Latch in a botched coup attempt in 1985. I had met Neil socially quite a few times and he was a lovely, laid-back, unpretentious character, with a wry smile and acute sense of humour. A true professional, Neil had been to all the hotspots in recent years, including incredibly dangerous work in Cambodia and Vietnam, but he was reluctant to talk about it. The documentary *Frontline*, about his coverage of the Vietnam War, is a good insight into Neil's philosophy on life. Nicknamed "The Fox" by his close friends, he had seemed indestructible. This sadly was not to be the case, but his spirit has remained close to everyone who knew him. One of his best friends was John McBeth, who provides a moving account of that terrible September day in his book *Reporter*.

During the mid 1970s I spent several years as features editor, succeeding Tony Waltham who had become deputy editor of our sister paper the *Bangkok World*. I really enjoyed this period, partly because it took me off the night shift, which meant I actually had a few evenings free and even rediscovered mornings.

An added bonus was that I also got to work with some extremely interesting people. It was at this time Sanitsuda Ekachai and Saowarop Panyacheewin joined our team fresh from

EVENTFUL TIMES AT U-CHULIANG

university. They were both very cheerful and talented reporters and gave me a lot of insight into aspects of Thailand of which I had been woefully ignorant. Saowarop went on to enjoy a spell with the BBC in London, while Sanitsuda developed into one of Thailand's most respected columnists. Her weekly *Bangkok Post* column is widely read in the kingdom and she should be commended for her bravery in tackling sensitive topics with insight and perception.

Also working with me at that time was Normita Thongtham well-known for her popular gardening column. It was Normita who taught me how to really appreciate plants, although her efforts to teach me Tagalog were less successful.

There was one particular week I will never forget in 1981, just before the *Post* was computerized.

On March 28 a group of Indonesian terrorists had hijacked a Garuda Airlines DC-9 plane to Bangkok with 57 passengers on board. For the next two days there was a tense standoff at Don Mueang airport. There were half a dozen hijackers and they clearly meant business.

On March 31, the newspaper received a tip-off that commandos would storm the plane around midnight. We were on full alert. But nothing happened. By 1 a.m. there was still no news and everyone began to drift off home. Unfortunately, I happened to be the chief-sub that night - that's the guy whose responsibilities include the front page - and had to stay on to wrap things up with the latest report on the situation.

I remember our sole remaining reporter, Vivat Prateepchaikul, saying goodnight about 2.30 a.m., remarking that it must have been a false alarm. Shortly after, the newsdesk telephone rang. It was from our man at the airport. It was a bit jumbled, but from what I understood the raid had started with quite a bit of shooting. Most of the hijackers were killed. I sprinted along the corridor and down the stairs at the U-Chuliang. Fortunately I caught Vivat stepping out of the lift and hauled him back to the newsdesk where he took over the phone. It was 2.45 a.m. and we were already way past our normal deadline of 1 a.m., but we had to change the front page.

Vivat did an admirable job dictating to me what our reporter at the airport knew, and I typed the story. It was totally disjointed, but by now the main concern was just getting the paper printed, mistakes and all. It's no good having a great story if you can't deliver it.

It was really frantic and my head was spinning. Suddenly, another sub-editor, M Hardy from Burma, who had been monitoring the teleprinters said: "Rog, you ought to look at this." I snapped at him not to bother me as we were way beyond deadline.

But Hardy persisted. "You really should see this," he said.

"What is it?" I barked impatiently. "It had better be important."

Hardy blurted out: "President Reagan has been shot!"

I couldn't believe it. "You're kidding me". Unfortunately he wasn't - and it was approaching 3 a.m..

We didn't know whether or not the shooting in Washington had been fatal. Whatever, it was a huge story. So, way after deadline we still kept the commandos as the lead story, but threw out the rest of the front page to accommodate the breaking news about Reagan.

It was near-dawn when I finally got home and my brain was totally scrambled.

Later that day I was woken up by a phone call from one of the senior editors. I immediately thought I was in deep trouble for what must have been the *Bangkok Post's* latest-ever print time. Instead the editor said: "There's been a coup in Bangkok. Can you come in?"

It was April 1, and I initially thought it was a joke. But it wasn't. And that was the start of what became known as the April Fool's Coup, which went on for several days and created a very tense situation, particularly in Bangkok. What a week!

Someone else not too pleased with the Reagan shooting was United Press International (UPI) bureau chief Sylvana Foa. She had been up all night working on the storming of the hijacked plane, which was almost a guaranteed front page story for the American newspapers - and the rest of the world. Unfortunately,

EVENTFUL TIMES AT U-CHULIANG

the Reagan shooting meant that Sylvana's report was immediately relegated to the inside pages.

As a postscript to those events, about a month later a British media magazine, the *UK Press Gazette*, carried a reproduction of the *Bangkok Post* front pages for that week, along with a caption that said something on the lines of "if you're looking for a job with a bit of excitement, this could be the place to go."

The April Fool's Coup, in which 'Young Turks' tried to overthrow Prime Minister Prem Tinsulanonda, was the most serious I had experienced. The military rebels were in control of Bangkok for a couple of days and we were under strict censorship. Rumours were rife. On a couple of occasions there were blank spaces where there should have been stories. However the military censors were not very adept at "reading between the lines" and the *Post* was able to give readers considerable insight into what was going on with careful juxtaposition of photographs, reports and cryptic wording of certain stories and captions. Satellite television and cell phones had yet to arrive in Thailand, so the paper was a hugely important source of news, particularly for expatriates.

It was shortly after the April Fool's Coup in 1981 that the *Post's* editorial department became computerized. We didn't have the most auspicious start. A few weeks after the system was installed, a direct hit by lightning blew the whole lot up. Nothing worked. So for three days we had to put the paper out with the leftovers of the old machinery, bits of which were literally held together by string.

The new technology also briefly created a problem of a more entertaining nature. For a few weeks, one of the international news agencies that the *Post* subscribes to had trouble with the letter "m" in its computer. Due to some high-tech malfunction the "m" came out as an "o". It led to some interesting news stories about bombs. Instead of "bomb", we had "boob". It was a nightmare for the proofreaders, who performed remarkably well to pick up most of the errors, but a few slipped through. Thus we had stories about "boob disposal units", a number of "boob alerts" and one item from Ireland in which "customers were recovering after a large boob exploded in a pub."

Of course, we blamed the "boob" on the computer. Previously, when mistakes appeared in print, we called them "gremlins", which was often a cover-up for human error, meaning someone was either incompetent or inebriated - the sub editor, the paste-up man, or probably both.

Despite all the modern-day technology, or perhaps because of it, mistakes will continue to slip into print, and long may they do so. After all, life would be boring without cock-ups. As the old saying goes: "Doctors bury their mistakes. Lawyers hang theirs. And journalists put theirs on the front page."

The emergence of emails sparked a significant increase in contributions to the Letters to the Editor column, known as *PostBag*. It was much easier and quicker to knock out an email compared to sitting down and writing or typing a letter, which then had to be posted.

It is said that the number of letters written to the editor are inversely proportional to the importance of the topic. That's the great part about it - people get excited or incensed over the most absurd things. Over the years, the *Post* has received passionate letters about overpriced doughnuts, fake crocodile shoes, mad cows, stuffed squirrels, grilled grasshoppers, topless trans-sexuals, spoiled rich brats (plenty of those), the first hearing of *Jingle Bells* and other matters of great import. And long may it remain that way.

In the early 1990s a reader who signed herself Edith Clampton (Mrs.) became a regular contributor to the letters section. She was the "Queen of Tittle Tattle", suffering infuriating problems with such things as electric toothbrushes and portable potties. She also took a firm stance on elephant dung. Edith's letters were so gripping, she even developed something of a fan club as readers eagerly awaited the next installment of her tribulations in Thailand, especially when she encountered awful "scruffy people". Invariably her letters also featured her trusted servants, the maid "Khun Hazel" and "Khun Parker", the driver. There was even a book published in 1996 of her collective correspondence and readers' responses.

Alas, in the mid 1990s Edith suddenly disappeared and the letters section has never been quite the same. There has been a lot of speculation over the identity of Edith. All I can say is that it wasn't me. I have met Edith on a couple of occasions, but that's as much as I will divulge. It's more fun to leave it in the realms of a mystery, which is just the way Edith would have liked it.

During the U-Chuliang days, one of the most popular items in the paper was the daily *Column Nine*, introduced by Editor Ian Fawcett, an experienced Australian who had worked in Fleet Street. Its name was derived from appearing in the ninth column on the front page, but the name stuck even when the paper's format changed to eight columns or less. Every day it featured four or five quirky stories, tightly edited down into highly amusing paragraphs. *Column Nine* was an instant success and quickly became something of an institution, providing a much-needed antidote to the often depressing news on the front page. Before long it had earned the reputation of being the first thing people read when they got the newspaper, even beating the comics. It became an important part of the *Post's* identity.

It was also hard work and because of his other duties, Fawcett quickly passed it on to the capable hands of sub-editors, John Sinclair from Scotland and Australian Kevin Meade. You needed a dry sense of humour to write the column, and the two subs did a masterful job. Other subs occasionally helped out, including myself, but John and Kevin were the backbone in the early days. After they moved on, Englishmen David Pratt and John Hayes kept up the good work.

Alas, *Column Nine* became a classic casualty of war, courtesy of a certain Saddam Hussein. After the invasion of Kuwait in 1990, the defenceless column's days were numbered. Sure enough, it was ousted primarily because the front page was swamped by air strikes, rumbling tanks and rambling rhetoric. The column was briefly relegated to an inside page, but suffered a similar fate there. Regrettably it eventually expired, disappearing into the sunset. About a decade later it made a reappearance on the inside pages with Aussie sub-editor Robert Johns gallantly at the helm, but this proved fairly short-lived. To work properly, it needed to be on the front page.

One of the most experienced and talented sub-editors I worked with was the aforementioned Sinclair, a proud Scot who happened to be allergic to Christmas. At the very first sound of *Jingle Bells* he would turn ashen-faced.

His idea of purgatory was being forced to attend the office party and wear a funny paper hat. Even worse was being given a noise-maker. Back then all the staff were given Christmas Day off, but someone was needed in the office to monitor the teleprinters. John would readily volunteer for this task. His reasoning? In his own words: "Well, at least that fills up eight of the ghastly 24 hours."

Once Christmas was over, there would be a spring in his step, for in a few days' time it would be Hogmanay, the real time to celebrate.

For much of my time at the *Bangkok Post*, Theh Chongkhadikij held a senior role, and was editor or editor-in-chief for many years. A veteran journalist, Theh was best-known for his political columns, but he also appreciated entertainment. During my time as features editor he would often come over to the desk, sit down and discuss the latest movies, books or music. He was particularly fond of music, inspired by his daughter Anchalee (Pu), who was to become a successful professional singer, and son Berm, who played the guitar and was also in charge of the *Post's* IT department. I remember Berm's band and Anchalee performing at one of the *Post's* Christmas parties in the mid 1980s.

Anchalee was particularly gifted, and the powerful title song from her first album *Nung Dieo Khon Ni (This Lonely Person)* was a huge hit in 1985. Naturally, Theh was very proud of her and on a couple of occasions I accompanied him to see Pu perform at the Montien Hotel nightclub, where she shared top billing with the talented Thongchai McIntyre, better known as "Bird", who went on to become Thailand's biggest-ever male singing star.

We were sitting listening to Pu perform one night, when political party leader General Chatichai Choonhavan and his entourage came in and sat in the next booth. Theh's journalistic instincts quickly kicked in and that was the last I saw of him that night as he spent most of the time in the adjacent booth picking up political titbits from Gen. Chatichai, who was soon to become Prime Minister. Anchalee, meanwhile, became an icon for many Thai women and went on to make a powerful Pepsi ad, sharing the stage with Tina Turner. For those not familiar with her voice, there are many clips on YouTube.

Anton Perera was another of the *Post's* remarkable characters. From Sri Lanka, he was the paper's sports editor from the early 1960s through to the late 70s. A trained economist and originally in the oil business, he was a familiar sight around Bangkok in his white shirt and tie. If you saw him outside the office, he was always clutching a pile of papers under his left arm. He was a unique sportswriter with a very distinctive style; for Anton, rain never stopped play, it was a visit by "Jupiter Pluvius". His filing system, especially in the Ratchadamnoen office, was legendary. At one stage his papers, notes, press releases and cricket paraphernalia covered five desks, but he always seemed to know where everything was. It was the Anton Filing System and God help anyone foolish enough to try and tidy things up.

Anton regarded himself as being on duty 24 hours a day and rarely seemed to get any sleep. One night in the early days I found him staring intently at the teleprinters. I asked him if there was some big breaking news, but there was no response. That's when I realized he was asleep standing up.

On another occasion, while covering a royal yachting event in Hua Hin, as he stepped from the quayside the boat was caught by a wave and Anton plunged into the sea. When they hauled him out, he was still clutching his customary pile of papers, which were now in a rather soggy state. Despite being totally drenched, he insisted on carrying on with his assignment as if nothing had happened.

Most of all, Anton was known for his incredible encyclopaedic knowledge of sport. If anyone at the office wanted to know about any historic event in the sports world, the immediate response would be "You had better ask Anton".

ROGER CRUTCHLEY

There have been many excellent writers at the *Post* over the years. When I first arrived, New York-born Harry Rolnick was always entertaining to read with his insightful movie reviews and wistful *Blue Monday* humour column, which invariably included some outrageous puns. When writing his column on a Saturday afternoon, he would be hunched over his typewriter, chuckling away as he thought of another good line. Harry enjoyed his work. After finishing the column, he would celebrate by having a few games of Scrabble with features editor Jim Kelly from Scotland. They were intensely-contested games with occasional eruptions, followed by Harry storming over to the newsdesk in search of a dictionary after his opponent had dreamed up another absurd word.

When *2001: A Space Odyssey* showed in Bangkok in 1969, Harry pointed out to the distributors that in the early showings two of the reels were in the wrong order, something that few people had noticed. Apparently, the cinema owner did not understand the opening scenes of the film, but liked the colourful descent into Jupiter, so he made that reel the beginning. Harry couldn't believe it and contacted director Stanley Kubrick in the US (not an easy task in itself). Kubrick naturally was furious and soon the cinema was showing the film in the correct order.

Harry once stunned everyone in 1967 - before my time - when he strolled into the office with Hollywood sex symbol Jayne Mansfield in tow. There was pandemonium and the whole office immediately ground to a halt - this was Tinsel Town royalty after all. The actress sadly died in a terrible car crash in Louisiana just a few months later. Harry also knew a number of famous authors; Norman Mailer and Gore Vidal were among those he brought into the humble office on Ratchadamnoen.

Some years after Harry left the *Post*, by sheer coincidence I found myself sitting next to him at the 1979 Hong Kong Film Festival, which was featuring the popular Thai film, *Kru Baan Nork* (Rural Teacher). It was one of the better Thai films of that era, but unfortunately after a while the English subtitles deteriorated badly and plunged into a world of hilarious anarchy. Harry and I could not help ourselves from collapsing with laughter as totally inappropriate subtitles appeared in supposedly serious moments on screen. We must have resembled a couple of naughty schoolboys giggling in church and were lucky not to have been thrown out.

Then there was Mom Ratchawong (MR) Ayumongkol Sonakul, one of the wittiest writers I have read and a great character. No Thai politician or bureaucrat was spared from his perceptive pen when "Uncle Ayu" was in full satirical flow. A graduate of Trinity College, Dublin, Ayu wrote for the *Nation* for much of his career before joining the *Post* in the early 1980s.

I happened to be features editor at that time and had the pleasure of editing his twice-weekly column. He sometimes had trouble meeting the deadline and quite often our messenger, who would ride his motorbike out to Ayu's house to collect the column, would have to sit and wait while the final paragraphs were being bashed out on his aging typewriter. It wasn't a major problem as Ayu's copy did not require much editing when he was at his eloquent best. In fact, it felt almost a crime to change anything he wrote. Ayu was a remarkable character and in conversation would talk in the same colourful way as he wrote, with all sorts of ideas bouncing around.

I first met Ayu in a small cocktail lounge on Gaysorn in the mid-1970s, where he was watching his colleagues from the *Nation* playing darts. He chatted away as if we were old friends and made me feel very comfortable. Ayu was a writer I had always respected and even when he was working for the *Nation,* he would send me occasional tips and notes of encouragement, simply addressed to "Crutch", which I valued highly.

I was fortunate enough to be named co-winner of the Ayumongkol Literary Award, presented at the old Siam Inter-Continental Hotel in 1994 by Her Highness Princess Vimalachatra. It was a proud moment for me, especially being the first non-Thai recipient of the award. It was all the more meaningful having met and worked with Ayu, and enjoyed his writing so much.

One person I am always asked about is Bernard Trink, who at the time of writing still contributes book reviews to the *Post*. Bernard was best known for his unique *Nite Owl* column, originally in the *Bangkok World* and then the *Post*. He truly was, and still is, a night owl.

In good company: The author sits with Her Highness Princess Vimalachatra after receiving the Ayumongkol Literary Award at the Siam Inter-Continental Hotel in 1994.

In the early 70s, for a period at the old office on Ratchadamnoen, I worked the "graveyard shift" from 10 p.m. until 6 a.m.. The only other person in the building would be Trink, who operated at night by choice, on the floor below. Because it would get a bit lonely sitting there through the night, I used to bring along a ghetto-blaster, which I would switch on after the rest of the staff had gone home usually around midnight. At the time I was very keen on the progressive rock group Yes, and one night I had a cassette of the group's *Close to the Edge* album blasting away at full volume. After all, I was the only one in the building... well, not quite. It didn't take long for Trink to appear at the entrance to the second floor to ask, politely, if I could turn the noise down. Considering he was working on the floor below, it must have been an appalling racket. We had a laugh about it and have remained friends, but Bernard never became a fan of Yes.

I have never come across a more prolific writer than Trink. There were certain days in the early 1970s when his work seemed to fill up half of the *World's* pages. He wrote voluminous copy on food and films, and had a weekly interview with assorted personalities, ranging from hotel chefs to visiting singers. But he is best known for his *Nite Owl* column, which was avidly read by friends and foes alike. It always puzzled me that some of his most vocal critics clearly read every word he wrote. Trink was also responsible for the naming of Soi Cowboy in the Sukhumvit nightlife area (see "Sukhumvit Sojourn").

I remember the sad day when the *Bangkok World* closed down on August 29, 1987. Its headline read "Goodbye and Thank You". The front page photograph in that last edition was of an understandably melancholy-looking staff assembled in front of the press at the U-Chuliang building. Among those in the picture were editor Anussorn Thavisin, who wrote an eloquent farewell article, news editor Prapaipan "Lek" Rathamarit and chief sub Songpol Kaopatumtip. Among the foreign staff was deputy editor Tony Waltham, later to become editor of the popular Post Database section, senior staffer Bob Boys and Bernard Trink, complete with his faithful pipe.

I am happy to report that after the last edition, in fine journalistic tradition, the *World's* staff all trooped off to the pub for a memorable wake.

We were to remain at U-Chuliang until 1992. Although we moved to the present location in Klong Toey more than two decades ago, I still call it the "new" building. Things started off at the Klong Toey office in splendid fashion when, on the first day, the security guard smartly sprung to attention and saluted me - mistakenly thinking I was someone important. He soon learned otherwise, and it wasn't long before I was saluting him.

9. THE DAY 100,000 STUDENTS MARCHED

Coups and curfews amidst tumultuous times

While this book focuses on the lighter side of life in Thailand, there were certain events that cannot be dismissed in a frivolous matter. Apart from the recent upheavals involving the Red Shirts in 2010, the most tumultuous time in modern Thai history is simply known as October 14.

It was 1973 and as the year went on, what had initially started as a dispute about the Constitution developed into a much larger-scale protest over just about everything. The targets were the ruling triumvirate of Prime Minister Thanom Kittikachorn, his son Colonel Narong Kittikachorn and Narong's father-in-law, Interior Minister Prapass Charasuthien, regarded as the "strongman".

A few days before the bloodshed began, an estimated 100,000 university students, immaculate in their uniforms of white shirts and dark trousers or skirts, filled up every inch of space on Ratchadamnoen Avenue as they marched peacefully. Many were holding portraits of Their Majesties the King and Queen. It was an eloquent protest and an unforgettable sight. Something had to give.

On that Sunday morning of October 14, word got through to our house that an already huge demonstration was escalating and it looked like there could be real trouble on the streets. None of this was on television or radio, which was totally censored. I raced down to Ratchadamnoen from my home on Sukhumvit Soi 8, in anticipation that something special might be happening. A few hours later I would be racing back in the opposite direction when panicking soldiers near the Royal Hotel opened fire. It did not seem a sensible idea to hang around.

It was about noon and I had been on the wide avenue a couple of hours. Thousands of curious onlookers had gone to watch the demonstrators - a mixture of students and civilians - set up roadblocks of commandeered buses across the avenue. For a while there was an almost surreal air of gaiety as demonstrators leapt onto buses waving the Thai flag and screaming anti-government slogans. Nothing like this had been seen before on the streets of Bangkok. Incongruously, there were lots of food vendors on the *sois* leading off Ratchadamnoen and they were doing a roaring trade.

Eloquent protest: The massive demonstration by mainly students on Ratchadamnoen Avenue led to the tumultuous events of October 14, 1973 and the subsequent overthrow of General Thanom Kittikachorn. - Bangkok Post photo

It was unprecedented open opposition to the military government and there was a sense of euphoria accompanying the new boldness. Then, a startling volley of gunfire soon put an end to any remaining feelings that this was a regular Sunday afternoon holiday outing. Men, women and children scattered into the lanes off Ratchadamnoen as the bullets began to fly, initially above the heads. Strangely, when the firing temporarily abated, the people came back into the main avenue, apparently to wait for the next response, before repeating the scramble for cover.

THE DAY 100,000 STUDENTS MARCHED

After one particularly scary moment I began to get that "what am I doing here?" sort of feeling. I didn't really know what was going on and that is a most uncomfortable experience in a big crowd with bullets sporadically whizzing overhead. When an unfriendly-looking helicopter appeared on the scene hovering above the Democracy Monument, the crowd started scattering in panic. It seemed an appropriate time to retreat to the safety of the *Bangkok Post*, so I headed back to the U Chuliang Building. A front-line correspondent I definitely wasn't. It proved to be a wise decision on my behalf, as the situation deteriorated badly after I left.

That afternoon was one of the rare times that the *Bangkok Post* resembled the way newspaper offices are usually depicted in Hollywood movies. The place was abuzz with people rushing to and fro, dazed reporters and photographers, many of whom had not slept for 36 hours, returning from Sanam Luang, hardly believing what they had seen. I remember one of the leaders of the student demonstrators, Thirayuth Boonmee (now a respected professor and political scientist), coming into our office looking totally exhausted and shaking his head as if he couldn't believe what was happening.

The office was noisy too, with the clatter of typewriters and editors shouting down telephones trying to make sense of it all as we battled to produce a special afternoon edition of the paper.

I was one of the contributors to that edition. It was one of the first articles I had ever written for the *Post*. I wish it had been in happier circumstances. The official death toll was 77, with nearly 900 injured, although many still believe the fatalities were considerably more. In those days the Weekend Market, now at Chatuchak, used to be located at Sanam Luang. Hence the headline on my article, which looks a little flippant in retrospect: "No Bargains at Sanam Luang".

It is impossible to forget certain photographic images from those tumultuous 48 hours. An old lady being carried by a student across Ratchadamnoen to safety; the monks on their morning alms rounds filing past tanks and burnt-out trucks and buses; demonstrators throwing themselves face down on the road to avoid the bullets; crowds scattering to escape tear gas as the tanks moved in; and the despair of those surrounding the body of a demonstrator who had been gunned down.

Then there was the police headquarters, which had been set ablaze, the thick black smoke drifting across the whole city. In fact, the police were conspicuous by their absence during and after the demonstrations. In the ensuing weeks it was left to students and other civilian volunteers to take over traffic duties at the intersections and they did a good job, too.

Someone else who will vividly remember October 14 is former *Post* colleague Norman Bottorff, who really risked his neck. A young man at the time, he had just started working for the American Broadcasting Company (ABC) and was ensconced at the Royal Hotel on Ratchadamnoen, which was in the thick of the action. He was attempting to do a sound bite, but every time he stuck his head out of the hotel window to see what was going on, the troops across the avenue opened fire at him.

A few days later he played his tape to a group of us: "There is automatic weapons fire coming from...AKAAKAAKAAKA (sound of gunfire)... there is automatic weapons fire coming... AKAAKAAKAAKA..." and so it went on. Thankfully, Norman survived unharmed and somehow eventually got his report out.

Three years later, on another dark October day, there was more bloodshed in the Sanam Luang area, this time of an even more disturbing nature. While October 14 was inspiring in many ways, I have no fond memories of October 6 at all.

After Thanom Kittikachorn's departure from Thailand following the 1973 uprising, the kingdom experienced a rocky couple of years of unstable democratic governments, featuring considerable labour and student unrest. When Thanom returned from self-exile in 1976 and was ordained as a monk, tensions soared between students and right-wing elements.

On October 6, bloody clashes erupted at the Thammasat University campus and the surrounding area of Sanam Luang. This time, in my capacity as a stringer for the *Daily Mail* newspaper in London, I approached Sanam Luang more nervously than I had three years earlier. I knew there had already

THE DAY 100,000 STUDENTS MARCHED

been some terrible violence, including mob lynchings, as well as university students being blown up by grenades.

Sanam Luang was an absolute mess, with debris from the earlier fighting all over the place. There were lots of people, some wandering around in what appeared to be a state of shock. Others, incongruously, seemed to be celebrating, feeling the students had rightly been put in their place. The only thing that was really clear was that something quite terrible had taken place.

Special warfare units eventually stormed the campus and rounded up the students, although some escaped on boats or by swimming across the Chao Phraya. A number were feared drowned.

The following paragraph comes from the story I filed for the *Daily Mail* later that day:

"Hundreds (of students) were herded onto a football field inside the campus, told to strip off their shirts and crawl on their hands and knees to a central location where they lay on the ground under guard. The women were forced to strip to their bras."

It became the lead story on Page 4 of the *Daily Mail* the following morning and covered two thirds of the page, but I derived little satisfaction from it. I've had a copy of that page hidden away in a file at home for over three decades and must have looked at it no more than a couple of times. It is not a day I particularly wish to remember.

During my time in Thailand I have witnessed nearly a dozen major political upheavals, including nine coup bids. Some of the coups had their entertaining moments, however. In the 70s and 80s, before satellite television, the first inkling most Thais had of something being afoot was when normal programming on the Thai TV channels was disrupted by the sounds of martial music and those John Philip Sousa marching songs. In those more straightforward days, the first target for any coup plotters was to take over the TV stations in order to control the dissemination of news. There was no Internet or satellite television to complicate matters. The same went for the radio stations in Bangkok.

You had to sympathise with the TV and radio newsreaders who suddenly found themselves reading out long announcements about the preservation of democracy without a hint of irony. During the failed 1985 coup, one announcer managed to escape from soldiers by going to the bathroom, picking up a mop and pail and passing himself off as a janitor.

A more poignant moment on the air occurred during the 1981 coup attempt. In the early hours of the third day, by which stage the coup had virtually crumbled, a "rebel" announcer, who had unwittingly left on the microphone, was heard to say nervously to a fellow announcer: "Oiee! Looks like we've had it." He was right.

There was a splendid moment featuring a tank in the 1981 coup attempt. The situation in Bangkok was quite tense and at one stage a tank was spotted trundling along Ratchadamnoen Nok towards a trouble spot. However, its commander must have been an ultra-conscientious motorist, because when the tank reached the intersection, it stopped at the red lights. Even though there was absolutely no traffic, the tank dutifully sat there for a couple of minutes before setting off again when the lights turned green. Maybe he was afraid of getting done by the cops.

Another rather surreal moment occurred during one of the 1980s coups when our office was at the U-Chuliang Building. As the situation was extremely volatile, everyone in the editorial department was deeply engrossed in their work, trying to establish who was trying to overthrow whom. Suddenly there was a commotion at the entrance to the office. Some people started running for the exits and a state of general pandemonium rapidly broke out. Had the coup spilled over into the *Bangkok Post's* offices?

Well, not exactly. It was far more serious than that - the office had been invaded by the newly-crowned Miss Thailand World and her considerable entourage, apparently blissfully unaware that the kingdom was in a state of crisis. Nothing stops these beauty pageant people once they get going. I would like to report that everyone just ignored the surprise visitors and carried on diligently with their work. However, at the first whiff of Miss

THE DAY 100,000 STUDENTS MARCHED

World perfume, computer terminals were abandoned, phone calls abruptly terminated and scoops scrapped, as normally sensible people scrambled to get a closer look at the beauty queen, who admittedly was quite stunning.

I confess that after studiously pretending to ignore the whole proceedings, I also succumbed and sneaked over to have a decent perusal of the lady in question. Miss Thailand had certainly staged her own coup of sorts… in our office. I hasten to add that once she departed, the journalists quickly returned to the less rewarding efforts of finding out which general was now in charge of the country.

In 1986 I had another close encounter in the office with Miss Thailand, although there wasn't a coup going on this time. Once again with a great sense of timing, the Miss Thailand entourage arrived unannounced. Unfortunately, there were no senior editors available to greet them - maybe they had been forewarned. So some sucker had to be found quickly. It turned out that I was the most senior - or more accurately the "oldest" - editor available.

Sod's Law meant I was wearing the tattiest shirt imaginable and some seriously faded jeans. Suddenly I found myself surrounded by beautiful women and overwhelmed by exotic scents. The flash lights went off as we went through the ritual of photographs, amidst embarrassed laughter. Actually, I was beginning to enjoy it.

The next morning one of the photographs appeared in the paper and I had to put up with a whole day of "Beauty and the Beast" jokes. The editor, possibly peeved that he had missed out on meeting Miss Thailand, mumbled something about me resembling an "unmade bed". Admittedly, I was not a sight of sartorial splendour.

Following the 1991 coup, I did not expect to witness tanks on Bangkok's streets ever again, except perhaps in a parade. Times had changed and the days of coups were over, or so I thought. Then in 2006, out of the blue, it happened again, this time with Thaksin Shinawatra being on the wrong end.

I will not go into the politics of all this, but it was a most unusual coup. The tanks that suddenly resurfaced didn't have anyone to shoot at and quickly became a tourist attraction, visitors and grinning tank crews posing with yellow roses. Not many tourists had been up close and personal before with real live tanks. Even the locals joined in the fun. Smiling soldiers were photographed lined up in front of tank barrels and holding rather bemused babies - a good one for the family album. Some kids even wanted to climb onto the tanks. It seemed more like Children's Day than a military coup.

In the TV studio things were a bit different in 2006. None of those awful marching songs for a start (although they did resurface in the 2014 coup). And for the first time a lady was reading out the coup announcements, which she did with some aplomb. It wasn't just any lady either, but a former Miss Asia beauty queen! Thai coups were adapting to the 21st century.

Hand in hand with coups came curfews. In the old days they weren't as lax as those witnessed in their latest manifestation in 2014. In fact, they could be a major inconvenience for the general public.

After the 1971 coup, what was called the National Executive Council issued a decree banning the sale of alcoholic drinks from 2-5 p.m. and it was also forbidden to drink in public after midnight. It was so vaguely worded that some diligent police districts interpreted the law as also meaning no eating on the streets after midnight, which was quite ridiculous in a metropolis like Bangkok. Almost inevitably, early in 1972, the *Post* carried the somewhat embarrassing front page headline "Korean tourists arrested for eating". The story went on to relate the sorry tale of these hapless visitors getting done for having a late-night roadside snack. There was quite an outcry and things relaxed a little after that.

Curfews are always a pain in the posterior, especially for night workers. That included those of us working on the night desk at the *Bangkok Post*. Most curfews thankfully lasted only a few weeks or so, but a couple times the curfew lingered on. I think it was in 1977 that a midnight to 5 a.m. curfew was strictly enforced for many months.

THE DAY 100,000 STUDENTS MARCHED

The *Post* did the practical thing and moved its print time forward so that the staff could get away by 11 p.m., just giving them enough time to get home. However, each night someone had to stay in the office to perform the copy-tasting and keep an eye on the teleprinters. We took it in turns and I recall having the job a couple of times a week. It was a little strange sitting in the large office at the U-Chuliang all by yourself and I sometimes brought along a ghetto-blaster for company. This time around it was Fleetwood Mac's *Rumours* and a couple of Neil Young albums that kept me going. It is amazing how good music sounds when you are sitting in an office all by yourself.

What was weird, though, was looking out over the normally bustling Rama IV Road just after midnight and seeing it totally deserted - absolutely no traffic. And that's how it remained for the next five hours. Occasionally an army pick-up or jeep would pass by, manned by a couple of soldiers with a machine-gun, but I don't think they ever had cause to use it.

I didn't have a car, so although the curfew ended at 5 a.m., there were no buses or taxis for at least another half-an-hour. I had to get used to arriving back home after dawn when most people were preparing for work. Eventually those of us who worked late were issued with curfew passes. But if you didn't have your own vehicle, the passes were not much use unless you fancied a very long walk in the dark as there was no public transport. A couple of weeks after receiving the passes the curfew was lifted, so it didn't really matter.

10. THE AWKWARD ENGLISH PATIENT

Dr. Ammundsen and an unscheduled visit to the Bangkok Nursing Home

When I began working on the *Post* on the night shift in late 1969, I also continued teaching at the commercial college. While I needed the extra money, I didn't want to let down the principal, Mr. Prayoon and abandon my teaching commitment. After all, he was responsible for giving me the opportunity to work in Thailand in the first place. After a while, however, the workload began to take its toll. My diary in mid-November had increasingly frequent references to being worn out and not getting enough sleep. One entry read ominously: "Feeling too tired to go out." That was a real worry, because I was never too tired to go out.

I was working from 9 a.m. to 4 p.m. at the college and roughly 5 p.m. to midnight at the *Post*. Although I was really enjoying life at the newspaper, the teaching was becoming increasingly hard work. Standing in front of a big class when you are feeling knackered is not a pleasant experience for the teacher or the students. On November 26 the lone entry in my diary was simply "feeling ill". I took a day off from both jobs, hoping that a good night's sleep might just do the trick. It didn't. I was still only 23 and had never experienced a serious illness, so I thought I could shake it off. I tried to keep working, but that only made me feel worse and realized I needed medical advice.

I asked Brett Bartos if he knew a good doctor and without hesitation he recommended Dr. Einar Ammundsen, a Danish physician who had been living in Thailand since 1946. The next day I staggered into the waiting room of the British Dispensary on Charoen Krung Road, feeling quite wretched. When the nurse called me in, I slumped in the chair and the doctor asked what was wrong. I replied that I felt ill, which was a pretty silly thing to say considering I was sitting in a doctor's surgery. He took one look at my face and announced immediately "Crutchley, you have jaundice (hepatitis)", my eyes having turned a curious shade of yellow.

THE AWKWARD ENGLISH PATIENT

He picked up the phone and promptly booked me into the Bangkok Nursing Home on Convent Road, where I was to remain for the next two weeks. Fortunately, although I had only been at the newspaper for a short while, the *Post* picked up much of the bill. This helped considerably in my recovery and, on looking back, was quite generous.

Dr. Ammundsen was ideal for someone like me. He usually had time for a joke, but more importantly knew what he was doing and always came straight to the point. I was very thankful for his swift diagnosis, as I might well have been heading for a premature date with the Grim Reaper.

For the next two decades, until he passed away at the age of 84 in Denmark in 1999, I was a regular patient of Dr. Ammundsen - not *too* regular I'm pleased to say. I always appreciated his pragmatic down-to-earth approach and dry humour. He never beat about the bush. I don't profess to have known Dr. Ammundsen that well, but after being my physician for almost 20 years, he certainly knew a lot about me.

While languishing in the hospital at the BNH, I always knew when Dr. Ammundsen was on his morning rounds because I could hear the matron greeting him in the corridor with, "golf again this morning, doctor?" He would enter the room looking immaculate in white shirt, khaki shorts, white socks, and practising his swing - which incidentally looked pretty good.

One morning he came into my room at the BNH and caught me struggling with a Thai-English dictionary. He looked aghast. "Crutchley," he said with a twinkle in his eyes, "in my day we had much more attractive dictionaries than that!" I apologized for clearly being less imaginative than him in my language studies.

On one occasion, when I had to receive treatment in another part of the hospital, the nurse made me sit in a wheelchair. On the way we ran into Dr. Ammundsen doing his rounds. He looked at me being pushed along by the nurse and snorted, "For heaven's sake, Crutchley, I know you're sick, but you're not *that* sick." In fact, I quite enjoyed being pampered by the Thai nurses and at the end was even a bit reluctant to leave the BNH, which, as the name and its colonial-style buildings suggests, felt more like a convalescent hideaway than a hospital. It was certainly more comfortable than the place I was living in at the time. Adding to the relaxed atmosphere were the sounds of gibbons (*chanee*) playing in an adjacent garden.

Footloose in Bangkok: After ending up in hospital following a football injury, the author dances with crutches during a Bangkok Post Christmas party at the Ambassador Hotel.

An indication of my recovery comes in the diary entry dated December 30, 1969, when I returned to the BNH for a blood test. "The nurse is absolutely gorgeous," I wrote. I was clearly getting better and finishing what had been a most eventful 1969 on an upbeat note.

A couple of years later, after another bout of hepatitis, I was back in the BNH again where I became the subject of mistaken identity. The Australian ambassador at the time was Mr. Tom Critchley. One morning there was a knock at the door and the minister from the adjacent Christ Church popped his head round the door. "Ambassador Critchley?" he asked, but quickly realized his mistake when he saw the ailing, longish-haired Crutch lying in the bed. I certainly didn't look like a diplomat, let alone a head of mission. "Oh, you are not the ambassador?" he asked apologetically. He had seen my name on the door and assumed it was simply a misspelling for the Australian envoy. Being a Man of God, he couldn't really turn on his heels and abandon me simply because I wasn't someone important. So we had a good chat about nothing in particular. By the time he finally left, I was even feeling a little guilty that I had only been to his church for funerals.

Over the years I periodically saw Dr. Ammundsen at his office and he always greeted me with a wry smile. On one occasion I was clutching a rather heavy-going Gunter Grass novel. He picked up the book and remarked in typically honest fashion, "I tried reading that once, but couldn't really understand it." I knew how he felt.

On a rare occasion when I saw Dr. Ammundsen outside his normal environment, it was on Soi Cowboy of all places, totally alien territory for the good doctor. It was in the late 1970s when the *soi* was very much a quiet neighbourhood bar area with little of the flashing neon lights that overwhelm the place these days. He spotted me having some noodles, came over and said "Crutchley, help me out. Do you know any decent places round here?" and explained he was with some visitors from Denmark who insisted on having a taste of the nightlife. I hopefully pointed him in the right direction and he waved a cheerful goodbye.

One topic I would have loved to have talked to him about was the mysterious disappearance of Jim Thompson, Thailand's "Silk King", in the Cameron Highlands on Easter Sunday 1967. It was still a big story in the *Post* when I arrived two years later. As well as being his physician, Dr. Ammundsen was a close friend of Thompson and was among those with him on that fateful weekend in Malaysia. I never plucked up courage to ask what he thought had happened to the American when he took that final walk down a jungle path, never to be seen again. An opportunity missed, perhaps, but in a way I'm glad I didn't ask. It would have been intrusive. I did read somewhere that the doctor didn't believe foul play was involved. Thompson's disappearance remains a mystery to this day and looks like it will never be solved.

I have Dr. Ammundsen to thank for helping cure me of two debilitating illnesses and he did the same for thousands of expats and locals during his five decades in Bangkok. Having fought in World War II (he was an active member of the Danish resistance) he was from a different era, but was someone who earned respect from everyone who came in contact with him, most of all his patients. He was someone I was proud to have met.

Apart from those early battles with hepatitis, I have been fortunate enough to have enjoyed reasonably good health in Thailand and kept away from hospitals. But there was a brief period in the 1980s when I suffered from bouts of asthma. I particularly remember one scary occasion in 1985. I was with Burmese colleague George Stevens at the old Pratunam market after finishing the night shift at the *Post*. It was about 2 a.m. and we were looking forward to a good meal and a few beers. At a nearby stall the owner was using a large *wok* to fry a particularly lethal cocktail of pungent chillies and peppers. The thick smoke was wafting across our table and I immediately began to have breathing difficulties. Within two minutes I was gasping for air and realized it was a full-scale asthma attack. Fortunately, George immediately sensed I was in distress and he quickly hailed a taxi, laying me down in the back seat. George jumped in the front and told the taxi driver to go to Bumrungrad Hospital on Soi Nana as quick as he could. I was lying in the back gasping for air, but conscious enough to remember a concerned George exclaiming: "Don't die on me!"

I vaguely recall lots of flashing lights and wailing sirens as the taxi arrived at the hospital. Then George helped me into the hospital foyer and nurses came running to our aid in a most impressive manner. I lay on the emergency bed and as the nurses gave me oxygen, my breathing gradually became easier. As I slowly recovered, I became aware that there was an enormous amount of activity in the hospital for so late at night, with nurses running around and sirens sounding. The nurse then asked the number of my room "in the hotel". I didn't understand,

THE AWKWARD ENGLISH PATIENT

explaining I had just come from Pratunam market. "You weren't in the fire?" she asked. "What fire?" I replied.

It turned out that our entrance coincided with a major fire at the Grace Hotel, which was almost opposite the hospital on Soi Nana. The hospital staff thought I was the first victim from the blaze, hence such prompt treatment. It probably saved my life - with more than a little help from George. Sadly, the fire claimed four fatalities.

I experienced one other untimely visit to hospital many years later, on the eve of the 1998 football World Cup in France. Out of the blue I was stricken with *eeh sook eeh sai*, which sounds a bit like an exotic Thai dish, but is better known as chickenpox.

Just why someone as ancient as me - I was over 50 - should succumb to an ailment normally associated with young brats, I really don't know. Penance for past sins, perhaps? I won't dwell on the malaise, suffice to say it was most unpleasant and a spotty Crutch was not a pretty sight. I was tempted to put a paper bag on my head. I felt really sick and even spent two days in Bumrungrad IC unit, which meant I missed the early World Cup matches on TV.

The nurses were charming as usual, but at times I felt like a delinquent schoolboy, regularly being reprimanded for having a quiet scratch when I thought nobody was looking. If you have chicken pox, the one thing you must not do is scratch yourself, which of course was the only thing I wanted to do the entire time I was in hospital. Talk about being an awkward patient. But at least I had learned the Thai word for chicken pox.

The ailment could not have struck at a worse time, as in my capacity as sports editor, I had been scheduled to have a one-on-one interview in London with a gentleman by the name of David Beckham. It had been set up by an international soft drinks company and I was anticipating boring everybody with tales about it for years to come. You can imagine that sinking feeling when the doctor came out with those magic words, *eeh sook eeh sai*, just a few days before I was due to fly to England. I was grounded. Being a highly contagious ailment, the only place I was travelling to was hospital.

One consolation about the whole miserable affair is what *could* have happened if these symptoms had not appeared until a few days later. It would have been even more of a disaster. I would have been on the plane, maybe feeling a bit groggy, and perhaps itchy, but determined to keep the appointment. Then what? Heaven forbid, I might have passed on the chicken pox to Beckham!

That would have been bad enough, a spotty Beckham out for the count. But even worse, half of the England team might have come down with it, bedridden by this unknown hack from Thailand. I would have been lynched. There might even have been a spotty Spice Girl.

As it was, colleague Atiya Achakulwisut took my place and she did a much better job with the interview than I would have managed. I'm also happy to say not one member of the England squad came out in spots.

11. ON (AND OFF) THE RAILS

Terrific times on Thai trains, even if they are a bit pedestrian

In 1969 and the 1970s I spent many enjoyable hours aboard Thai trains, in fact *too* many hours, as the combined words of "express" and "train" in Thailand are something of an oxymoron. If you couldn't get on the express, then there was always the "rapid", which was anything but rapid. You definitely did not want to travel "ordinary", a neat Thai understatement for going very slowly, possibly backwards. Mind you, after experiencing the trains in Pakistan and India, the railways in Thailand were quite sublime, if a bit on the pedestrian side. At least you didn't have to dive through the windows to get a seat. And they usually got you there in one piece, which is more than can be said of the buses.

Full steam ahead: Elegant steam engines were still active on Thailand's main rail routes in the early 1970s.

In England during the 1960s, the most common announcement at Reading General station began: "We regret to announce…" followed by a litany of woe from British Rail featuring late or cancelled trains. So I was always quick to defend Thailand's rail system. For a start it didn't serve stale sausage rolls. Unfortunately, in the past two decades things have deteriorated badly with frequent derailments and complaints of poor service. The State Railway of Thailand has become the butt of jokes, rather like British Rail back in the old days.

In 1969, Thailand still used steam engines, which made it more enjoyable for me, being a great fan of these old locomotives, which were kept in fine condition. You would see the drivers lovingly polishing them during extended stops. There are still a couple of the original locomotives in the sheds at Thon Buri and I am pleased to say they occasionally get a deserved outing on national holidays.

The Thai railways were also more friendly than most. On a journey in 1970, as I was about to board the Bangkok-bound train at Chiang Mai station, the engine driver leaned out of his cab and shouted: "Hey you, *farang*, where you go?" As he was supposed to be driving the train, you might have thought he should know where we were going. Still, you would be unlikely to get that sort of greeting at Waterloo or St. Pancras.

Many of my rail journeys in the early 1970s were visa runs, when I was off to Penang, Vientiane or Cambodia every couple of months. The trips were fun at first, and an essential part of the Thai cultural learning experience, but they did become bit of a chore after a while. And there was always a nagging fear that there might be something wrong with your visa application.

I spent many hours trundling southwards on the express to the Malaysian border, from where I would go to either Penang or Kuala Lumpur to renew my Thai visa. The train was incredibly slow and took ages getting out of Bangkok, as if it was reluctant to leave the big city behind. There were always plenty of delays, almost inevitable with Thailand's single-track system. All it needed was for one train to be a bit late, or a minor derailment, and it mucked up the entire network. Sometimes it took as long as six hours just to get to Hua Hin, where it required considerable self-discipline to resist the temptation to get off and settle for a few days at the seaside.

But there was a pleasant diversion awaiting at Thung Song junction in Nakhon Si Thammarat, where Clarence and I were acquainted with the stationmaster's daughter, whom we had earlier met as a student in Bangkok. She would greet us, boarding the train loaded down with southern delicacies and we would stuff ourselves all the way to Hat Yai.

On the northeastern route to Laos, the regular time of arrival at Nong Khai terminus was about dawn. You would then take a *samlor teep* (pedicab) for five baht from the railway station to the immigration post and ferry. There was no Friendship Bridge, or any other bridge for that matter, across the Mekong in those days.

The outstanding memory of those excursions to Vientiane was of magnificent sunrises reflected on the water in the early morning as, bleary-eyed, you crossed the mighty Mekong River to the Laotian embankment at Tha Dua. The river was a most impressive sight, even 2,000 kms from its mouth. But the real treat at the end of the journey was breakfast at a pavement café in Vientiane with delicious freshly-baked French bread and hot aromatic coffee. It made you forget that you hadn't slept properly for the previous 36 hours or so.

Vientiane was a quiet place and a most pleasant contrast to the frenetic activity of Bangkok. It must have been a candidate for the most laid-back capital city in the world … and probably still is. The first thing of note was the welcome lack of cars. Just as it is now, the city was dominated by its own "Arc de Triomphe", known locally as *Patuxai*, the Victory Gate. It was jokingly called the "vertical runway" since the cement used in its construction was originally destined to build the airport and came from American funds. In an unfortunate choice of words, the official sign referred to the monument as a "monster of concrete".

There were very few tourists in Vientiane in those days, apart from the odd person like myself making visa runs. There was a smattering of foreigners around, some of them spooks involved in the Vietnam War. Vientiane was peaceful in that respect, although the Pathet Lao had a compound in the city, which served as a reminder that there was a conflict going on. The communists eventually took control of the whole country in December 1975.

Before the Pathet Lao took over, in the evening you could seek out the Vientiane nightlife in the Don Phalane area and its environs. The most celebrated spot was the White Rose, possibly the smokiest bar I have ever been in. This establishment had developed a well-earned reputation for "exotic shows" and was something of an institution in Southeast Asia, as was another popular watering hole, Madame Lulu's.

You were likely to meet some intriguing people on the Laotian visa runs. On one overnight rail journey from Nong Khai to Bangkok, I spent the whole time chatting with a genial soul brother. He was "doing something in Laos", almost certainly linked to Air America, the US airline operated by the CIA which was active in Laos at that time.

We were joined by an unusual young man. He had Asian features, was well-groomed and claimed to be a Laotian prince, but couldn't speak, read or write Lao - or Thai for that matter. He openly apologized for his lack of Asian linguistic skills, explaining he had lived nearly all his life in Europe, mainly Paris. To make up for it, however, he spoke very cultured English and fluent French, and came up with a lot more fascinating tales than I could muster.

This unlikely trio spent the entire overnight journey back to Bangkok in the restaurant car. In those days they didn't throw you out at 10 p.m., or whatever time they shut up shop now. In fact, it was almost like having our own private party as the train rattled through the night. The time just flew by, as did the Singha beers, and we couldn't have been a pretty sight as the train pulled into Hua Lamphong station as dawn was breaking. The American probably told me a lot more about his Laotian exploits than he should have done, considering I worked for a newspaper. However, I had forgotten it all by the next morning, aside from his entertaining adventures at Madame Lulu's. We staggered out of Hua Lamphong a trifle the worse for wear, but it was another visa run accomplished and some new friends made.

Not all train journeys were visa runs. On one occasion some years later, I was coming back from a trip to the southern border in Narathiwat province with *Post* colleague Colin Hastings (who went on to publish the successful *Big Chilli* magazine). We were travelling from Hat Yai on the express, which was scheduled to arrive in Bangkok the next morning. It was late evening and we were ensconced as usual in the restaurant car, when the train ground to a halt in the middle of the jungle. This was nothing new on Thai trains, but after half-an-hour it became apparent that this was no ordinary stoppage. Then word drifted down the carriages that a goods train had derailed in Surat Thani and we could be delayed "for some time".

This was the signal for everyone in the restaurant car to order another round of Singha or Mekhong whisky. For the next SIX hours the train didn't move and the restaurant car developed into something like a Thai nightclub on wheels. Of course, the more drinks that were consumed, the more sociable everybody became. Being the only two foreigners in the restaurant car, Colin and I were the subject of considerable attention as assorted friendly policemen, students and railway officials practiced their English with memorable enthusiasm, but varying degrees of success.

The scene was made all the more bizarre by hundreds of moths and insects attracted by the lights in the normally pitch black jungle. Soon giant moths were dive-bombing the soups and beers, while the train's resident cockroaches emerged to join the party with some spirited tap dancing on the tables. It was quite a scene. Unfortunately, although it was probably just as well, the alcohol ran out and with dawn approaching we escaped to our bunks for some much-needed sleep.

We eventually arrived at Hua Lamphong the following afternoon about eight hours late, a little bit weary but appreciative of a memorable journey, courtesy of the SRT.

My favourite railway route in the early days was a much shorter distance, going just 130 kms west to Kanchanaburi and a further 50 kms up the Kwae Noi Valley to the terminus at the small town of Nam Tok Sai Yok. The appeal of Kanchanaburi was partly the convenience, being one of the nearest places to Bangkok with mountains and fresh air, making it an ideal destination for relatively brief trips. But equally important was its history, the infamous "Death Railway" built in 1942-43 by the

Japanese, with a huge loss of life amongst the forced labour and Allied prisoners-of-war.

Like most people of my age, I had enjoyed the 1957 film *Bridge on the River Kwai* starring Alec Guinness and could whistle the "Colonel Bogey March", but knew little of the grim realities involved in building the line. A more recent film, *The Railway Man* (2014), starring Colin Firth, gives a much more personalized account from the point of view of a British PoW.

Standing in the immaculately maintained Kanchanaburi War Cemetery for the first time, late in 1969, was an incredibly moving experience. It seemed impossible that those unimaginable horrors were going on in such a beautiful part of the country less than 30 years earlier. It was a sobering experience seeing the young ages of the Allied troops - primarily British, Australian and Dutch - who had perished during the construction of the railway. Many were teenagers. An estimated 16,000 Allied troops and 90,000 Asian labourers, mainly Malayan, perished.

Paradoxically, the graveyard was an incredibly serene and eloquent monument to the dead. Anyone who has experienced tropical heat will understand why so many died working on the railway. Without proper food and medication, many died of disease (mainly cholera and malaria), starvation and sheer exhaustion, in addition to those who were actually killed by the brutal Japanese guards.

The rail journey only really got interesting as the steam train chugged its way west of Kanchanaburi town towards Myanmar along the Kwae Noi Valley, via the impressive wooden Wang Po viaduct, which was constructed by the PoWs. After the train wheezed into Nam Tok station, it required a walk along the disused track (later reopened) a further 1.4 kms to the Sai Yok Noi waterfall. There was no road access in those days and Nam Tok had just the one hotel where I recall one particularly sleepless night in the early 1970s.

I was with English colleague Mike Boydell, and we were quite weary after spending most of the day tramping around the jungle near the waterfall. Shortly after we retired to our respective rooms about midnight, there seemed to be an unusual amount of noise in the corridor outside. I had a look to see what was going on and there were half-a-dozen Thai people, a couple of them young women, sitting outside Mike's room settling into a game of cards, assisted by a bottle of Mekhong whisky and with a radio blasting.

I returned to bed, but as the noise from the card party increased, I knew it wouldn't be long before Mike had something to say about it. Sure enough, 10 minutes later there was an abrupt silence, quickly followed by considerable laughter. I opened the door to see an exasperated Mike standing in the corridor clad only in an ill-fitting towel, desperately gesturing to them that he was trying to sleep. The card players thought this was hilarious and one of the girls misinterpreted his actions, thinking he was looking for some female companionship. She slid past him into the room, but was quickly dispatched by Mike.

In faltering Thai, I explained that we needed to sleep and asked if they would kindly try to keep the noise down. They promised they would finish in five minutes and so we retired. Nearly an hour later the noise still hadn't gone away. Then I heard Mike's door open, followed by an almighty and very English "SHUT UP!" This certainly ended the card game, but started the hotel dogs barking, sparking the town's entire canine community to join in, creating a racket that went on until dawn. There's nothing like a quiet night in the country.

In Kanchanaburi town itself, I stayed in a small wooden hotel on a quiet street overlooking the river. The room cost 30 baht a night and the Thai-Chinese family who owned it was so pleased they had a foreigner staying at their humble abode that they invited me to join them at the family table for supper every night. It was a humbling experience sitting at the round table with mum, dad, grandma and a couple of kids. My Thai wasn't too clever, but we still had lively conversations and the father always produced a bottle of Singha beer, something I don't think normally appeared at their evening meal.

It was yet another example of the wonderful Thai hospitality I enjoyed during those early years. On subsequent visits in the

1970s, I always made a point of staying there even though there were much better hotels available.

One of my more memorable New Year experiences occurred in the village of Wang Po, just down the line from the famous viaduct. It was New Year's Eve 1981, and Tony Waltham and I had just returned from a most enjoyable trek through the jungle to the Myanmar border. We were staying with a Thai boatman on the river and in the evening went up the steep bank to the "town" for some refreshment. It was a chilly night with very few people about, except a cluster of men in a sala who appeared to be tucking into a big feast. As soon as they spotted us, they insisted we join them. They turned out to be Border Patrol Policemen.

They had a battered old record player and even older vinyl records of ancient pop songs by the likes of Cliff Richard, Elvis Presley and Paul Anka. Once the food was finished, it was time to dance. There was one minor problem - there weren't any females present. But Thais are a practical people. Although there weren't any women, there *were* two foreign men. So for the next couple of hours we had to do the honours, dancing with all these guys with guns. I recall one of the songs they particularly liked was *Lipstick On Your Collar* by Connie Francis, which was played over and over again. It was actually tremendous fun, although I admit to politely declining on the slow dances.

All those visa trips in the early days required regular excursions to the Immigration Department as it was called then, which was in North Sathorn Road. The visits weren't something you exactly looked forward to, but once you got used to the procedure it wasn't so bad. After just six months my file was as thick as the feasibility study for Suvarnabhumi airport. The various rooms you had to visit were packed with yellowing files, which looked as if they had been collecting dust since World War II - probably true for many of the files. The rooms had ancient overhead fans, but it will come as no surprise that they were not particularly effective, especially in the debilitating heat of April and May.

ON (AND OFF) THE RAILS

There weren't so many foreigners about in those days and you soon got on nodding terms with the immigration staff. Life was made easier for me in that the fellow who dealt with the British passport holders was an affable young gentleman and as polite as they come. He would always greet me with a smile and a *wai*, despite the mountain of paperwork on his desk. And he would be almost apologetic as he handed over yet another form to fill in. On a couple of occasions at lunchtime he insisted on buying me noodles at the little place downstairs, where we chatted about meaningful things like Manchester United and Charles Bronson. He's probably retired now. I've always hoped he did well for himself, as he certainly made my visits to Sathorn more bearable.

In those early days you also had to trudge over to the Foreign Ministry for the final stamp in your visa, so the process sometimes stretched into a few days. There was a lot of hanging around, so it was always advisable to bring along a decent novel or the *Bangkok Post* crossword - a golden rule I follow to this day when visiting government departments and embassies.

In those days Sathorn Road was quite picturesque, with a *khlong* down the middle lined with beautiful mango and flame trees, something it is hard to imagine now. Then in 1979 there came the Great Sathorn Tree Massacre as thousands of them were cut down in the name of progress. It still makes me mad just thinking about it. They didn't have to wipe out all the trees. But, admittedly, if there had not been some sort of tree cull, the traffic on Sathorn would be even worse than it is today - not a pleasant thought.

12. CAMBODGE - THE WAR NEXT DOOR

An eventful trip to beleaguered Siem Reap in 1970

One of the more memorable visa runs I experienced in the early days was an eye-opening excursion to Cambodia. Very few people had crossed from Aranyaprathet to Poipet, where the border had been closed for many years owing to the poor relationship between the two countries. It had only just reopened in 1970 with Lon Nol coming to power in Phnom Penh after ousting head of state Norodom Sihanouk, who had fled to Beijing.

On one trip in October 1970, I was travelling with colleague Tony Waltham. The train journey from Bangkok to Aranyaprathet was uneventful, but departed Hua Lamphong station at 6 a.m., which meant you were dog-tired even before you had started, especially having worked the night before. At the border, the Cambodian officials were not used to processing westerners, which soon became apparent. The young immigration official scrutinized Tony's British passport with commendable thoroughness. This would have been a little more convincing had he not been holding the passport upside down for much of the time. Handing it back to Tony, he said with a big smile: "You American?"

We duly trudged across the border into Poipet, a ramshackle town, but bustling with activity. With unmade roads, wooden shacks and dozens of mangy dogs, it resembled more a frontier town in one of those old spaghetti westerns. You half expected to see Clint Eastwood or Charles Bronson stepping out of a saloon, gun smoking. It was the sort of place where, upon entering, you really wanted to keep on going. So we headed straight for the railway station.

We took the train from Poipet to Battambang, which was the end of the line. It was unsafe to travel on to Phnom Penh owing to frequent Viet Cong and Khmer Rouge ambushes, so the railway was closed. However, that relatively short journey was an experience in itself. The platform at Poipet was a hive of activity, as befitting a border town, while the train prepared for departure. It was a mixture of ancient carriages and goods wagons, all absolutely jam-packed with Cambodians, many of them sitting on the roof. Everyone was carrying boxes, bags and battered suitcases. Unfortunately, the ancient steam engine in charge of transporting this motley band of passengers had seen better days. When it strained to pull away from the platform, it was totally enveloped in steam and made such extraordinary noises, I honestly thought it might blow up.

Eventually the train rattled off and we managed to squeeze into a carriage. The fellow passengers, all Cambodian, were incredibly friendly. Fortunately Tony's command of French was much better than mine and he soon learnt that the Cambodians could not understand why we would want to venture deeper into their war-ravaged country when we could stay in blissful Thailand with all its charms. They did have a point.

Battambang Express: It was not exactly first-class accommodation aboard the train from Poipet to Battambang in war-torn Cambodia in October 1970. - Tony Waltham

There were quite a few young female soldiers aboard the train and I must say they looked appealing in their camouflage uniforms. They all sported big grins, belying the fact they were in the middle of a war. In fact, a lot of the passengers were women, an unusually high proportion of whom appeared to be pregnant. However, all was explained as the train approached Battambang station, when the women gave birth to bags of sugar and other necessities and began tossing them out of the window to accomplices waiting by the tracks. There was a huge smuggling operation going on, another reminder there was a war in progress. I suspect we were the only two people on the entire train not running contraband of some sort.

Battambang was a bustling town and relatively safe, which wasn't saying much as nowhere was really secure in Cambodia at that time. Like the rest of the country, the place was later to suffer terribly under the Khmer Rouge. The underlying nervousness was reflected in an 8 p.m. curfew which was strictly enforced. But that did not stop them having a nightclub, which operated from 2.30 p.m. to 7.30 p.m., which Tony and I felt obliged to experience. It was the first time I had ever been in a nightclub in daylight hours.

It was a funny place, with a big dance floor and a band playing old fashioned music associated with the likes of Frank Sinatra, Dean Martin and their ilk. It was strictly ballroom dancing and I recall an elegantly dressed Cambodian gentleman performing a splendid foxtrot with a lovely- looking lady, a true "Satin Doll". It all seemed so incongruous with the reality of what was happening outside. Although there weren't many customers, a few hostesses were on hand to sit at the tables and it was all operated in a calm and sophisticated manner considering the circumstances. It was also quite cheap, but then it wasn't exactly the Ritz.

The nightclub closed at 7.30 p.m. on the dot to give staff and customers just enough time to beat the curfew home. Tony and I squeezed onto a lone pedal *samlor*, which whisked us back along the rapidly emptying streets to a hotel that had seen better days. It was an eerie atmosphere as the town suddenly closed down. It was another of those "mum would never believe this" moments.

In Battambang we foolishly purchased some bizarre, almost grotesque, anti-Sihanouk posters issued by the recently installed Lon Nol Government. This did not reflect our political views, but the posters looked so weird they felt like collector's items. However, we didn't keep them very long. On being told by the taxi drivers in no uncertain terms that the road between Battambang and Siem Reap, our next destination, was prone to being cut off by the Viet Cong, or even worse, the Khmer Rouge, if felt prudent to dump such propaganda in the trash.

It turned out to be a nerve-wracking ride in a packed and dilapidated Peugeot taxi from Battambang to Siem Reap. From the small town of Sisophon alone, we counted 15 checkpoints on the 100-kms journey into Siem Reap, which was basically surrounded by Viet Cong forces. The Viet Cong had their headquarters at the majestic 13th century Angkor Wat, which they had overrun a few months earlier. The airport was being fought over on a daily basis, with one flight from Phnom Penh ferrying in essential supplies - if the fighting was not too intense.

In the beleaguered town, uniformed soldiers outnumbered civilians by about three-to-one and the five hotels in Siem Reap had all been commandeered by the Cambodian Army. The rooms were curtainless and carpetless. The hotel bars and lounges had become army quarters, stocked with rows of camp beds. The largest of the hotels, the Grand, looked anything but "grand" and had become the regional Cambodian Command Headquarters. Guns adorned the reception desk, while forgotten posters, half-covered by army notices, advertised elephant rides to Angkor.

We managed to get a room for almost nothing in one of the hotels hosting the soldiers. On the wall there was a notice asking tourists not to climb or deface the ruins of Angkor Wat. We hoped the Viet Cong had read the notice.

It was a strange experience in Siem Reap, a town under siege, with constant reminders in the form of bombed-out buildings and battle-weary government soldiers. What were once tourist buses rattled by, jam-packed with troops. Some pedal *samlors* struggled past with as many as four fully-armed soldiers aboard, going out to the front. Their uniforms appeared to be whatever they could pick up at the market, but they all wore the same colour scarf around their necks.

We discovered a rare shop still open, selling handicrafts and Angkor temple rubbings. Not that far from the shop were the trenches and bunkers marking *"La Premier Ligne"*, the front line of the town's defences. Valuable rubbings were scattered across the floor and marble carvings wrapped in newspapers were stacked in large wicker baskets, awaiting possible speedy evacuation.

The townspeople tried to continue normal life as much as possible. Amazingly, kids were still going to school, although most likely they were only being taught what to do in the event of an attack. Children not old enough for school followed us all over the place, waving, laughing and shouting "bye-bye". I wondered if they knew something we didn't.

You could only admire the defenders of the town who were fighting a losing battle and probably knew it. The Khmer Rouge eventually overwhelmed the place within a few years. One officer in command of a section of the front line passionately condemned *"Le aggresseurs Communistes"* and vowed to fight to the end, and he meant it. His final words to us were a defiant *"Toujours Cambodge* (Always Cambodia)". In retrospect, it was all rather sad - these people didn't have a hope when the Khmer Rouge took over.

Ironically, despite the communist soldiers surrounding the town, it turned out the biggest threat we faced during our visit was from an inebriated Cambodian government soldier. We were having a noodle lunch outside what had been a popular French restaurant before the war, when a soldier sat himself down at the same table. He proceeded to place a Chinese stick hand grenade on the table and to our horror began unscrewing the top. A little boy who had earlier been giggling at us fled in terror, which is what we should have done.

But we sat it out, fearful that any sudden movement might make him drop the grenade he was playing with. Much to our relief the drunken soldier eventually disappeared into an adjacent shophouse. Seconds later gunfire erupted from the building and plaster came crashing down. The soldier then staggered out with one of his arms badly bleeding. Apparently he had accidentally shot himself with his automatic rifle. Never had a war wound been more deserving. At that point we made a rapid exit, not wishing to experience an encore.

Steady hands: An inebriated Cambodian government soldier in Siem Reap in October 1970 plays with his new acquisition - a stick grenade. – Tony Waltham

We didn't get much sleep that night, listening to the machine guns clattering away a bit too close for comfort for my liking and the occasional mortar lighting up the adjacent jungle.

I was up at dawn determined to get out of the place, although I think Tony would have liked to stay on for a few more days. He did bravely return at a later, more dangerous time. I could imagine that Siem Reap had been a beautiful place in peacetime, but my next visa trip was going to be somewhere a little less hazardous.

We found the obligatory, ageing Peugeot taxi and as usual we were stuffed into the vehicle along with eight other people, all Cambodian, with accompanying ducks and chickens. The driver seemed a little reluctant to leave Siem Reap and a few minutes later we discovered why.

We had ventured no more than a kilometre to the west on the road out of town, when gunshots erupted from the rice fields either side of us. All hell broke loose. Farmers, their wives and children fled from their huts, soldiers dived for cover, some rather alarmingly sheltering behind our taxi. To say I was scared would be off the mark - "terrified" would be far more accurate.

Mercifully, after a few minutes the shooting died down and we rattled off down the potholed highway towards the relative safety of Sisophon and then on to Battambang. The other passengers, all Cambodian, seemed to take it in their stride. For them it was just another day. But that's a close as I ever want to get to any war.

A couple of days later, news agencies reported that the highway to Siem Reap had been cut, isolating the town which was cut off for the next month before government forces retook the road. We had been very lucky to get out when we did.

Those Peugeot taxis were about the only way you could move around Cambodia at that time. Tony recalls that on a later trip from Sisophon to Poipet, there were so many people crammed into a Peugeot estate he decided to do a head count. There were 22 people aboard the taxi, consisting of three rows of six (including the driver), two babies in the arms of their mothers and two armed soldiers sitting on the roof!

It's funny the odd little things you remember from such a long time ago. The following morning after we left Siem Reap, Tony and I had to catch the train from Battambang back to Poipet as I had to be at work at the *Bangkok Post* that evening. There didn't appear to be a specific departure time, the train no doubt waiting until all the smugglers were ready to board. Because we were unsure what time it would leave, we sat outside a noodle shop on the other side of the square across from the station, where we could see the train waiting.

The owner was a delightful woman who was clearly quite excited about having a couple of foreigners drinking colas at her establishment in such hard times. Suddenly the whistle went and the locomotive burst into a cloud of steam and began chugging off. Tony and I grabbed our rucksacks and sprinted for the train, managing to clamber aboard one of the last carriages as it eased out of the station.

CAMBODGE - THE WAR NEXT DOOR

A couple of minutes later, I realised that in our haste to catch the train, we had forgotten to pay for our drinks at the noodle shop. It was only a few *riel*, but I couldn't help feeling that we had betrayed the woman's trust - she must have thought we had simply done a pre-planned "runner" to avoid paying. Silly though it may sound, I still feel guilty about this accidental misdemeanour more than four decades later.

It was on that same trip to Cambodia that I had a rather embarrassing experience at the Poipet border crossing. To get across the border required a lengthy walk. By the time we reached the crossing point I was dying to take a leak, so I discreetly nipped round the back of a wooden house on the Thai side. Not discreetly enough, as it turned out.

I was engrossed in watering the weeds when a sweet voice called out *"acharn"* (teacher). I looked around, but couldn't see anyone. Then came *"Sawasdi* Khun Roger. What are you doing?" Somewhat alarmed, I glanced up to see a familiar face leaning out of the upstairs window. It was a female student from the college in Bangkok where I had been teaching.

To say I felt foolish would be an understatement. But she didn't seem concerned at all and promptly invited Tony and me into her house for a welcome soft drink. It turned out she was the daughter of an immigration official at Aranyaprathet and had spotted *"Acharn* Roger" acting rather suspiciously in her back garden. That was just another reminder that you can't go anywhere in Thailand without the chance of someone you know spotting you.

It must have been the following year, 1971, when Tony and I along with colleague Wayne Morrison briefly returned to Cambodia in an unscheduled and somewhat unorthodox fashion. We had travelled from Bangkok to Khlong Yai in Trat Province, which is flanked by the Cardamom Mountains and the very last place in Thailand on the coast before the Cambodian border.

In the town we got talking to a Thai-Cambodian lady, who said she was a guide and could take us to a beautiful untouched beach nearby for a small fee. So we dutifully followed her through a forest, which eventually opened up on a pristine deserted beach, just as she had promised.

We walked along the beach for a further kilometre until we came across some wooden huts set back from the beach. It was then we saw a company of soldiers performing drills… under a Cambodian flag. They were, fortunately, Cambodian *government* troops and we were obviously no longer in Thailand. Our initial thoughts were to retrace our steps pretty quickly, but the guide told us not to be alarmed and suggested we have a swim while she talked to the soldiers.

And so we did. The swim was most welcome as we had worked up bit of a sweat with all the walking and the water was absolutely beautiful. We were the only souls on the beach, which stretched for many kilometres. It was so incredibly peaceful and idyllic, it was hard to imagine we were in a country torn apart by a savage war, which was about to get an awful lot worse.

After the swim we emerged to find the Thai lady sitting in the middle of a circle of Cambodian troops, who were also sitting, listening politely as she held court. It was a peculiar, but at the same time, reassuring scene. On our way back across the border I could only think it was just as well we had run into Cambodian government soldiers. Those from the other side, who were active in the area at the time, most definitely didn't take kindly to strangers.

I should state here that despite being in Thailand during the Vietnam and Cambodian conflicts, I was never by any stretch of the imagination a war correspondent. Much braver souls were doing that job.

13. FROM NAKHON NOWHERE TO TAMBON TOO FAR

Riding buses in Thailand is not for the faint-hearted

During the early 1970s, whenever I could string together a couple of days off, I would head for one of the Bangkok provincial bus terminals and hop aboard an "Orange Crush", the name given by travellers to the cramped, orange-coloured people-movers. It was in the days before air-conditioned buses and there was no such thing as a comfortable seat. On occasions the journeys were something of an ordeal.

The express buses from Bangkok were a law unto themselves. Their crews, which usually included a couple of boys hanging out of the doors directing traffic in flamboyant fashion, displayed a gung-ho camaraderie with a simplistic policy of "thou shall not pass" concerning anything else on the road. By contrast, tour buses I have taken in recent years seem relatively sedate, although they are still far too accident prone. The buses would scream down the highways at a terrifying speed, often with unfortunate results. You were putting your life into their hands - something that has not really changed over the years.

On one of the early visa runs to Laos, rather than take the train, I foolishly clambered aboard the express bus to Nong Khai on what they called the *"roht gaew gaew"* (Number 99). But never again. The Orange 99 had the reputation of being the fastest bus around, something I would not dispute. It was 12 hours of sheer terror and zero sleep. Seeing the wreckage of accidents on the main highway didn't help my confidence much. By the time we reached Nong Khai, I was absolutely shattered, yet still had to get to Vientiane. All future trips to Nong Khai were by train.

One of my more disturbing Orange Crush excursions was on a journey from Korat (Nakhon Ratchasima) to Khon Kaen in the mid 1970s. At Korat bus station, being the only *farang* aboard, I was given the dubious honour of sitting in the front-left seat - a place often reserved for monks to ensure an auspicious journey - and quickly wished I had declined. It was a blisteringly hot day in May and as we thundered along what was then an old-style highway, unlike the present dual carriageway, it soon became apparent the driver was either drunk, exhausted or both.

It didn't take long to notice he was having severe problems trying to stay awake. These fears were quickly confirmed when the bus boy periodically prodded the driver with a long stick whenever he started nodding off. Each time the bus boy performed this act, he turned to me and grinned. It was hard to reciprocate the cheerfulness, with 10-wheel trucks and other buses hurtling towards us on the narrow highway. The further we went, the more frequent the prodding. I looked around for some moral support from the other passengers, but in true Thai style they were all blissfully asleep.

I never took my eyes off the driver once on the entire journey, ready to alert the bus boy as soon as the man at the wheel went on the nod. It was the longest three-hour journey I had ever experienced. The relief I felt getting off at Khon Kaen bus station was akin to that feeling on a plane after a particularly difficult landing.

One thing I was to learn in the early days from bitter experience was to avoid travelling in the provinces on public holidays. It was always a nightmare, the buses and trains packed with passengers going to or from Bangkok.

There was one particular horror bus trip during the 1971 Songkran holiday from the southern town of Chumphon to Bangkok. It was another scorchingly hot day and I was with colleague Peter Finucane. All the decent buses were full, so we had to squeeze onto the back seat of an aging Orange Crush. To say it was jam-packed was not entirely accurate - it was brimming, overflowing, bursting. This was unpleasant in itself, but there was an additional hazard. The seat had somehow separated from the rest of the bus, so that every time the driver braked, the seat continued its forward momentum and fell off, dumping us all on the floor. We laughed the first time it happened, but the joke wore thin pretty quickly.

The discomfort was exacerbated by popular Songkran activities. All along the highway kids chucked plastic bags full of water through the windows, which were open because of the stifling April heat. For the next 10 hours or more, we sat there wet, uncomfortable and exhausted. Then we had to face a night shift on the *Post's* newsdesk. We were definitely not in a festive spirit and I don't think I wrote any intelligible headlines that evening.

How it should be done. The author (left, with the silly long hair and even sillier shirt) and colleague Peter Finucane receive a polite Songkran splashing from children at Wat That Phanom in Nakhon Phanom province in 1975.

In stark contrast to the express buses that plied the main highways, their country cousins used to amble along in almost leisurely style. The whole atmosphere on these buses was totally different. Unaffected by the rigours of city life, time seemed to be of secondary importance governing their operation. They would leave when the driver showed up and the arrival time was anybody's guess. If you were told that the bus was leaving "about 8", that could mean anything up to 10 o'clock.

My most unnerving experience on a country bus was on the Loei-Lomsak route in 1972 when it was still a dirt road, although a very picturesque ride. It was the rainy season and the meandering mountain track was a sea of mud. This probably explains why the bus boy, when asked in Loei what time the bus would arrive in Lomsak, grinned and answered "yes". Every time we took a bend, I grew increasingly nervous as the bus slid nearer the edge of a ravine with a considerable drop.

We were stuck for several minutes on one particularly bad stretch. As the driver revved the engine, the bus began sliding towards the edge. The driver finally swung the wheel round and the bus slid to a halt, with the back wheels dangling in space over the ravine.

The other passengers seemed to think it was great fun and much to my alarm, leaned over to look at the drop below them. At that point I leapt off, convinced the bus was doomed. Partly to save face, I proceeded to take photos of the bus, even though I had virtually run out of film. Much to my embarrassment the bus boys halted their rescue attempts when they saw the camera and posed to have their pictures taken, spades in hand and sporting big grins. We were finally rescued half an hour later by a bulldozer, which towed the bus to safety. Nevertheless, I hesitated to climb aboard until I was convinced we were back on terra firma.

In those days before mass tourism, foreign visitors were a constant source of entertainment when they ventured out into the provinces. I was on a local bus from Lampang to Chiang Mai in 1973 when a French traveler boarded at a village. His appearance caused quite a stir amongst the passengers, who were mainly villagers. Bald *farang* men are a common sight now, but in those days it was quite rare. The fellow was totally bald on top but had long wisps of hair dangling down his back, and he was dressed in the classic Thai image of a "hippie".

At first he was eyed rather suspiciously by the other passengers. However, at a brief stop things changed. I could see him leaning out of the window gesticulating at a lady selling eggs. He was jabbering away and waving his arms about, which only went to confirm the Thai passengers' suspicions that he was totally mad. Then the bus went quiet as he grabbed an egg and proceeded to bash it on his bald head. The passengers erupted into unrestrained laughter. The fellow had only been trying to establish whether the egg was raw or hard-boiled. Fortunately for him it was the latter and after paying the lady, he went on to satisfy his appetite. The passengers agreed that he was the best comedian they had seen in a long while.

One country bus I took in the early 1970s went to the Laos border from Amnat Charoen (then part of Ubon Ratchathani province) to Khemmarat, by the Mekong River. Nobody could figure out why a westerner could possibly want to get on the bus and admittedly I wasn't sure myself. I was just going to a place I had never been to before. There was still some communist insurgency going on in the area and it was not recommended for casual travelers.

It was one of those buses that as soon as you have boarded, you knew it would break down. And it did, several times. Suffice to say, it took the entire afternoon to trundle less than 70 kms. When we finally reached our destination, the only place in Khemmarat calling itself a hotel was full. After the tortuous journey that was all that I needed, but a guardian angel in the form of a local government official whom I met in a noodle shop came to the rescue. He took me to a compound and put me up for the night in a small wooden bungalow normally used by visiting government officials. Supper was a tasty fish from the nearby Mekong. Not for the first time Thai hospitality had saved the day.

I was to receive more help from the locals on another trip to the Northeast in the mid-1970s on a visit to Ubon provincial town. I had a ticket for the night sleeper train to Bangkok scheduled to leave Ubon early evening, so decided to take a day trip out to the newly-built Sirindhorn Dam, close to the Lao border. Not a good idea as it turned out. There weren't any buses after we reached Phibun Mangsahan. This meant using pick-up trucks, so it took much longer to get to the dam than I had envisaged. Time was at a premium, so after a quick look at the dam, I decided it was best to head back to Ubon and walked back down to the road.

I waited and waited and waited. There were no buses and in fact, virtually no traffic at all… no people to offer friendly advice, either. By this time it was mid-afternoon, desperately hot, and I was seriously concerned about missing the train. So, for the first time since that early trip to Malaysia, I had to hitchhike. This was all very well, but there was hardly any traffic. Finally, an old truck belonging to the local water authority rolled up and stopped. When I told the couple of fellows in the cab I wanted to go to Ubon town, they said okay, and I hopped aboard. Saved again... well, not quite.

We had only gone a few kilometres, when the truck turned off the road and stopped at a ramshackle farmhouse, where we all got out. One of the fellows then emerged with an ancient motorbike and a couple of live roosters, which he proceeded to tie from the handlebars so the birds hung upside down. He indicated to me to hop on the bike and for the next 90 minutes, I was perched on the back as we headed for Ubon. Understandably, the big birds did not appreciate dangling upside down on the bike, so before long my jeans were covered in (excuse the expression) chicken shit. We eventually arrived just 10 minutes before the train departed, thanks to this kindly gentleman, who refused any money I offered for the ride. However, the state of my jeans did prompt a few funny looks from other passengers.

The frequent upcountry trips necessitated numerous overnight stays in hotels, none of which would merit more than a one-star status. Many were just plain seedy and worst of all... noisy. It has to be really quiet for me to sleep and I would regularly wake up to the sound of other people's alarm clocks or anything that goes bump in the night.

In the 1970s, the cheap hotels always seemed to be located as close as possible to every conceivable noisemaker - the ice factory that grinds into deafening action at 7 a.m.; the timber mill with the piercing electric saw; the cinema truck barking out promotions for its latest epic from ear-shattering loudspeakers.

It was a long tale of woe. I'll spare the grim details, but there was the panting peeper in Phetchabun who kept drilling holes through the wooden wall in an adjacent room; a deafening night in the border town of Sungai Kolok with Malaysian tourists running rampant down the corridor chasing screaming young ladies; the Indian fortune teller in Suphan Buri who kept knocking on my door promising I would experience "wonderful happenings"; and finally the conscientious room boy in Khon Kaen who periodically tapped on the door enquiring if I would like some female company, genuinely puzzled that all I wanted was a good night's sleep.

On these expeditions I didn't spend all the time sitting on buses. Now and again I actually got in a bit of walking - I hesitate to go as far as calling it trekking. In the Thai countryside you always had to keep an eye on the weather. I must confess to quite enjoying the drama of tropical storms and the accompanying heavy rain, but sometimes the conditions can change without warning.

In the early 1970s I was with a friend in Nakhon Nayok and we hiked for hours up a narrow stream in the forest, near one of the waterfalls. It was more of a brook really; apart from a small trickle of water, it was bone dry. After an exhausting ramble, we sat down for some much needed rest and sandwiches. When the wind began to pick up, we did not take much notice and in fact were enjoying the cooling breeze. Then a huge gust suddenly blew our sandwiches away. When the bough of a large tree came crashing down near us, we realized it was time to make a hasty departure. The sky had suddenly turned pitch black and within minutes the rain was lashing down in torrents. It was shades of the Kathmandu misadventure all over again.

In most undignified fashion we bolted back down the stream, which was easier said than done. The rocks underfoot were now wet and slippery and I took several tumbles. Branches were crashing to the ground around us as we scrambled downhill. Even more alarming was the lightning, which was striking far too close for comfort. The once placid stream was transforming into a raging torrent and there was a clear danger of a flash flood. It was with considerable relief we finally got back to the relative safety of a bamboo noodle shop, totally drenched and looking quite pathetic. I always remember the lady owner with a big grin, asking these two bedraggled foreigners, "*sanuk mai?*"("Did you have a good time?")

As you may have gathered, I am not exactly a Jungle Jim, but have on occasions made occasional forays into the jungle bordering Myanmar. On one expedition with Tony Waltham and a Thai ranger, we set off along a mountain trail to see a waterfall, which sounded straightforward enough. We seemed to have been going for ages, but after exerting a bit more energy than I had bargained for we found the waterfall. I settled down for a relaxing hour or so with the beer and sandwiches.

I was then informed that we had only reached the first stage of the waterfall. "Well, how many stages are there?" I asked somewhat warily. "Oh, six altogether," Tony casually replied and began following the ranger, who was already scuttling up a steep track into the jungle. By the time I reached the top in a state of disarray, Tony and the ranger were already preparing to return to the bottom. The descent was something of a haze, but presumably the law of gravity played a part, for eventually I ended up at the foot of the mountain.

The next morning, despite aching in every bone, having a running nose, gravelly cough and collapsing chest, I foolishly agreed to enjoy the delights of a "nice mountain view". There was one condition from me - under no circumstances would I get my feet wet. Two hours later I found myself standing waist-deep in water in the middle of a stream in the middle of nowhere. We weren't *looking* at a waterfall - we were *in* it.

Walking up a mountain stream can seem quite a romantic notion until you actually try it. My progress was of the "advancing sideways" category, a lurch here, a plunge there. It was a veritable water ballet. I eventually caught up with Tony and the ranger sitting contentedly on a rock as if on a Sunday picnic. "I'm afraid we can't go any further," said Tony, "we haven't got enough time." Never before were words such music to the ears. "Oh, really?" I replied in most disappointed fashion, "what a shame!"

On many trips to out-of-the-way places, the BBC World Service radio was a regular companion, especially in the days before satellite television had found its way to the kingdom. For years I possessed a handy pocket-sized Sony short wave with its

FROM NAKHON NOWHERE TO TAMBON TOO FAR

precious BBC, which accompanied me to virtually every province. It was particularly comforting at night, sitting in some remote part, to hear the familiar refrains of *Lilliburlero* come wafting through as a prelude to the news. And, of course, there were the chimes of Big Ben. Even the beeps of the time signal and the strains of the London church bells ringing out *"Oranges and Lemons"* were comforting. It was also quietly satisfying and somewhat bizarre listening to a ball-by-ball Test cricket commentary from England, while spending the night in a hilltribe village hut near the Myanmar border.

Back in Bangkok, the buses were not without adventures either. When I was newly arrived, Brett Bartos recommended learning the bus routes. It turned out to be sound advice and a money saver, as I could not afford taxis on a daily basis. The bus fares were 50 satang and I travelled all over the city in assorted rattletraps, often ending up in totally the wrong place. It was a cheap way of getting to know the city and a good experience, if you could get a seat. But it was a nightmare if you had to stand, especially with those low roofs. Sometimes the buses were so crowded, it seemed that even the driver was standing up.

One problem with city buses was that they had an annoying habit of hitting other vehicles, especially *samlors*. When this happened, everyone had to get off and it was a real pain having to stand there in the heat or the rain waiting for another bus to show up. It was also quite hazardous simply trying to get off. Many drivers were paid on the basis of how many journeys they could complete in a day, so once they got some speed up, usually at night, they were a bit reluctant to stop.

In one incident on Sukhumvit, a passenger I knew pushed the buzzer for the bus to stop, but was totally ignored and the vehicle accelerated down the road. As they approached the next stop, the passenger buzzed again and once again was ignored. In a foolish fit of bravado, the exasperated passenger grabbed the conductor's coin box and threatened to throw it out of the window unless the bus stopped. This had the desired effect - the conductor screamed and the driver slammed on the brakes. The passenger wisely decided to flee the scene and sped off down the road, pursued by an angry driver who simply abandoned the bus in the outside lane.

It will come as no surprise that over the years there have been many complaints about reckless bus driving in Bangkok. Fortunately the heavy traffic in the city usually negates any serious attempts at speeding. But give the drivers a bit of open road and they love to put their foot down, sometimes with disastrous results. The *Post's* picture files are full of Bangkok buses ending up in *khlongs*, going through shop windows and dangling precariously from bridges.

Some years ago BMTA officials recommended that bus passengers should ask drivers to slow down if they thought they were going too fast - well meaning, but totally impractical. A few days later a terrified passenger sitting on a bus hurtling through the suburbs put this advice into use and requested the driver to slow down. The passenger was rewarded for this display of public spiritedness by being hit on the head by the bus conductor wielding the tin ticket holder.

Another passenger in Bangkok who took matters into his own hands did not fare much better. After waiting more than an hour for a bus, he became extremely irritated when he saw an empty bus park by the side of the road and the driver get out and wander off. That was when the commuter decided to drive himself home, self-service if you like. So he climbed aboard and drove off in the direction of his residence, much to the consternation of the bus driver, who was sitting at a nearby noodle stall. The fellow at the wheel was arrested a few kilometres down the road after being pursued by the driver and a gaggle of policemen in a chase befitting the Keystone Kops. The police, in fact, praised the fellow's driving skills, as he had succeeded in manoeuvring the large bus for some distance without hitting anything. It was even suggested he be given a job as a bus driver. He certainly won full marks for initiative.

It will come as no surprise that a couple of years ago, it was reported that many Bangkok buses were suffering from old age and falling to bits. I know the feeling well. Apparently one of the oldest buses had been trundling around Bangkok since 1955. I

FROM NAKHON NOWHERE TO TAMBON TOO FAR

bet that vehicle could tell a few stories - it would have experienced nearly a dozen coup attempts for a start.

Some of the buses certainly look like they would be more at home in a museum, while others should have been dispatched to the knacker's yard years ago. But they are still the cheapest way of getting around Bangkok - all it requires is just a bit of patience. And a sense of humour.

14. DANCING IN THE DARK

A first taste of Bangkok's nightlife down by the docks

Owing partly to limited finances, my introduction to Thai nightlife in 1969 was on the sporadic side, which was probably just as well. Tourism had yet to really take off in Thailand and internationally there wasn't that much written about the nightlife. But in Bangkok we had Bernard Trink's unique *Nite Owl* column in the *Bangkok World*, while Louie Morales, an amiable Filipino, had a more upmarket weekly offering entitled *Nights 'N Daze* in the *Bangkok Post*. Add to that my basic naivety and it is safe to say my early taste of Bangkok's entertainment scene was very much a matter of trial and error… mainly error.

The first Thai-style nightclub I experienced was Le Moulin Rouge, quite close to the *Bangkok Post* on Ratchadamnoen Avenue. Despite the location it was not a hang-out for *Post* employees, as it was a bit on the expensive side, something journalists always find quite unsettling. It was also fairly sophisticated, another scenario that newshounds struggle with. I was taken there in May 1969, before I joined the *Post*, by a Thai teacher who I suspect also couldn't afford it, but he insisted on paying.

An old fashioned band played equally old fashioned music, which my mother might have appreciated, but wasn't much to my taste. There was also a "crooner", the less said about him the better. I ended up dancing a waltz with a lovely Thai lady hostess in a silk gown, well, I think she was a lady. She soon learned I wasn't any Fred Astaire, as I stumbled through the dance and her poor toes took a bit of a battering. My only excuse was that, as in most Thai nightclubs, it was so dark you couldn't see a bloody thing. Just as well by all accounts. These clubs also often had carpeted steps in the most unlikely places; owing to the darkness it was not unusual to see unwitting customers taking a sudden tumble.

Silly though it might sound, I was actually quite nervous because I didn't know how the hostess system worked - we didn't have that sort of thing in Reading. Also I only knew a few words of Thai. I could count to ten, say *"sawasdi"* and order a *"kowpat"*, but that was hardly a recipe for sparkling conversation, especially of a romantic nature. It wasn't the most uplifting experience, but at least it was a start.

Over the years I've usually tried to avoid Thai-style nightclubs, not always successfully. After all, you are in Thailand. In some small provincial towns there wasn't much choice. One thing you could always rely upon, however, was a plate of stale and very salty peanuts, which you never asked for and invariably cost nearly as much as the drink. And the nuts made you very thirsty. It's something of a generalization, but in the same way you don't see many foreigners in Thai-style nightclubs, you find very few Thais, apart from the staff, in western-style bars. It is an unspoken cultural thing.

One of the first Bangkok bar areas I visited in 1969 was down by the docks in Klong Toey. An American friend loved it there because of its sheer rawness, and referred to the whole place as "The Harbour", usually with a twinkle in his eye as he related colourful past experiences.

There were up to a dozen bars altogether in Klong Toey, but four main hang-outs catering almost entirely for merchant seamen plus a few expats. I think the whole area was off-limits to GIs, who were encouraged to frequent the many bars on New Petchaburi Road (more of which later). Several of the Klong Toey bars were upstairs, with noodle shops downstairs where you could watch the world go by... and there was plenty to watch. Klong Toey after dark was quite a strange world. It was the sort of place the great Italian film director Federico Fellini would have loved. The girls were "earthy", but then so were the customers.

The most well-known establishment was the Mosquito, which was one of the few bars in Bangkok that lived up to its name - you always got bitten in one way or another. The bar had live bands, which often appeared to be fighting a losing battle with the songs. One group had a signature tune, *Strangers in the Night*, and that's exactly what they sounded like.

It was run down, but exciting in its own way, inevitably prompting comparisons with those smoky old joints which surfaced in Humphrey Bogart movies. Ancient ceiling fans and the distinctive smell of stale beer all added to the "atmosphere". There would be some splendid punch-ups there too, featuring primarily drunken merchant seamen from the old Eastern bloc. It was a reminder of how much the Russians were resented by many eastern Europeans, especially the Poles. When they started laying into one another, it was really quite a scene.

To get into the Mosquito you had to climb some steep stairs, which were also particularly useful for disposing of the drunks who sometimes disappeared down the stairs in unorthodox fashion, courtesy of some tough little Thai bouncers. But generally it was a good laugh, although some might feel "sleazy" a more appropriate description.

Somewhat incongruously, I recall dancing the *ramwong* at the Mosquito with a Thai hostess who was definitely no spring chicken, but had a certain quaint charm that was quite appealing. She kept requesting the band play her favourite song, *River of No Return*, made popular by Marilyn Monroe. It was a hit in 1954, which admittedly dated her a bit. On subsequent visits I always called her "Marilyn", which she thought was quite witty.

The Mosquito advertised itself as "The most modern and elegant bar in town... with charming hostesses." Well, there's nothing wrong in having a sense of imagination.

A few doors down was the popular Venus Room and I fell in love with the moon-faced noodle vendor outside, who always looked so cheerful. Unfortunately I suffered some stomach upsets in a futile attempt to win her heart. She was a bit liberal with the chillies and I wondered afterwards if she deliberately made the food super-hot to ward off my clumsy advances. Upstairs, the Venus Room was much the same format as the Mosquito, but smaller and often featured what an acquaintance called "the worst magic show in Bangkok." As I recall, the magician sometimes suffered a bad case of the dropsies with embarrassing results. On occasions the rabbit escaped out of his top hat and scampered off, while the dove also was prone to flapping around the bar. It didn't matter one iota, as it was all very entertaining. Other much quieter establishments were the Okay Bar and the Ship Inn.

Across the road, below another upstairs bar called the Golden Gate, stood the Copenhagen restaurant, which had the best *"frikadiller"* (minced meat-balls) I have ever experienced and was a pleasant little oasis down by the docks. It was in a nearby noodle shop, close to the river, that I saw a flickering tape of England getting beaten by West Germany in the 1970 World Cup quarter-finals in Mexico. As distressed as I was by this football disaster, after retiring to the Mosquito for a couple of hours, the England defeat didn't seem to matter in the big scheme of things.

Speaking of football, I played one of my first games in Thailand in 1970 for a team called the Cosmopolitans in a field behind the Mariner's Club in Klong Toey. Our opponents were the crew of a visiting British minesweeper and I was crunched on the ankle by an overweight sailor, putting me out of sporting action for three months. At least the fellow bought me a beer in the Mariner's Club after the game.

Away from the doubtful delights of the docks, there was one small pub I frequented in those days called the Yard of Ale, on the corner of Convent Road and Silom. The place was run by a talented pianist Sam Scott, who would perform anything from Noel Coward to Gilbert and Sullivan. It boasted a dartboard, which helped attract expats, including a number of *Post* colleagues like Stuart Judd and Jim Kelly. It was also home to some very large rodents. One of the more serious dart players became so enraged at the rats scurrying around below the board, he threw his dart at one, scoring a direct hit on the rodent's backside. The rat and dart disappeared down a drainpipe, never to be seen again.

The establishment later had a change of owner and name, being known simply as The Pub, run by an amiable American, Art Hubbs, before being transformed into a trendy boutique called John Fowler's. Just an early example of how fleeting nightlife establishments can be in Bangkok.

After that there was an absence of British-style "pubs" for a few years until Bobby de Cozier opened Bobby's Arms at the back of Patpong in 1975, which became very popular. It was one of the few places you could take your wife or girlfriend at night without them feeling uncomfortable. In 1980, just round the corner on Silom Road, came the Toby Jug, a friendly little pub and restaurant run by Annan, where it was easy to spend a few hours relaxing after work.

Patpong was quite different in the early 70s - there was no naff street market for a start, and you could even park outside a bar. It was still quite a business hub in the daylight hours, with airline offices and the like. The news agency United Press International was also based there, in the thick of things - a true "hardship post." When UPI eventually moved to the U-Chuliang, its old office became a bar, known as the UP 1 (Up One). There was also a large upstairs nightclub called the Aladdin, which was to succumb to the boom in a-go-go bars a few years later.

There was only a smattering of a-go-go bars with pole dancers on Patpong at that time, but this was to change significantly. In the mid-1970s Patpong really began to pick up steam and would regularly feature in international news reports highlighting Bangkok's "naughty nightlife". There were frequent changes of name, but certain bars stood the test of time. They all had their special appeal, although the common denominator was stunning dancers.

One of my favourite spots, at the Silom end of Patpong, was the Bad Apple, which was later to become better known as the Safari, one of the most successful establishments on the strip. The Bad Apple played great rock music and was one of the few bars I ever patronized during daylight hours. This was not an early sign of alcoholism, but there was a table tennis room at the back, where some afternoons I took on Sri Lankan colleague Edward Thangarajah, later to become *Post* sports editor. I always ended up being well and truly thrashed.

The Bad Apple was the perfect forerunner to the Safari, which was special in that the DJ only played music from vinyl albums and you were guaranteed hours of top music. Remarkably it retained its "vinyl-only" policy with considerable success until just a few years ago.

Superstar, run by Frank Allum, was perhaps the trendiest and most popular bar, always playing the latest music. I remember going there after work late one night in December 1980 and informing Frank about the killing of John Lennon in New York. Frank played nothing but Lennon songs for the remainder of the evening. During one crackdown, he even put barbed wire on the stage to protest a ban on dancers and early closing.

Night Out: Coming across former Post cartoonist "Nop" and other Thai colleagues at the old Superstar bar on Patpong in the early 1980s.

Another popular spot which I really enjoyed was The Mississippi Queen, which specialized in soul music and produced some energetic dancers, who performed on platforms above the bar. It was quite a small place, designed to look like a steamboat, but they crammed a lot into it. Two of the most popular dancers were twins, and I couldn't tell them apart - their nicknames were Joy and June. But most of all, the Mississippi Queen had a great atmosphere. Even the sign outside had a certain style - a sketch of a Mississippi river boat and below it the enticing words, for me anyway, "blues, soul, jazz".

Mississippi Queen also gained fame for providing a scene from the 1978 Oscar-winning film *The Deer Hunter*. One of the Patpong dancers, Noi, famously secured a brief speaking role in the production, which elevated her to number one in the street's pecking order for a while. Around that time I was invited to be a judge in the Patpong Mardi Gras beauty contest, sponsored by the Rotary Club. It was Noi who went on to win the crown, Miss Patpong. I hasten to add that the judges were not influenced by Noi's brief taste of film stardom.

Then there was the Grand Prix run by Rick Menard, who introduced pole dancing to the street. The bar became a meeting place for journalists, diplomats, Vietnam vets, spooks and just about anyone who had spent a long time in Asia and had a tale to tell. A number of international celebrities passed through the Grand Prix, especially boxers as Rick was mad about the sport.

When it was time to eat late at night, I often headed for the Madrid cocktail lounge with its unsurpassed pizzas that proved lifesavers on many a night out. It wasn't unusual to spot senior corporate executives rounding off their evening munching on a "pepperoni with extra cheese" to help prepare themselves for the rigours of the next day's board meetings.

One establishment which was a bit different was the Napoleon, more of a restaurant lounge than a bar. There were no dancers, but some pleasant hostesses. During the week it showed movies, but its main attraction was the Dixieland Jazz Club sessions every Sunday afternoon, at that time Bangkok's only regular jazz outlet. The place was always packed with a comfortable blend of expats and Thais. When it was bouncing, it was arguably the liveliest place in town. Led by Vic Luna (trombone) and Laurie Gooding (clarinet), the band played the whole range of traditional jazz and occasionally blues if they felt in the mood. Visiting international musicians sometimes joined in for memorable jam sessions. Popular British doctor Paddy Dickson, a great blues piano fan, was often seen tickling the ivories to good effect. The *Bangkok Post* even had a representative, American sub-editor Joe de Rienzo, who played a mean banjo.

Sunday Special: The popular jazz band packed out the Napoleon on Sunday afternoons in the late 1970s.

Another reasonably sophisticated establishment and a favourite spot amongst expats was Club 99 just around the corner from Patpong on Silom Road. Particularly popular with the Scandinavian community, it featured a combo which played old standards for the relatively mature clientele. Some of the hostesses were fairly well-seasoned too, but very genial and added to the comfortable atmosphere. It was an ideal place to relax and have a chat, away from the brasher Patpong bars.

Almost anyone who has been to a Bangkok bar or nightclub will have witnessed the "candle show", in which the female dancers let the hot wax from the burning candles drip onto their bodies. I have never been quite able to fathom what is remotely entertaining about this particular performance, but it has always been popular.

However, one incident I observed does stand out. In the early 1980s at a Patpong establishment, a girl was performing the candle routine to a fairly disinterested audience, with the exception of one Middle Eastern gentleman who was enraptured, jumping up and down and absolutely loving it. He was also totally drunk. This can only explain his next act, when he tried to extinguish the burning candles the dancer was holding by spraying them with beer from his glass. Not a good idea.

For a moment the dancer just stood there motionless with the beer suds running down her body along with the candle wax. Then she leapt off the stage and landed on the fellow who was still clapping with glee at the accuracy of his beer spraying. The next couple of minutes there was total pandemonium, culminating in the beer-thrower leaving the bar in horizontal fashion, covered in candle wax.

Another unscheduled incident occurred in an adjacent bar, when the python co-starring in what was billed the "exotic lady-snake show" became a bit bored and slithered off the stage into the audience. Suffice to say, the entire bar's customers fled the scene, if only into the next bar.

Something that always impressed me about Patpong was that although it was the centre of western-style nightlife and relatively expensive bars by local standards, the restaurants in the vicinity were extremely good value. There were many excellent places to eat, like the Red Door and Tip Top, but two that really stood out were the Thai Room, with the very attentive waiters, and Mizu's Kitchen, which is still there on Patpong 1 and highly recommended.

It was in Mizu's in mid-1969 that I was first introduced by Brett Bartos to *Bangkok Post* sports editor Anton Perera before I joined the paper. Anton immediately ordered several plates of sashimi and insisted on paying for everything, a typical gesture from a man I was to get to know quite well. For the next two hours we talked sport, but mainly cricket, and little did I know at the time that very soon I would find myself playing for the *Post* team, which Anton captained.

Over the years I visited Patpong less and less, partly because it became increasingly mercenary, but I was also getting weary of the scene, although managed occasional trips to Limelight and Goldfinger, two of the livelier bars. The introduction of the night market in the early 90s certainly did not help matters and the place became a far cry from the dynamic strip of the 1970s and 80s. For me it had lost its sense of fun and spontaneity, or maybe I was simply spoilt... and getting older.

15. GOOD VIBES ON THE STRIP

Escaping the Vietnam War on Bangkok's 'Golden Mile'

The wildest, most entertaining nightlife area for foreigners up to 1975 was definitely the New Petchaburi Road strip, sometimes known as "The Golden Mile", which stretched roughly from Asoke to Ekamai on both sides of the road. Behind the bars on the eastern side there was nothing but fields and swamp. The "Strip" catered primarily for raucous GIs on R&R from the Vietnam War and those fortunate enough to be based in Thailand. There was also a smattering of expats and newshounds who couldn't afford the hotel nightclubs and who were possibly just as noisy as the GIs after a few beers. Tourists were almost non-existent.

The bar names were not exactly a source of creativity, with such offerings as California, Las Vegas, San Francisco, Hollywood and Miami. They all had a basic format of live bands, booze and birds, not necessarily in that order. In reality, they acted like dance halls. All the ladies wore numbers, although by the end of the evening it was not uncommon to see inebriated customers wearing them too. Suffice to say, these watering holes were considerably more entertaining than any of the present-day pole-dancing establishments around the city.

Most of the bars had dance floors, which were always a source of entertainment and amusement, considering the wretched state of some of the customers. There was also a plentiful supply of rodents and cockroaches, which would get into the spirit of things by performing some commendable break-dancing.

Admittedly the quality of the music left a lot to be desired. But it didn't really matter. The US servicemen, especially those fresh from the horrors of Vietnam, were not too bothered if the band didn't play in key or couldn't sing, just as long as the music was loud and there were lots of guitars blasting away… and of course, plenty of girls lurking. But there were also some very talented bands. Everyone seemed to be intent on having a good time, although there were inevitably occasional punch-ups, usually involving disputes over bills or girls. The waiters invariably won on points and were not averse to using tables and chairs as impromptu weapons. Nothing has changed in that respect.

One watering hole that was particularly popular was Thai Heaven, which lived up to its name if you had just come from battling the Viet Cong in the jungle and rice paddies. It was a cavernous establishment, with an estimated 200 hostesses, where you were charged the grand sum of 20 baht for a large bottle of Singha beer - a cheap way of getting a horrendous hangover. A colleague took an Australian nurse there on one occasion and she wondered why there were so many "waitresses".

Most nights the Thai Heaven had a quaint show featuring an old-fashioned stripper, usually a buxom, slightly overweight, not-so-young lady. She would dance to the strains of *Tea for Two Cha Cha,* a sort of compulsory song for Thai strippers in Bangkok at that time, although sometimes we were treated to *Besame Mucho*. It was all a bit camp, but the American servicemen loved it and would whistle and cheer like they were at a gridiron game as the dancer divested herself of assorted bangles and beads.

Understandably, many of the Americans coming from the battlefields in Vietnam had somewhat fragile nerves. This was highlighted one night in the Las Vegas bar when there was an enormous explosion as the air conditioner blew out. This was followed by an even louder crash as about 50 US soldiers hit the floor, thinking it was an incoming round. Tables and beers went flying and it even got a mention in the *Post* the following day.

Down the far end of the strip there was a small cluster of bars catering almost entirely for black GIs, particularly the Soul Sister and the somewhat smaller Jack's American Star Bar. Colleague Peter Finucane and I were both great fans of soul music and became frequent visitors. American friends thought two white guys like us were crazy going into such places and looking back on it, they were probably right. But the music was superb - James Brown, Marvin Gaye, Otis Redding, Aretha Franklin - and so was the atmosphere.

Both bars had excellent bands, particularly the group at Jack's called Salt 'n' Pepper. Two of the group's members were usually the only white people in the place, apart from us. When the black lead singer launched into Brown's anthem, *Say It Loud (I'm Black And I'm Proud)*, he would sometime strut across the small dance floor and with a big grin gesture at us "honkies" sitting in the audience. I think he was genuinely amused at seeing these two white dudes sitting there, enjoying it so much. We never had a problem at Jack's or any of the other soul bars, although admittedly some people did. It probably helped being British - our accents sounded funny for a start.

Jack's also had an upstairs coffee shop where a jukebox played all the latest soul music. I could sit there for hours just absorbing the sounds while tucking into some "soul food".

Not far from Jack's, was a small massage parlour, curiously named Stephen Ward Massage, presumably after the osteopath involved in the dramatic Profumo Affair featuring Christine Keeler, in England a few years earlier. It seemed an odd name for a Thai massage joint.

One soul bar I particularly liked was Whiskey and Jazz, which required climbing some steep stairs. As the name implies, the music was a little more jazz oriented and featured a laid-back, but very accomplished, sax player called Kurt Watkins. His standout number was a tremendous version of *My Favourite Things,* inspired by John Coltrane's classic interpretation. I suspected he might have got a bit fed up with us, as we always requested that song. The Whiskey and Jazz manager, a tall, balding soul brother, seemed to know only two words - "Right on!". When we arrived he would greet us with "right on!", when he walked past our table it was "right on!" and as we were leaving it would be "right on!" He was also a master of the elaborate handshake called the "dap", something I could never master.

Unfortunately there was a darker side to the scene. The manager of Jack's, an amiable retired serviceman by the name of Jimmy Smedley, turned out to be part of a heroin trafficking operation. When he was arrested in October 1976, after a large heroin shipment had been intercepted in Bangkok, I was quite shocked. In fact I was stunned, as only a couple of nights before I had been chatting with him in the Thermae coffee shop after finishing work. I had even mentioned to him about the huge heroin bust the *Post* was carrying on the front page as its lead story in the next day's edition, blissfully unaware that he was in any way involved. He was later sentenced to life imprisonment and after some delay was flown to the US to serve out his term.

My favourite establishment on the Golden Mile was a bar called the Green Dragon, primarily because of the Apples band, which played lots of Beatles, Hendrix, Animals and even Dylan.

I recall sitting in the Green Dragon one night in October 1969 during a major thunderstorm. Being in a low-lying area with little drainage, the floodwater simply poured into the bar until it was about a foot deep. To their credit the band, who were on a raised stage, kept playing despite there being a safety risk with all the electrical equipment. As for the customers - well, we just put our feet up on the tin chairs and ordered another beer. We were stranded anyway because outside, New Petchaburi Road had transformed into a *khlong*. It truly was Venice of the East. The Apples got into the spirit of things by playing Buddy Holly's *Raining in My Heart*.

The band specialized in the Beatles and would play anything, from *With A Little Help From My Friends* to *Strawberry Fields Forever* or *"Sa-trawberry Phil"* as it sometimes came out. I was impressed at the quality of their interpretations and could listen to them all night ... and sometimes did. One of their most frequently requested numbers was the iconic *A Day in the Life* and they made a good job of a rather complex song. They also displayed a nice touch of humour. When it came to the line "the England Army had just won the war", they changed the lyrics to "Thailand Army", which prompted much mirth. To accommodate the GIs they would repeat the line, this time with "American Army" and were greeted by loud applause and a bombardment of free beers from the assembled military men. However, I remember one GI sitting at the next table with a couple of girls draped over him shouting out: "Ain't no f------ way we are going to win this war man." He was right.

We became friendly with some members of the Apples band, most of whom were Thammasat University students and a very pleasant bunch of lads they were, too. I would attempt to write the lyrics in English for them when none were available. The only way to achieve this in those pre-internet days was through a tedious process of playing a cassette tape, or even worse a vinyl record, and listening over and over again.

The organist and lead singer of the Apples, "Eed", was mad keen on Dylan, but not surprisingly struggled with the lyrics. We spent hours listening on vinyl records to Dylan tracks from *Highway 61 Revisited* and *Blonde On Blonde* albums, trying to decipher what he was singing. As any Dylan fan knows, the singer's enunciation often left a lot to be desired and on occasions we had to simply guess what he was singing. Not exactly a high-tech operation, but it was great fun and actually helped me appreciate Dylan more, especially some of the intriguing lyrics he came up with. What made it worth the effort was seeing the reaction of some of the Americans in the bar when they heard this Thai lad coming out with difficult Dylan numbers. They absolutely loved it.

Like all good groups, the Apples broke up after a couple of years and Eed went on to play with the Royal Sprite, which became very popular, but the music was middle-of-the-road pop. Eed had few opportunities to indulge in his Dylan repertoire.

Not long after I had first met him, Eed took me to a small shop near Sanam Luang to buy a record player - yes, it was still in those vinyl LP days. During the bargaining process an argument erupted between the shopkeeper and Eed, but eventually a reasonable price was agreed upon. As we left the premises Eed told me the shopkeeper couldn't understand why he wouldn't agree to an inflated price and get 10% commission to fleece the *farang*. Eed explained that we were friends, which apparently the shopkeeper found quite puzzling.

The "Golden Mile" was always going to be a temporary set up and the end of the Vietnam War, effectively when Saigon fell on April 30, 1975, also marked the beginning of the end for the New Petchaburi Road bars. The final rites came pretty quickly. A few bars tried to keep going, but without the American servicemen these places were doomed. But my goodness, they were buzzing while they lasted.

During those seven years on the strip I heard all sort of extraordinary tales from helicopter pilots, medics and the regular "grunts" who manned the patrols that trudged through the Vietnam paddy fields and jungles, always with the fear of an ambush or being blown up by Viet Cong booby-traps. While the alcohol was doing a lot of the talking, I'm sure much of it was the truth. After all, there was no need to exaggerate. And after their seven days of getting plastered in Bangkok, all they had to look forward to was more close encounters with the Viet Cong. I wouldn't have swapped places with any of them.

16. SUKHUMVIT SOJOURN

From the Joker Club to the early days of Soi Cowboy

While most nightlife areas tended to be hidden away, the main thoroughfare of Sukhumvit Road featured quite a few bars in the early 1970s, although the establishments were small and relatively discreet. You certainly didn't have girls parading outside them, unlike more recent times.

Many of the bars had the same format, but some tried a few innovations. One such establishment, between Soi 7 and 9, was the Electric Shadow, regarded as a hangout for "cool dudes" who appreciated Jimi Hendrix, Led Zeppelin, Crosby, Stills and Nash and so on. Backpackers, or "hippies" as they were called by Thais in those days, couldn't afford the prices, so it was mainly patronized by a few expats and the more senior students from the International School of Bangkok (ISB), which at that time was based on Soi 15. The students from ISB, mainly American, are probably now middle-aged pillars of society.

Apart from good music, the Electric Shadow's main attraction was a giant water bed, which was something of a novelty at the time. Unfortunately, it eventually sprung a leak, creating quite a mess. When Hendrix died in 1970, a coffin appeared with the singer's name on it in the middle of the dance floor. Having a pole dancer performing on top of the coffin was a bit bizarre, but certainly became a talking point and Hendrix would probably have approved. Unfortunately the bar didn't outlive Hendrix for very long, as it was located on some prime real estate.

Something a bit different was the Cock 'n Bull restaurant and the Joker Club above it, on the corner of Soi 19 (now the site of Westin Hotel), run by Chris Huie and Peter Ernhjolm. Both places did well. The restaurant used to run old films on reel to reel, which went down very well in the pre-video era. Upstairs, the Joker Club was particularly popular with oil and construction crews on leave from the Middle East, offering the most comfortable armchairs in Bangkok where you could listen to versatile Filipino Freddie and the band doing their thing on stage.

SUKHUMVIT SOJOURN

I swear I saw ace British guitarist Jeff Beck jam there one night. I wish there were a few more places like the Joker these days.

There was a particularly entertaining period at the Joker when Peter adopted a pet piglet which he thought might become a talking-point at the club. It did, but not in the manner intended. The porker was given a "kennel" on the building's flat roof above Peter's room. Tucking into the daily restaurant leftovers, the piglet soon transformed into a full-size pig. Unfortunately attempts to house-train the porker failed miserably and it never became the bar celebrity as Peter originally hoped.

The pig hated rain and would make horrible squealing noises when the heavens opened. So when it rained Peter would put the pig in his bathroom next to his bedroom - not a great idea. One rainy night after the bar had closed, Peter went out for some after hours entertainment, forgetting he had left the pig in the bathroom. He returned later that night with a girlfriend and once inside his room the girl headed for the bathroom. The next thing Peter heard was a loud shriek. The girl had opened the bathroom door to be greeted by this giant porker grunting at her and wagging its tail. She rushed out, gave Peter an earful and fled the scene.

The staff never thought the pig was a good idea anyway, so when Peter went back to Sweden for Christmas, the opportunity was taken to have a festive season special in the restaurant, featuring roast pork. No need to say where the pork came from.

There was a small stretch of little bars on the main Sukhumvit Road from Soi 14 to Soi 16, before it was transformed into the Ratchadapisek highway. We used to refer to them as the "Roses" bars, as they had names like Three Roses, Rosemary 1 and 2, while there was also the El Toro and Rainbow. If you were feeling a bit rundown or weary walking along Sukhumvit, they were convenient spots where you could slump into a corner and be pampered at no great expense. Most of these bars transferred to Nana Plaza in the early 1980s.

Nana Plaza hadn't really taken off in those days, although the spacious Woodstock bar and restaurant was always very reliable, with good food and solid rock 'n roll music. Woodstock was also one of the first places to hold a-go-go competitions, featuring dancers from assorted bars in the city. They were always pretty lively evenings and the place was packed to the rafters.

I remember viewing the English 1987 Cup Final at the Woodstock, when Coventry upset Tottenham Hotspur. It was a rather strange environment in which to watch a football match as the place was full of Australians and Americans, who didn't have the slightest interest in soccer and were listening to loud rock music. I was the only person watching the match and I suspect the other customers thought I was a bit weird, especially when I asked the pole dancers on the stage to get out of the way as they were blocking my view of the game.

A regular haunt on Sukhumvit, occupying a prime spot on the corner of Soi 16, was one of my favourite restaurants, Mitch and Nam's, which specialised in "soul food". It was run by Vietnam War veteran Mitch, assisted by his friend Josh Gaines. Nam, who was Mitch's wife, could not get out of Vietnam. The restaurant's speciality was spare ribs, which were absolutely spot on, along with some mouth-watering cornbread. The restaurant had a great jukebox full of soul music, although I still associate the place with the Rod Stewart song *Hot Legs*, possibly influenced by a slinky waitress.

The restaurant sadly fell victim to the Ratchadapisek extension. Where Mitch and Nam's once stood is now a huge office block, Exchange Tower. After Mitch died, Josh ran the place, but later moved to Soi Cowboy, where he ran J's Soul Food restaurant for several years. I was a regular customer and sometimes ran into Bernard Trink taking in a movie and demolishing some "toothsome" spare ribs at the same time. Unfortunately ill-health struck Josh and he passed away a few years later.

This brings us to Soi Cowboy, a little street which to my surprise has become a major attraction in recent years. As a nightlife area it didn't really surface until the late 1970s and experienced humble beginnings. Long before it became known as Soi Cowboy, it was just a small nameless *soi* with a few neighbourhood bars, friendly and quite amateurish, which was part of its appeal. It was occasionally referred to as Soi Gold Label after the first proper bar of that name opened in 1975. Run by someone calling himself "The Sheikh", it was more of a cocktail lounge, although it had a couple of dancers and being the only place on the street, was something of a hideaway. At the time of writing, Baccara bar is on the original Gold Label site, a very different kind of establishment.

I first came across the *soi* completely by accident one New Year's Eve in the mid-1970s along with colleague Tony Waltham, while taking a short cut from Asoke to Sukhumvit 23. It was just a quiet little street of dull shophouses, but halfway down on the left we spotted a little place with fairy lights named Ratree, which was enough to appeal to our curiosity.

It was just a shophouse with metal tables and chairs and a couple of serving girls - nothing naughty and no dancing. There were no other customers and we had good fun practicing our Thai with the staff, who were all from the Northeast (as is still the case for most Soi Cowboy workers). We must have whiled away a couple of hours and by the time we ordered the bill, Tony and I had got through quite a few Singha beers. To our surprise they asked us if we could remember how many beers we had consumed. It was then we discovered they didn't really have a cashier and had kept no record of the beers we had drunk. They had taken the bottles away and we could only guess as to our consumption. They seemed quite happy with our somewhat conservative estimate. It was no rip-off, in fact just the opposite. They were hopelessly incompetent, but in the nicest possible way.

Not surprisingly, we returned every now and again, by which time they had discovered the necessity of bills. There slowly developed half-a -dozen bars, all of a similar laid-back nature, although some had a smattering of dancers

On one occasion I was in a quiet little place called Chitra's aimlessly munching away at some peanuts, when I became aware of an alien object in my mouth. It felt like a very stale peanut. I eventually extracted the rogue peanut, only to discover it was a false tooth - and not mine. When I presented the tooth to the bartendee, she did not seem in the least surprised and had a perfectly logical explanation. Apparently Auntie Jum, the cleaner, must have taken out her false tooth earlier in the day and deposited it in its regular resting place, one of the peanut bowls which was empty at the time. She had simply forgotten where she had put it.

As is commonly known, Soi Cowboy is named after an African-American former US serviceman, T.G. Edwards, who went by the nickname "Cowboy" and frequently wore a cowboy hat. He didn't ride to work on a horse as legend has it, although admittedly it makes a good story. Just imagine riding down Sukhumvit on a horse, even in those days.

Cowboy and his Thai wife, who I knew as "Anong", opened the original Cowboy bar a little way down from the Gold Label in around 1977. It was just a single shophouse bar, but very lively and soon became popular, partly because of the gregarious nature of Cowboy, while his wife could also be pretty entertaining after she'd had a few.

Unfortunately they split up, with Cowboy establishing his own Cowboy bar on the opposite side of the *soi,* while his former wife went on to open Loretta's bar, named after the couple's daughter. It was a double shophouse and became a regular haunt for many Cowboy denizens. I attended quite a few farewell parties there for expats who had been posted elsewhere, but didn't really want to leave. There was a definite "upcountry" flavour to the place and you could be forgiven for feeling you had ended up in Buriram or Roi-Et. She later opened Milanos, identical to Loretta's, further down the street.

Anong was very patriotic and on the royal birthdays she would organize the girls from Loretta's and other bars to line the *soi* at 8 p.m., all holding lighted candles and singing the royal anthem. It was quite a sight.

Cowboy was a tall man, quite loud and frequently drunk, but in a friendly way. He also had quite a few tales to tell, all of which I have forgotten. It was because of his gregarious nature that Cowboy became friendly with the *Bangkok Post's* nightlife correspondent, Bernard Trink, who paid weekly Sunday night visits to the *soi*. Trink heard much of what was going on along the *soi* from Cowboy, and it wasn't long before he was referring to the place as "Soi Cowboy" in his widely-read Friday *Nite Owl* column. The name stuck and has long been an officially accepted address in the Bangkok metropolis. If it was not for Trink, Soi Cowboy would be called something totally different. I shudder to think what that might have been.

Field work: With fellow journalists running into Bernard Trink on Soi Cowboy during the late 1970s. (From left) Trink, Geoffrey Goddard, Julian Spindler, Julian's nephew, Crutch and Norman Bottorff.

Owing to financial problems, it wasn't long before Cowboy left the *soi* named after him and opened a couple of places further down Sukhumvit, neither of which were very successful. His final offering to Bangkok's nightlife came in 1986 when he opened the New Cowboy Bar and Restaurant on Sukhumvit Soi 22. Cowboy left Bangkok shortly after and is believed to have passed away somewhere outside of Thailand. For someone with such an outgoing nature, it was a rather subdued and sad way to bow out.

Cowboy was not the only character on the *soi*, but he certainly had the highest profile. None of the bars from that early period exist in name now, but to get a flavour of that time other places included My Lady, Pam's, Shuffs, Honeymoon, Gallery and Red Diamond.

One thing that Soi Cowboy was lacking in the early days was decent music, although Cowboy's bar itself wasn't too bad, with a smattering of soul sounds. There were no live bands on the street at that time and few proper deejays. You had to put up with cassette compilation tapes of the blandest hits of the time, often selected by the female cashier or some other staff member. So in nearly every bar you would be subjected to songs like *Yellow River, Sugar Sugar, Yummy Yummy Yummy, Save Your Kisses For Me, Disco Duck* and whatever Boney M song happened to be popular at the time.

On one occasion I was sitting in a bar chatting to a sweet young lady. But the music was even worse than usual - a tape featuring Thai cover versions of the aforementioned songs... absolute purgatory. I said to the girl that although the bar was pleasant enough, it would be a lot better if they did something about the music. She completely agreed and shook her head knowingly. The music was quite dreadful, she said. Thankfully the tape came to an end. Then she excused herself, explaining she had to change the music as she was the deejay. Not my first or last experience of foot in mouth.

Just around the corner on Soi 23 was the George and Dragon pub, run by a Geordie called 'Doc', ably assisted behind the counter by his loyal Thai staffer "Miss Piggy". She loved talking about the time former England football star and manager Kevin Keegan, himself a Geordie, visited her pub and bought her a drink. The pub was renamed the Ship Inn by Barry Cable and his wife Doi, and proved to be a very pleasant oasis from the bar scene until it closed in 2013, replaced by yet another brash a-go-go joint. A little bit further towards Sukhumvit was the Offshore, helmed by Ray from Preston, which also closed after a commendable 30-year run.

One of the older bars on Cowboy that is still in existence is the Moonshine Joint, a friendly place run by Aussie Steve Hatherell and Thongsorn. Known for its decent music and accompanying videos, it attracts a lot of expats. On the wall inside the Moonshine is a striking image of Steve dressed as a magician, pulling out of a top hat, not a rabbit, but a frightened-looking dog which became a legend in its own lifetime.

The dog, named Half-Hard, featured in my previous book, *Forgotten, But Not Gone*, but deserves a brief mention here. Half-Hard was a fairly ugly-looking stray mongrel, which had wandered down Soi Cowboy on its last legs. It looked in such bad shape that a couple of bar owners, Steve at the Moonshine along with Dave Adams and Tuk from the Hare and Hound pub opposite, felt sorry for him. So they cleaned him up and began feeding him, pork chop being his meal of choice.

After a few months of care, Half-Hard developed into a healthy hound, although they could do nothing about its looks. For the most part the dog was a friendly little fellow and the staff at the bars loved him, as did most of the customers. Unfortunately Half-Hard had a mean streak in him, having no time for vendors, the ice man and policemen. One quick sniff and he would dash out, take a nip out of their ankles and beat a hasty retreat. It got so bad, some of those on the receiving end of his attention made it clear that the dog's days were numbered. That's why, when Half-Hard disappeared one night, everyone feared the worst. He had last been seen after closing time having a quiet nap and there were any number of candidates who were capable of committing the unthinkable.

After a couple of weeks, with no sightings of the dog, his many two-legged friends on the *soi* reluctantly accepted he had gone to the Great Kennel in the Sky. Some were so distressed they held a small wake for him in the Hare and Hound, featuring a wreath and a plaintive eulogy. A few tears were even shed and special Half-Hard memorial t-shirts were made to commemorate the occasion.

The following evening, customers were discussing the previous day's wake, when to their astonishment who should they see wandering down the *soi*, but none other than the familiar wet nose and ugly face of Half-Hard, appearing without a care in the world. What had taken place in the previous few weeks only the dog knows, but suffice to say, if he had shown up 24 hours earlier Half-Hard would have walked in on his own funeral.

The dog became something of a celebrity after that escapade and was even known to climb onto the a-go-go stage in the Moonshine and strut his stuff to the sounds of the old Rolling Stones hit, *Walking The Dog*. He would get particularly animated when Mick Jagger started whistling.

In the late 1980s, a slightly more upmarket bar scene emerged on Sukhumvit Soi 33, otherwise known as "Soi of Dead Artists", with bars bearing the names of French Impressionist painters like Renoir, Monet, Gauguin and Degas. It was a promising idea and an added attraction was that these establishments did not bother with the otherwise ubiquitous pole dancers. They more than made up for it with a plentiful supply of hostesses, purportedly a bit more sophisticated than their counterparts on Soi Cowboy, although some might dispute that. In addition, expats probably felt more comfortable telling the wife they had spent an evening of interesting conversation at Renoir or Degas as opposed to say Pussy Galore on Patpong.

I was only an occasional visitor owing to my late working hours at the *Post*. The Soi 33 bars had a reasonable "Happy Hour" up to 9 p.m., but after that prices soared. By the time I finished work the joy of "happy hour" had long evaporated and the *soi* lost much of its appeal unless you had deep pockets. However, many businessmen appreciated the cerebral atmosphere of the Soi of Dead Artists, as opposed to more basic attractions of Cowboy, Nana Plaza and Patpong. Recently, however, many of the traditional establishments on Soi 33 have struggled and at the time of writing there was only one bar left bearing an artist's name, Goya... and he wasn't even an Impressionist. However, the *soi* is evolving and the arrival of the popular Check Inn 99, which has moved from its long-time abode on lower Sukhumvit, may well inject new life into the street.

Soi Cowboy looks like being the main draw in the Sukhumvit area for a while, although things can change very rapidly in the nightlife business. It is amazing how this once quiet little backwater, which has been through some very hard economic times in the past three decades, is now such a popular tourist haunt, with all the garish neon lights and brash commercialism that has come with it. Several times in the past I thought it was on its last legs, like some of its customers.

It is somewhat ironic that one unexpected boost to the *soi* came with the ban on smoking in bars and restaurants in 2008. Just about every bar on Cowboy responded by setting up an outside area for smokers. The outside seating also proved very popular with non-smokers, who felt more comfortable observing the nightly pageant on the street, rather than being confined inside. Some would argue there is considerably more entertainment out on the street than inside. One thing for sure, anyone wearing a really silly fancy dress outfit will end up on Cowboy before the night is over.

The success of the movie *Hangover 2* in 2012, which was partly filmed on Soi Cowboy, has no doubt helped in the street's popularity and there are a number of "Bangkok Hangover Nightlife Tours". You can watch tourists of all nationalities parading up and down the *soi* every night. Most of them look quite amused, if somewhat embarrassed, others seemingly a trifle bewildered and a few who don't appear too impressed. It will come as no surprise that I preferred Soi Cowboy in the old, quieter times. However, it can still be a fun place to watch the nocturnal world go by and serves a reminder that there are all sorts of shapes and sizes in the world. And some ghastly tattoos.

17. BASES LOADED

Nakhon Phanom, U-tapao, Bob Hope and the B-52 bombers

When I arrived in Thailand, the Vietnam conflict had been going on for more than a decade, with US involvement escalating in the mid-1960s. Their numbers peaked in 1968, with 537,000 troops on the ground during the Lyndon Johnson administration. The war was to continue for another six years until the fall of Saigon in 1975. Coming from England, where there was little support for the war, more a feeling of general apathy, I was not aware of how heavily involved Thailand was, hosting a number of bases which were crucial to the US effort.

From 1969 to 1976 I visited all the Thai towns with US bases - Korat, Udon Thani, Ubon Ratchathani, Nakhon Phanom, Takhli and U-tapao, all but the last two in *Isan* (Northeast Thailand). The bonus at these towns for casual visitors was that the nightlife was pretty lively - the US servicemen certainly knew how to party.

Every year in December, the *Bangkok Post* carried stories concerning the visiting USO Christmas Show, which performed at all the bases from 1964-72. The show starred Bob Hope and it is probably the only time that anyone of international acclaim had ever visited, let alone performed in Takhli, a small unremarkable town near Nakhon Sawan. There were accompanying photographs of Hope riding in pedal *samlors*, coming face to face with buffaloes, making funny faces at Thai babies and generally putting smiles on people's faces, Thais and Americans alike. He was the perfect match for the Land of Smiles.

Hope loved performing in the shows, which is quite understandable because they featured some of the world's most attractive women at that time, including Ursula Andress, Raquel Welch and Ann-Margret. The GIs all spoke highly of Hope. In a way, he was a kind of talisman for the troops and a much-needed one at that.

It wasn't all fun and laughter for Hope, however. On his last Christmas tour in 1972 he performed at U-tapao and found the audience uncharacteristically subdued. U-tapao was the home of the B-52 Stratofortress bombers, which in the weeks before had suffered many casualties on bombing missions over North Vietnam. Hope was informed by the base commander that they had lost 15 of their B-52s in just a few weeks and morale was very low. The comedian wrote later: "If they ever needed a morale-booster, it was then." To cheer them up, Hope made a point of chatting with the B-52 crews and telling them jokes before their mission, which was aptly named "Operation Hope". He later admitted he didn't get too many laughs, but they at least returned safely.

The B-52s were the most intimidating aircraft I had ever seen. Nicknamed "Buffs" by the American servicemen, they were simply called *"Bee Hasip-sawng"* (B52) by the Thai populace. "Buffs" stood for "Big Ugly Fat Fellow", although you don't require much imagination to figure out that "fellow" was usually replaced by a well-known expletive.

I remember sitting outside the base on the Sukhumvit highway in Rayong, watching the B-52s taking off on their bombing missions. It was both awesome and scary; the noise was deafening. They carried huge payloads, averaging 108 bombs of 500 and 750 pounds per mission. You wondered how they ever got off the ground... and how anyone on the ground could survive such a barrage.

Equally dramatic was watching the bombers returning, some of them a bit shakily, limping in after having bits shot off them over Vietnam. It wasn't all happy landings and there were plenty of dramatic scenes at U-tapao in the last two months of 1972 at the height of the bombing.

With all that going on, the Air Force personnel needed somewhere to let off steam, which they did in no uncertain manner at a couple of areas not far from the base - Kilo Sip and a place with the uninspiring name of Newland, especially set up for US military entertainment. The bars were uniformly sleazy and bit of an eye-opener for someone like me, who was more used to sitting in a countryside pub in Berkshire discussing the latest cricket scores.

The first time I went to Newland, I asked a passing serviceman which bars he could recommend. He looked at me as if I was an idiot: "They're all the f------ same man," he replied as he wandered off, and he was right. Just like the New Petchaburi Road strip in Bangkok, many of them had Thai bands. The most requested song was *Sky Pilot*, the hit about military chaplains by Eric Burdon and the Animals. The airmen just loved that song, as they did Cream's *Sunshine of Your Love*.

One of the more intriguing American military units based at U-tapao was the 556th Red Horse Squadron. Red Horse stood for Rapid Engineer Deployable Heavy Operational Repair Squadron Engineers, so you can understand why they felt an acronym was necessary.

The squadron arrived at U-tapao in 1966 and elements also went to five other US bases in Thailand. Known in Thailand as "*Ma Daeng*", they had their own live mascot, a small horse called "Step-n-Half", a name derived from radio call signs in Vietnam, from where the horse originated. According to RG "Andy" Anderson on his informative website www.angelfire.com dedicated to the Red Horse Squadron, Step was flown to U-tapao from Da Nang and was a popular figure at the base, reportedly developing a taste for Thai beer.

Although the squadron was deactivated in 1969, the horse remained at U-tapao until 1976, when it was transported to the Philippines, where it lived out its days. Step was buried at Clark Air Force base.

Just down the road from U-tapao was the small resort of Pattaya. Although hard to imagine now, at that time Pattaya was a sleepy coastal village with little night-time entertainment. On my first visit in mid-1969 there were no buildings higher than three storeys. The only hotel of note was the Nipa Lodge, a low-rise affair and very relaxing. The Pattaya Palace Hotel, constructed in the early 1970s, actually became a tourist attraction because of its size, even though it was only six storeys high. For several years it was major landmark on Beach Road.

Along with friends, I would stay at some wooden bungalows by the small beach in North Pattaya called Moonlight-on-Sea or another spot called Rock Cottages. Both were very pleasant, relaxing places, too.

In South Pattaya there was a large tamarind tree situated in the middle of Beach Road at the entrance of what is now Walking Street, which in those days featured the occasional restaurant and not much else. The tree acted as a natural roundabout and survived all sorts of vehicles slamming into it until, after many years, it inevitably got the chop. The tamarind was something of an institution and gave the place a bit of character, so its demise was a real shame. It was particularly handy if you were giving directions to anywhere in Pattaya - "When you reach the big tree, turn left and…". Mind you, if you turned right you would end up in the sea.

Almost adjacent to the tree was one of the few international restaurants of note, run by Dutchman Dolf Riks. On my first visit to Dolf's in late 1969, I was near broke, with only a couple of hundred baht to my name. Dolf served us himself and I sensed he was rather disappointed that I selected one of the cheapest dishes on the menu, a 75 baht pork chop. That still seemed expensive in those days. It was almost sacrilege to order something bland like that when Dolf had so many splendid Indonesian dishes available, like *rijsttafel*, with their rich and spicy flavours.

Little did either of us know as I sat there munching on my pork chop that some years later I would have the pleasant task of editing Dolf's cookery column for the *Post*. It made my mouth water just reading it. Sadly, Dolf passed away in 1999. He was one of the great Pattaya characters and a wonderful story teller.

I had my introduction to Nakhon Phanom while waiting at a bus station in neighbouring Udon Thani province, 210 kms to the west. There are probably worse places to be than Udon bus station at six in the morning, but none immediately spring to mind. "Nakhon Phanom?" I enquired of an ancient fellow, flicking flies from his coffee cup. "Where?" he asked, looking quite blank. "Nakhon Phanom," I repeated, struggling to remember if I had got the tones right. I was getting frustrated that after a couple of years in the kingdom I still could not make myself understood even for a common place name. After another series of tortuous attempts, the old man's face lit up in recognition with a toothless grin: *"En Kay Pee"* (NKP) he said with a chortle, and pointed to a dilapidated orange bus.

The unusual nomenclature given to Nakhon Phanom came as the result of the American base on the outskirts of the "city". When the Americans arrived at the base in 1963, Nakhon Phanom was little more than a sleepy border town on the bank of the Mekong River. When they left in 1976, it reverted to being a sleepy border town once more. But in between it was mighty "NKP City".

In 1972, during the daytime NKP was as quiet as anywhere else in rural Thailand. But at night the place transformed as the US servicemen headed into town. The names of the bars were the usual mixture, ranging from familiar promises of paradise such as Thai Heaven, Blue Hawaii and Lucky Star, to one simply called 123. A more interesting establishment was the ABC Wee House, about which many tales have been told over the years. However, I remember it primarily as the place where I heard for the first time on the jukebox Pink Floyd's, *Money*.

It may have been the relaxing influence of the mighty Mekong River that, despite the inevitable culture clash, the atmosphere in NKP seemed to be more pleasant than the other base towns, not that it was particularly bad in the other places. You would hear a unique bastardised language from the GIs on the lines of *"phom eat kowpat"* followed up by *"khun me cigarette?"* The girls were quick to catch on as to which servicemen were on *"Tee-Dee-Why"* (TDY - temporary duty) and used the standard bar girl English like "my friend you" and "same same monkey house".

I went on the base at Nakhon Phanom on a couple of occasions, the last time being in 1976 in an official capacity for the *Post* when the Americans pulled out. I've still got a moth-eaten "Fly The Friendly Skies of Thailand 1975-76" t-shirt purchased in Nakhon Phanom with a Jolly Green Giant helicopter emblazoned on it. NKP was primarily the monitoring station for the Vietnam War and the most popular t-shirt at that time was "In God We Trust, Everyone Else We Monitor".

Another t-shirt with a more sobering message reflected the growing disillusionment of US servicemen the longer the war went on. It read:

"Join the Air Force
Travel to exotic distant lands
Meet exciting, unusual people
And kill them."

It was at a restaurant-cum-nightclub on the banks of the Mekong in Nakhon Phanom that I first saw Thai rock guitarist Lam Morrison in action with the VIP band. They were young guys then and quite brilliant. The American servicemen loved them. They could play all the latest rock music, including songs by Led Zeppelin, The Doors and Jimi Hendrix. If you stepped out the backdoor of the club and looked across the river to Laos, with rock music blasting away, it was a very surreal experience to realize there was a war going on.

Lam and his band went on to tour Europe in the late 1970s, where they played many concerts. I last saw Lam a few years ago doing his thing in Pattaya, though he didn't have quite such a spectacular backdrop as the mighty Mekong and the Laos mountains.

During the daytime in the restaurant the radio was permanently tuned in to the local American Forces radio network, which, with all due respect, was a bit more entertaining than Radio Thailand. I would look over to Laos and wonder what the Communist Pathet Lao troops, who could easily pick up the broadcast, would make of it all. At eight every evening, legendary disc jockey Wolfman Jack, of *American Graffiti* fame, came howling forth on the radio shouting all sorts of nonsense, which must have confirmed any lingering suspicions the Pathet Lao held that all Americans were totally insane. That same restaurant featured dramatic photos on its walls of bombs being dropped on the Laotian side of the Mekong by the US bombers a few years before. Villagers used to gather nightly on the Thai side of the river to watch this most unusual light show.

R&R: Taking time out in the Northeast with Peter Finucane at a Nakhon Phanom hotel poolside in the mid 1970s.

The American forces are long gone, but Nakhon Phanom remains one of my favourite spots on the Mekong with its spectacular backdrop of the limestone mountains in Laos. When there is a full moon, it can be equally seductive as the moonlight dances off the water. I happened to be there during the Loy Krathong festival one year and it was a magical night watching all the *krathong* and their lighted candles bobbing about on the Mekong. As usual, mine unceremoniously sank a few seconds after releasing it on the river.

While Bangkok was not exactly a base town, it hosted thousands of Americans on R&R from Vietnam, who spent much of their time in the bars of New Petchaburi Road (as mentioned in Good Vibes on the Strip). However, during the daytime they had to be alert for assorted scams or semi-legitimate operations, designed to relieve them of their money.

One of the more sophisticated operations involved selling real estate to the servicemen. However, in most cases the prime real estate was little more than a piece of swamp in the Florida Everglades. They would send young Thai "spotters" out onto the street to look for vulnerable GIs and invite them to a nearby respectable hotel for a free meal. After that it was up to the foreign salesmen, mainly American, to do their pitch.

I was walking along Ploenchit Road one morning in 1970, when a smart-looking Thai youth approached. After a brief conversation he gave me a ticket, which said I would get a free buffet and a chance to buy cheap land if I attended the lunch. I was not in the habit of responding to approaches in the street and knew I wasn't the sort of customer they were looking for. But, knowing a couple of the salesmen involved, I was aware of the operation and thought it would be a laugh to show up. After all, it was my day off and lunchtime was approaching.

There were a number of tables in the function room, each with an American salesman in a suit. I was shown to one table where one of the salesmen I knew was sitting. When he looked up, he almost choked: "What are *you* doing here?" he asked, his face dropping. "I was invited," I said chirpily, showing him the ticket. "Well, bugger off!" he replied, knowing full well I had hardly enough money for a cinema seat, let alone "prime real estate". More importantly, he was worried I would tell the GIs the realities about their swamp. I kept quiet and stuffed myself at the buffet.

While the Vietnam War was going on, I was picked up on three separate occasions by the US Military Police in Thailand on suspicion of being AWOL. I can only think there must have been an AWOL GI who fitted my description.

On one occasion in 1970, I was walking along Ploenchit Road outside the British Embassy at about 7 a.m. after staying the night at a friend's apartment, when a jeep pulled alongside with two US MPs and a Thai cop. I didn't have any ID, although with my longish hair and English accent I thought it was fairly obvious I wasn't a runaway GI. Apparently it wasn't obvious and they wanted to see my passport, which was in my home. So I hopped aboard the jeep and was driven to my residence at the bottom of Sukhumvit Soi 1, by the *khlong*.

My arrival with three policemen naturally created quite a stir amongst the neighbours and a large crowd quickly gathered.

Matters were not helped when I discovered I didn't have my keys to the house. But after hammering on the door I awoke a journalist colleague who was none too pleased at being disturbed at an uncivilized hour after a night's work. I duly produced my British passport and one of the American cops politely apologized for bothering me.

I actually gained a bit of street cred for that little brush with the law. When I went to the local noodle shop for a coke shortly afterwards, the kids gathered and gave me the thumbs up as if I had achieved something. Also for months I had to put up with jokes from the Thai neighbours asking if I had been arrested lately.

18. SOUTHERN COMFORT

Experiencing the 'Deep South' in happier times

In the early 1970s, I usually spent my two-week annual vacation with colleague Peter Finucane exploring the "Deep South" of Thailand. We travelled around Yala, Pattani, Narathiwat, Songkhla and Satun. Sadly, with the exception of Songkhla and Satun, that would be inadvisable for westerners these days.

Our choice of destination was regarded as a bit odd, even in those times, by our Thai colleagues at the *Post*. Few people from Bangkok went south for their holidays - Hua Hin was the furthest many had ventured. But Peter was tired of being told that Chiang Mai was the best place to visit; he wanted to go in the opposite direction and asked me to join him. After what I had seen of the South on my hitchhiking experience in 1969, I jumped at the opportunity.

We didn't hitchhike. I'd had enough of that, eventful though it undoubtedly was. We hopped on the "express" train at Hua Lamphong in the early evening and arrived in Hat Yai late the following morning. Much of the trip was spent in the restaurant car and may well have involved a few beers to wash down the *kowpat*. Hat Yai is definitely not the prettiest place in the world, but it's a lively, bustling town with a heaving nightlife, much appreciated by Malaysians, who pour across the border at weekends.

I much preferred Songkhla as a town, which was far more attractive, quieter and relaxing, enhanced by the splendid Samila Beach, where it was all too easy to enjoy an extended sundowner session - something I experienced on a number of occasions over the years. I had first been to Songkhla in 1969, on the way back from the hitchhiking trip to Malaysia, looking for a boat to take Clarence and myself back to Bangkok. Not speaking a word of Thai on that initial journey, I recall drawing a child-like sketch of a boat with a funnel and showing it to a passing Songkhla local. He pointed us in the right direction to the port, although he did chuckle at the immature drawing.

I still associate the place with the haunting Steely Dan hit, *Do It Again*, as I first heard the song on a Songkhla noodle shop jukebox in 1972. Every time I hear that tune it conjures up an image of that noodle shop and wandering along Samila Beach, even four decades later.

Songkhla was also a great place to play beach volleyball, as related by American author James Eckardt in *Waylaid by the Bimbos* and his hilarious contributions to the *Bangkok Post*. Eckardt's heroic performances with Boontong's Bombers made gripping reading. Many years later, on Christmas Day in 1991, I felt quite privileged playing with *Post* colleague John Leicester against the Bombers on Samila's sacred sands. I can't remember too much about our performance, partly because the celebratory session on the beach after the game involved far too many Singha beers.

On one of our early expeditions Peter and I headed into Yala, the only landlocked province in southern Thailand. I was impressed by the wide streets in the provincial town and also the cleanliness. There was a small separatist movement at the time, but it was not regarded as a major problem. Of more concern were the communists, who were still active, especially in the vicinity of Betong on the Malaysian border. The Vietnam War was still going strong and the Red elements in the south had not yet given up the cause. The Yala-Betong road was not totally secure and off limits at night, which immediately made Peter want to travel on it. So we hopped on a dilapidated bus in Yala and rattled our way down the 150-kms road towards Betong, the southernmost town of Thailand.

On the bus journey I found myself looking out of the window, half expecting communist guerrillas to emerge from the thick jungle that lined the road. But there was no excitement of that nature, thank goodness. There were regular military roadblocks and we got a few funny looks from soldiers, not impressed by our explanation that we were simply "*bpy teeo*" (just looking around).

Betong, which means "bamboo" in Malay, was a busy little town with an abundance of Chinese restaurants. The Chinese influence was very strong with at least one-third of the population ethnic Hokkien. In the surrounding hills there were hundreds of Mandarin-speaking Chinese, who were members of the Communist Party of Malaya. In the mid 1980s they all surrendered to the Thai authorities.

I clambered up a small hilltop overlooking the town and was startled to come face-to-face with a bear. Fortunately it was of the stuffed variety, which had a place of honour in some rundown ornamental gardens. According to locals, a few of the bear's relatives still roamed the hills nearby.

While Pattani, Yala and Narathiwat are all predominantly Muslim, there were few outward signs of unrest at that time and no obvious safety fears. Pattani was arguably the most strikingly different province to the rest of Thailand, with a strong Malaysian atmosphere. In the provincial town, night entertainment consisted of sitting in Chinese noodle shops, the only places which served alcohol, and settling in for a very long but satisfying meal, assisted by a few slurps of Singha.

Satun was an intriguing place, as the majority Muslim population was much more assimilated into Thai society than those provinces further south. There wasn't an awful lot to do, however, and to kill a few hours one day Peter and I decided to board one of the regular long-tail boats full of locals. We said we wanted to go to *"pak nam"*, the mouth of the river where there was usually some sort of village. They all agreed this was the right boat.

We duly climbed aboard the packed boat and off we went. Before long the long-tail was threading its way through assorted mangrove channels, but there was nowhere to get off. After a while we found ourselves alarmingly in open sea and that's when I began to wonder just where we were heading. However, that was the least of our concerns, as we got hit by a squall. It soon became evident that our little boat was not fit for the sea.

Fortunately the storm quickly blew over and the boat settled down as we hugged the coast to our left. One little girl on the boat hardly took her eyes off me the whole journey and I wondered whether she had ever seen a *farang* before. It was more likely she was thinking "these two idiots haven't a clue where they are going" and she would have been right.

Eventually, the boat began to head towards the mainland and a few buildings could be spotted. As we pulled up into what was a small port, I noticed a large Seven-Up sign on the jetty which read "*Manum-Lah!*". We were in Malaysia - Perlis to be exact. This was all very well, but for one minor point - we had no passports on us or any other form of identification. After all, we thought we were just getting a ride to a village at the mouth of the river.

We quickly established that another long-tail boat would be making the return trip to Satun in a couple of hours. So we took an unscheduled stroll around Perlis. Fortunately they accepted Thai baht, so we had a snack and soft drinks, and made sure we avoided any policemen.

It was with some relief that we boarded the boat destined for Satun. On the way back we got talking to a pleasant Thai gentleman who spoke good English. He seemed quite impressed that we worked for the *Bangkok Post*. As the boat approached Satun, he reminded us to get our passports stamped at the immigration post when we got off the boat. That's when we should have said nothing, but instead foolishly explained to the fellow we did not have passports.

The poor chap was quite horrified, but not nearly as horrified as we were when he identified himself as an immigration officer. Understandably he wanted to know how we had gone to Malaysia and back without any passports. We explained, quite truthfully, that it was all a big mistake. We had only intended to visit the mouth of the river. It must have sounded very unconvincing, as people don't just go to another country by accident.

The official spent the remainder of the boat journey deliberating over whether to have us arrested for illegal entry, or illegal exit, or both. Eventually I think he realized we were going to cause him more trouble that it was worth - just imagine the paperwork for a start. So he just told us to get out of Satun as quickly as possible, but not by long-tail boat. We took his advice.

Many years later, in 1984, there was another long-tail boat ride in the South I wouldn't forget in a hurry. I was with Tony Waltham and a Thai family who lived in the southern provincial town of Trang. We were heading for a small island called Koh Sukhon (Pig Island) in the Andaman Sea, just off the Trang coast.

At the small port of Palian one afternoon we boarded an overloaded long-tail boat that didn't look fit to negotiate a *khlong*, let alone the ocean. My worst fears were confirmed about 20 minutes later, when the engine spluttered to a halt and expired. For the next hour, the boat with 30 passengers crammed on board just sat there bobbing about. Fortunately it was a relatively calm sea. However, I was feeling really uncomfortable, or more accurately my bladder was beginning to regret the couple of lunchtime beers I had consumed before boarding.

Suddenly there was bit of commotion down the front of the boat and an old chap sitting in front of me, turned and announced *"johm nahm"* (we're sinking). And he was right. Water was definitely building up in the boat. I remember looking around to see if there was any small island nearby that would offer a chance of escape and didn't require the efforts of an Olympic swimmer. But there was nothing and no other boats in the vicinity either. Passengers all began scooping the water out with whatever they could find and I joined in as it was better than just sitting there.

To add to the discomfort, dusk was closing in and I had visions of us being stuck there all bloody night - if we didn't sink. Never have I been more relieved to hear the "chug-chug" of another small boat emerging from the gloom and coming to our rescue. It attached itself to us and nudged our boat towards the island. What was supposed to have been a journey of less than an hour had taken three-and-a-half hours. Judging from the way all the other passengers sprinted for the bushes lining the beach, they were equally relieved to have made it onto dry land.

But the trip was worth it. Despite its name, 95% of the island's population was Muslim. It had earned its name from the wild boar that used to roam the island. The islanders were extremely friendly, and Tony and I even got on nodding terms with the many buffalos. I did have certain problems, however, understanding the ear-mangling southern dialect, while the islanders smiled and pretended to understand as they listened to my wretched Thai.

The island, which was basically coconut trees and beaches with a bit of jungle, was small enough to walk around in about six hours. We managed that one day, starting off early in the morning with a delicious beachside breakfast of raw *"goong dten"* (dancing prawn), which were still wriggling, fresh out of the sea.

We stayed overnight at several different farmhouses on the island and the people could not have been more hospitable. One of the houses belonged to an elderly widow. Early one evening she began rummaging around in a trunk and finally found what she was looking for. She proudly presented what appeared to be the sole material item to remember her late husband by - his set of false teeth. As we began the evening meal, she passed the teeth around and we all reverently inspected them. A very fine set of gnashers they were, too.

I also had the pleasure of visiting Phuket in the early 1970s with some *Post* colleagues, including Paisal Sricharatchanya (later to become editor), Suthep Chawivan, Norman Bottorff and Thai photographer Satharn Pairoah. We travelled by car from Bangkok and the journey was quite exhausting in itself. Phuket was vastly different then, with very few resorts and even fewer roads. We stayed at a modest hotel in the town. In those days Phuket had a reputation as a place where nobody needed to lock their doors at night because there was no crime. Oh, happy days.

We got to see quite a bit of the island and it was a hugely enjoyable experience.

It was my first time to see Patong Beach, which was rightly regarded as a treasure, probably the finest beach on the entire island. In those days there was not even a road to Patong, the last stretch being a frightening dirt track down a steep hill. The only buildings were a few huts and there was an odd shack where you could get a bottle of warm beer. That was it. The beach was deserted with the exception of a couple of kids playing with a dog. You needed a few more people around to share your enjoyment of the place.

SOUTHERN COMFORT

(On a subsequent visit with Norman only a few weeks later. our arrival coincided with a massive storm even by tropical standards. We spent the next two days wading around up to our waists in Phuket town as everything came to a standstill. At that time it was the worst flooding I had ever experienced.)

In the wet: Norman Bottorff and friends in flooded Phuket town in the early 1970s.

On the earlier trip we were also lucky enough to visit the Phi Phi Islands when they were truly pristine, beautiful and yet to be discovered by the outside world. The water was absolutely crystal clear with magnificent views of colourful coral banks. The towering limestone cliffs only added to the atmosphere. Phi Phi Don was the paradise island you imagined from those childhood books. You half expected Long John Silver to come hopping up the beach with his parrot.

The only inhabitants were a few Muslim fishermen. Even by village standards it was small. We arrived there from Phuket aboard a leaky fishing trawler, which kept breaking down. Our intention was to return to Phuket that night as there was no accommodation on Phi Phi. However, a storm blew up and we had to stay the night on the island, which was not exactly a hardship. In fact I was secretly pleased - a night on a truly untouched tropical island.

The only buildings on Phi Phi Don at that time were a few fishermen's huts and there was no electricity. Not surprisingly, supper that night was fish and raw prawns, washed down by coconut juice fresh off the palms - and very tasty it was too. The village headman kindly allowed us to sleep on the matted floor of his hut, right on the beach and not far from where the current pier is located. While we were there I recall going to a huge cave on the neighbouring smaller island, where we watched locals climbing up bamboo "scaffolding" to collect swallows' nests from a terrifying height. It was a most extraordinary sight.

Sadly the Phi Phi Islands and Patong were among the many places hit by the terrible tsunami that caused such devastation on Boxing Day in 2004. It was a numbing thought that such idyllic places where we had relaxed without a care in the world would witness such tragic scenes.

Another beautiful spot I visited in the South suffered a tragedy of a very different nature. In 1980, I was fortunate enough to spend a few days in Tak Bai, a quiet and picturesque small town in Narathiwat on Thailand's southern border.

Along with colleague Colin Hastings, we were guests of a Thai family who lived in the town. We enjoyed a most restful stay after the bustle of Bangkok, more than 1,100 kilometres away. The place was so peaceful and tranquil, while the local people were friendly, without being intrusive. The lush tropical vegetation and pristine pine-fringed beaches, untouched by tourists, just added to the serene atmosphere. Evenings were spent sitting in a *sala*, gazing across a lake, drinking a few beers and chatting, mainly about how relaxing it was. We couldn't believe how fortunate we were to be in such a placid place.

Unfortunately, more than two decades later in 2004, Tak Bai was the scene of a protest, which led to 85 deaths. Most of the casualties needlessly suffocated after being dumped aboard trucks. No one has ever accepted responsibility for the tragedy. I could never have imagined anything so awful happening in such a beautiful place.

I visited Koh Samui in the early 1980s when it was still relatively, but not entirely, untouched. There was no airport at the time and we got there via train to Surat Thani and then ferry to Nathon, the island's only town. The two main beaches, Chawaeng and Lamai, were okay, but there was a lot of construction work going on… a sign of times to come.

I was with Tony Waltham and in Nathon we rented a couple of small motorbikes as it was the only way of getting around the island. A policeman rented us the bikes and spent some time assuring us there was absolutely no crime on the island. As we were about to set off, the cop came out with: "If someone steals your motorbike, you'll have to pay for it."

I hadn't ridden a motorbike for years and was extremely cautious the first few days. As my confidence grew, I began to go faster and almost paid the price. I was belting down a deserted road when dozens of chickens suddenly ran out in front of me. With no time to brake I just hung on for dear life. By a miracle I missed hitting the chickens, although I collected a few feathers. It gave me such a fright that the rest of the journey proceeded at a snail's pace.

Shortly before we were to return the bikes, we decided to stop off at an isolated beach. I was still mentally congratulating myself for not having any major mishaps, which was really tempting fate. To get to the beach required going through a coconut plantation. I was proceeding very slowly on a narrow dirt path when the front wheel hit a tree root, the bike came to a halt and I fell off in slow motion. It must have looked ridiculous.

I landed a bit awkwardly and cut my hand on a palm frond, but that was the extent of my injuries. However, my pride was definitely hurt. Fortunately the bike did not suffer any significant damage apart from a couple of the faintest scratches and a minor dent on the mudguard, which hopefully the policeman wouldn't notice - fat chance. Upon returning the bike to the cop, the first thing he asked was "accident?" I shook my head. He examined the bike and glanced at my bloodied hand and repeated "accident". This time it was not a question, but a statement of fact.

I tried to explain it wasn't really an accident, but that I had simply fallen off when the bike stopped moving. Now try explaining that in English, let alone Thai. To my relief a couple of hundred baht later everything was resolved. One suspects it would be a little more costly these days.

19. THE LEGEND OF THE MIGHTY MITR

On location in Thailand is not exactly Hollywood

There is a day in October 1970, which I remember quite vividly. I had travelled back to Bangkok with very little sleep after an exhausting overland journey from Battambang in Cambodia (as related in The War Next Door). I was already late for my shift at the *Post*. As we approached Lan Luang Road not far from the office, we were caught up in a massive traffic jam. There was total mayhem on the streets with thousands of people milling about. My initial thoughts were some sort of uprising - not beyond the realms of possibility.

Then the taxi driver explained. The previous day, Thailand's biggest-ever film star, Mitr Chaibancha, had plunged to his death while filming a helicopter scene for *Inseethong* (*Golden Eagle*), in which he insisted on performing his own stunts. Mitr had been clinging to a rope ladder dangling from the helicopter and apparently could not hold on.

The reason for all the chaos at Lan Luang was that they had taken Mitr's body to Wat Sunthorn Thammathan, close to our office. It was reported that 100,000 mourners showed up at the temple, which explains the gridlock. Primarily because of the huge crowds, the *Bangkok Post* called it "the most trouble-plagued funeral rite in living memory."

Mitr was sometimes called the "Clark Gable of Thailand" and during his 13-year career made more than 300 films. His popularity was such that when he died he was working on 18 different films, all of which had to be scrapped as he was the main star in every one. It was quite normal for Thai stars to be involved in several films at the same time. Racing from set to set it was amazing that Mitr could remember which film he was working on at any given time, let alone the script. Mitr didn't have to worry too much, however, because most of films were very similar. He always played the hero and generally fell in love with a country girl if he was a city boy, or a city girl if he was a country boy. The love interest was usually Petchara Chaowarat

171

and they made an amazing 165 films together. The two names, Mitr and Petchara went together like Tracy and Hepburn, mango and sticky rice, salt and pepper… well, you get the idea.

For a newly arrived foreigner like myself, it was extremely useful to be aware of the existence of Mitr and Petchara, and later Sombat Methanee and Aranya Namwong, another golden duo. This was especially true while travelling in the provinces. Just mentioning their names won you immediate acceptance and gave you a kind of street cred. People would say you spoke good Thai even if the only words you knew were "Mitr" and "Petchara". I saw their films on occasions in provincial towns, where there was little else to do. They were fun, but a bit fluffy and far too long - the sort of film in which you could wander off for 10 minutes to get an a ice cream or bag of crispy grasshoppers and return without having missed anything.

Then there were the outdoor movies, *nang klang plaeng* (movies in the middle of a field) that were particularly popular in the provinces, primarily because they were free. Witnessing hundreds of villagers, sometimes thousands, sitting in a meadow watching the film on a huge artificial screen was a sight to behold. It was often a comedy and the whole field would erupt with laughter as one of the actors is pushed into a *khlong* or hit on the head with a frying pan.

Alas, there was one occasion when it wasn't so entertaining. Many years ago I was in Mae Sae, the northernmost town in Thailand, in Chiang Mai province bordering Myanmar. There was little to do in the evening, so I opted to watch the open-air movie showing in an adjacent field. There were hundreds of people seated on the grass and they all seemed to be having a good time. Suddenly there was a big bang and everyone fled, the giant screen also being dismantled in a matter of seconds. I was a bit slow off the mark, but when I saw the dead body sprawled on the grass nearby, I joined the fleeing throng and scurried back to my hotel. The receptionist had already heard about the shooting and said firmly, "We have bang! bang! No go outside. You go bed!" I didn't need any persuading.

THE LEGEND OF THE MIGHTY MITR

Maybe it was the grounding in Mitr and Petchara classics, but in 1973 I became one of the *Post's* movie reviewers, assisting chief reviewer Tony Waltham. It was in the days before multiplex theatres and the cinemas were larger than present times. Some, like the Lido, Siam and Scala, all in Siam Square, were relatively modern and more comfortable than any I had experienced in Britain. Others, in the Pratunam area, such as the Metro, Paramount and Hollywood, were a bit more basic, but cheap - six baht in the front row, while the good seats cost a massive 20 baht.

I was a little surprised at how many Thais went to the cinema during the daytime, but in the absence of shopping malls, it was an inexpensive way of beating the heat. I kept a diary in 1969 and in just eight months I went to the cinema in Bangkok 52 times, which was admittedly a bit over the top. One suspects the air-conditioning played a major role. I did see the odd decent film, however. The pick of the bunch was *Butch Cassidy and the Sundance Kid*. Others worth the six baht were *Rosemary's Baby* and the great spaghetti western, *Once Upon A Time In The West*.

Because of their large size you could doze off without anyone noticing, which could be rather useful if you were reviewing a boring film. At least in those days you didn't have to worry about cell phones going off in the middle of a sensitive scene, which had become a big problem in recent years. The major menace in the older cinemas was the large rodents that would scurry along the rows once the lights went down. Sometimes an excursion to the bathroom made you realize how the Pied Piper must have felt.

Occasionally there were delays during the middle of a film. This was because one cinema franchise was showing the same movie, but sometimes only had one copy and would send the reels by motorbike from one cinema to another while the shows were running. All it needed was for one of the cinemas to get out of sync, or the motorcyclist transporting the reels having an altercation with a truck or bus, and the audience was left waiting in the darkness, fending off the rodents.

It was a film review that led to one of my more embarrassing moments at the *Post*. The film in question was the re-release of *Those Magnificent Men in Their Flying Machines,* starring Stuart Whitman, Sarah Miles, James Fox, Robert Morley and a whole host of celebrities. It was an entertaining film and I gave it a favourable review, but as an afterthought added that I wasn't very impressed by Whitman, who seemed a bit wooden.

The day the review was published, I had just got to work when the phone rang. The ensuing conversation went something like this:

"I am the man who wasn't magnificent in the flying machines."

"'I beg your pardon?"

"You said I wasn't magnificent in the flying machines."

"I'm sorry, I don't understand, this is the *Bangkok Post*."

"Yes, I know. My name was in the *Bangkok Post* this morning. You said I wasn't any good."

(Beginning to sense the worst, I still thought that, maybe it was friends having a joke).

"Is that Bob? Peter? Norman?"

"No, it's Stuart. Stuart Whitman. You said I couldn't act."

"Ah Mr Whitman! How nice of you to call. I didn't actually say you weren't any good did I?...er..."

There was no wriggling out of it. Of all the stars in the film, I had to criticize the one who, unbeknown to me, happened to be in Bangkok. Served me right. Actually he was very decent about it. He said he was staying with friends and was delighted to see a review of one of his old films... until he started reading it.

I was fortunate enough to go on location with some Thai film productions, which proved to be an eye-opener on just how difficult it is to make a movie, especially on a tight budget. It was through writing the film reviews that I got to know Thai filmmakers Santa Pestonji and Lek Kitiparaporn, and watched them at work in the mid 1970s.

Early in 1976 I found myself in a beautiful lakeside village in Chiang Mai on the set of *The Pot*, better known as *Mae Nak America (American Wife)* directed by Lek. I always associate this film with American singer Linda Ronstadt. It was the time of her big hit, *You're No Good,* and on the set we heard it half a dozen times a day drifting across the lake from a noodle shop jukebox in an adjacent village.

Essentially a Thai film, as a special attraction it featured a budding American actress called Lisa Farringer. She was a very sweet person and fortunately possessed a good sense of humour, because she needed it. Lisa had flown from the US by herself. She must have felt very strange to be the only westerner on the set and not know a word of Thai.

American actress Lisa Farringer during the filming of Mae Nak America (American wife) in Chiang Mai in 1976.

In the film she is married to a Thai war veteran (Krung Sivalai) and one scene required her to gaze forlornly out of the window of a typical wooden house on stilts during a rainstorm. Unfortunately there wasn't any rain and being a low-budget project, no sprinklers. What they did have, however, was a large watering can, which looked like it had served time in the museum. This was dutifully filled and the actress had to keep a straight face while a member of the crew climbed up a stepladder and watered the air in front of her. Inevitably, each time they were ready to shoot, the water had been reduced to a dribble and the fellow had to clamber down the ladder to refill the watering can. Not surprisingly Lisa struggled to fight off the giggles at the absurdity of it all. When the film was finally released, in that scene you can see her shaking with emotion, although it was more likely her brave efforts to avoid bursting out in laughter.

In another difficult scene, Lisa had to lie down in a coffin while her bereaved husband Krung kissed the corpse. There was no air-conditioning and it was not exactly fun lying in a box with the temperatures pushing 40° Celsius. Once again, Lisa had a fit of giggles and the scene required several takes before the director was satisfied that he did not have a laughing corpse. Lisa explained to me later: "I felt kind of stupid".

A few days later we were at an old village temple to shoot a ghost scene and the place was swarming with people from miles around. Word had spread that it was not any old ghost, but an attractive lady *farang* ghost from America, i.e. a ghost with MAKE-UP. Lisa finally emerged, dressed in flowing white robes and looking extremely pale, probably brought on by all the villagers gawking at her. There were gasps from the onlookers and some of the kids scurried away to safer vantage points.

The highlight of the special effects was "the hand", a horror prop consisting of what resembled five large condoms lodged onto the end of a long stick to provide the ghost with a "super-arm" which did unspeakable things. That caused a considerable stir amongst the villagers - "*oh ho!*" - who were still trying to come to terms with the ghost's *farang* nose, let alone a seven-foot arm. The arm also gave the film crew an opportunity to play ghost tricks on the villagers and throughout the proceedings there were intermittent shrieks as "the hand" did the rounds. It was all tremendous fun.

One thing I grew to appreciate was just how much work goes into making a movie, even of a low budget variety. Those involved in the production are nearly close to exhaustion by the time it comes to the final takes. Santa once commented that when he started a production, he wanted it to be the best ever, half-way through he would be satisfied if it was just okay and by the end, he simply wanted to finish it, whether it be good, bad or ugly.

Later that year I found myself on another set with Santa directing. The film was *Santi-Weena*, a remake of a production made two decades earlier by his father, Rattana, a highly respected film-maker. It was a simple story of an ill-fated love affair between a girl and a blind boy. But if the story was simple, filming it in Phetchaburi's magnificent Khao Luang cave most certainly wasn't, as I quickly discovered. I made an unceremonious entrance slipping down the steep, muddy steps, much to the amusement of the local urchins.

In the cave, which Santa affectionately referred to as the "big hole", I watched the crew with the unenviable task of sorting out dozens of extras, all local villagers, for a crowd scene. There was an understandable buzz of excitement as visions of fame flashed across some minds and despite constant pleas of "don't look at the camera", everyone looked at the camera. All the girls, mostly farmers' daughters, were in their most devastating sarongs, the shafts of morning sunlight in the cave highlighting a dazzling array of purples, pinks, yellows, greens and blues. In his excellent book *Guide to Thailand*, Achille Clarac describes the cave as having a "Wagnerian atmosphere". Goodness knows what he would have made of this scene.

Later in the day, while I was munching on a sandwich in a dark corner of the cave, a bunch of local youths moved in on me. Immediately my defensive mechanisms went on high alert, but the lads were smiling and simply wanted to make friends. I suspect they mistakenly thought I was an actor. They fired the usual questions, wanting to know my opinion on Thai girls and how much I earned, a common enquiry in those days. I answered in the usual non-committal way. Then the leader of the group asked me if I liked guns.

"No, I don't like guns," I replied. They seemed genuinely puzzled. "Why not?" the leader asked. Now how do you answer a question like that without sounding sanctimonious? He then offered to show me some real bullet wounds. "Well, no thanks," I said. But another young man promptly pulled up his "Carpenters" t-shirt and showed off two deep scars on his back, about four inches apart. "Bang, bang" he said grinning, shaping his fingers like a gun. I made a face to show I was highly impressed by his wounds and quickly changed the topic back to pretty girls, which seemed a safer subject.

A few years later, in 1981, a group of mainly journalists were lured into being extras for a film called *Angkor* - later to have *Cambodia Express* added to the title - again directed by Lek. Among the cast were Robert Walker Jr., Christopher George, Woody Strode and the exquisite Nancy Kwan of *The World of Suzie Wong* fame.

It was set in Cambodia in the days of the Khmer Rouge and we found ourselves roasting on the tarmac outside a hanger at Don Mueang airport. This particular scene required us to sit on a plane, supposedly at Phnom Penh's Pochentong Airport for "just a few minutes" while the hero, Walker Jr., was arrested by Khmer Rouge soldiers and hauled off the plane. Of course, we were working on Thai time and those few minutes became a few hours, eventually consuming the whole day. It was swelteringly hot and matters were not helped by the old Dakota DC-3 not having any air conditioning. It gave me time to ponder whether it was the same Dakota on which I had flown from Chiang Mai to Mae Hong Son on a white-knuckle journey back in 1970. I was thankful we were not about to take off.

The word "extra" is certainly very appropriate, because that's exactly what you are, superfluous to requirements, spare, inessential, leftover. There was an awful lot of hanging around doing nothing, although being journalists we were quite adept at that. While we were loafing around, we bored one another with tales of other films that had been shot in Thailand, like *The Man with the Golden Gun* (1974) and *The Deer Hunter* (1978). Inevitably there was discussion about the lovely Patpong dancer Noi, who featured in *The Deer Hunter*.

There was also the secret hope that, like Noi, if the director thought you had the right-shaped nose - most unlikely in my case

THE LEGEND OF THE MIGHTY MITR

- or a suitable receding hairline (I had a chance there), we might be extracted from the herd and actually be given a speaking role. This could lead to fame and fortune. Alas, all it led to was fatigue and frustration. Well, okay, it was fun... sort of. It will come as no surprise that after sitting in that wretched Dakota for hours, when the film was finally released, we appeared on screen for no more than five seconds. Fame at last, albeit very fleeting.

Hollywood beckons: An eclectic gathering of journalists on the set of Angkor at Don Mueang Airport in 1981. Far left: Post design editor David Pratt; second left, Jon Hail of dpa; far right, author and journalist Steve Van Beek; former Bangkok Post Database editor Tony Waltham. At the back, right, Crutch with receding hairline and photo-journalist Gustav Dietrich. - Pix courtesy of Jon Hail

I have to confess that I was heavily involved in writing the screenplay for *Angkor*. So it was a trifle embarrassing when one of the extras got hold of the script while we were hanging around, and not knowing my links to the film, said something like: "This script's a bit rough, isn't it?" Of course, I thoroughly agreed with him, commenting to the effect that they must have got someone on the cheap.

Morale wasn't improved when the reviews came out the following year. There were references to a "cliché-ridden script", while one reviewer observed "the storyline is somewhat incoherent". So much for a career in Hollywood!

Someone who came considerably closer than me to Hollywood was colleague Tony Waltham. Tony was involved in the *Man with the Golden Gun,* starring Roger Moore, when the crew came to film in Thailand in April 1974. Tony had his own long-tail boat at the time and was originally hired to show Moore how to handle such a boat. However, when he showed up at the Ancient City, where they were filming, the assistant took one look at Tony and said: "You're the right height and build, you'll be Moore's stand-in." Tony, who had longish hair at that time, was told to get a haircut, shave off his moustache and report at The Oriental Hotel to be fitted with a Moore wig.

Tony duly rolled up at the "James Bond Suite". The door was ajar and he walked in to find a beautiful blonde (fully dressed) reclining on the bed. Being a gentleman, Tony immediately apologized for his intrusion, but the lady smiled and said, "Hi, I'm Britt Ekland" and held out her hand. Tony admits to wobbling at the knees for a brief moment as he explained he was "just a stand-in" and was there to get a wig fitted.

Unfortunately, showing a horrible sense of timing, the wig-fitter arrived, and Tony was unable to pursue his tete-a-tete with the delectable star, who played the quaintly named Mary Goodnight in the movie. But it was nice while it lasted.

20. THE PERILS OF POSTSCRIPT

It all began with a particularly unpleasant ghost

I was not a reporter, but a sub-editor, so I normally didn't go out getting the news. However, occasionally they let me loose to write the odd offbeat feature no one else wanted to do. One of those unexpectedly became a bigger story than I could have imagined.

It was October 25, 1978. A few days earlier a story had surfaced, originally in the Thai-language papers, about the ghost of an old lady that was haunting an equally old house next to Khlong Rangsit, just north of Bangkok in Pathum Thani. She was known as "Phi Khem" and all subsequent residents had fled the house in terror because she kept reappearing. The last occupants had jumped into the *khlong* in fright, which had prompted the *Post* to get interested. What made it more creepy was that she wasn't any old ghost, but a particularly nasty type of spirit known as a *"phi grasue"* - that's the one with just a head and lots of intestines, tubes and entrails hanging from it, which survives by drinking human blood.

It was decided that the *Post* should send a team to stay in the house overnight to prove whether or not there was a ghost. Inevitably, most of the Thai reporters came up with strong reasons why they were unavailable for the assignment... baby's sick, granny's funeral, dog unwell etc. The truth was, of course, that there was no way they were going to spend the night in a house supposedly haunted by a ghost, especially a blood-sucking variety.

Seeing the opportunity of having a night off my regular job and away from the office, and definitely not out of any sense of bravado, I volunteered. Reporter Suthep Chaviwan and photographer Rungruang Jinakul also agreed to come along. So off we went, accompanied by a couple of reporters from Thai-language newspapers. Northern Bangkok was badly flooded at the time and we reached the house by long-tail boat. It was approaching dusk and with the thunder, the stark silhouette of the house certainly gave off a haunted aura.

181

We proceeded to sit in this ancient wooden house by the *khlong* all night. There was no electricity and we just had an old oil lamp. A portrait of the old lady, Phi Khem, was hanging on the wall and the Thai journalists dutifully gave the portrait a *wai* just to let her know they didn't mean her any harm. After some thought, I gave her a *wai* too... well, you never know.

I must admit that initially it was a bit creepy. Noises at night take on a much more sinister feeling than their daytime equivalents - a cat miaowing becomes a wailing demon, a dog howling is the baying of a werewolf, a twig falling on a corrugated roof is the rattling of unholy bones. For a while we were a pretty jumpy crew.

We must have spent 12 hours sitting there, making idle chatter, eating Thai snacks. The ghost had been a musician in her earthly life and previous residents had said her spiritual entrance was usually accompanied by the sound of traditional music. So when music suddenly erupted about midnight, we all jumped. But the song, coming from a neighbour's house, turned out to be *Ain't Gonna Bump No More With No Big Fat Woman,* not exactly ghost music. As the night wore on, we didn't meet any ghosts, but we did get bitten by squadrons of mosquitoes that attacked us constantly. I was half hoping Phi Khem might put in a sneaky appearance to liven up proceedings, but alas she apparently had stage fright.

Eventually we were saved by the approach of dawn, when we all gathered eagerly on the landing outside the house awaiting the first long-tail boat. The boat arrived, but Rungruang was a bit too eager to get aboard and he plunged into the flood-swollen *khlong*, fortunately minus his camera. We hauled him out and he looked like he had seen, well... a ghost. He was convinced he had not accidentally fallen into the *khlong*, but was pushed in by the ghost, which was upset by our intrusion.

As far as I was concerned it was all over, but when we returned to the office that morning there were extraordinary scenes. Apparently reports of our overnight excursion, including the plunge into the *khlong*, had been on breakfast TV. The photographer and I were mobbed by staff wanting to hear first-

THE PERILS OF POSTSCRIPT

hand accounts of meeting a ghost. I had planned to write a small tongue-in-cheek feature on the ghost hunt for the Sunday edition at the end of the week. However, seeing all the fuss in the office, the editor, Graeme Stanton, came over and said that I had better knock it out straight away for the following morning's paper.

And that's how I got my first front page story. I think it was also probably my last. The Thai-language newspapers continued with the story for some time after and actually had me languishing in hospital, stricken by the Curse of Phi Khem. Sometimes I suspect I'm still suffering from it.

About that time the *Post* carried an occasional op-ed column featuring photographs by veteran German freelance photo-journalist Gustaf Dietrich. Gustaf was a lovely good-natured old chap and had an eye for amusing photos from Bangkok's streets, like holes in the road, upside down *samlors*, ankle-breaking pavements and people sleeping in odd places. One of my more enjoyable tasks was attempting to write frivolous captions to go with Gustaf's photos.

We received favourable feedback from readers, most of whom suggested there was not enough light-hearted material in the paper. It was partly with this in mind that in late November 1979, I submitted a sample column I had written to then deputy editor Peter Finucane. I had been at the *Post* for 10 years by this time and there were a lot of thoughts bottled up in my head demanding to be set loose.

Peter rightly slashed out a couple of the sillier items, but gave the go-ahead for the rest of it -and that was how *PostScript* was born. In fact, the very first column, published on December 2, 1979, was called *PostMortem*. But that sounded a bit grim for a supposedly humorous column, so we reverted to *PostScript*... and that's the way it stayed.

For the curious, topics in the first column included Thai superstitions, a hopelessly inept but charming waitress, bungling cops and mayhem at the opening of the blockbuster *Star Wars* at the Lido cinema.

I often get asked about the dog in the logo and an explanation is required. In the old days, *PostScript* got away without any mug

183

shot, but when the newspaper changed its format in 1992, a decree came down from above that all columns must have an accompanying photo of the writer. For a while there was a photo of a youthful-looking Crutch adorning the column - too young for some, however. A few readers had the temerity to suggest it was not an entirely up-to-date picture. Among the observations were: "Congratulations on your column with the photograph of your son in it" and "please tell me the name of your photographer. I also want to look 10 years younger." Then there was the cryptic "Judging from your photograph, you have decided to remain anonymous." But at least my maid, Ms. Yasothon, said it looked like me and that was the most important thing. You can't beat loyalty like that.

However, a change was felt prudent and as more contemporary photographs were deemed not very appealing, it was decided that the new mugshot should be something that fitted the writer's image - an orang-utan. It was generally agreed that the new mug shot was a great improvement, especially the ape's cute nose. Although it was a little podgy around the jowls and the haircut looked a bit dodgy.

The orang-utan was put into retirement at the start of 1994. As it happened to be the Year of the Dog in the Chinese calendar, the ape was replaced by the hound that has graced the spot to this day. The original plan was to change the mug shot annually to coincide with the calendar. But as the next year was Year of the Pig, followed by Year of the Rat, I decided to remain faithful to the dog, having myself been born in the Year of the Dog. Besides, the dog had even developed a sort of fan club with letters and emails enquiring about him, which is more than can be said of the writer.

I received one letter from a reader who said that when he first came across *PostScript*, he totally ignored it - not an uncommon reaction, I might add. Seeing the mug shot of the dog, he assumed it was some kind of 'animal advice' column. It was not until he accidentally started to read it that he discovered it tackled all sorts of serious issues, like men with bald heads, pedestrians plunging down holes, singing chickens and dancing policemen.

THE PERILS OF POSTSCRIPT

Admittedly wildlife has cropped up now and again over the years including heart-rending revelations on squashed lizards, pickled parrots, break-dancing rodents and misbehaving dogs.

The column has always been fun to write, but on occasions you can come out with something trivial which escalates out of hand. That was the case when I wrote in *PostScript* a brief item about Soviet President Mikhail Gorbachev.

In 1987, Gorbachev announced that the Soviet Union would stop jamming the BBC radio broadcasts to his country. This was regarded as a major breakthrough as the jamming had been going on throughout the Cold War. As a joke - and purely as a joke - in the column the next Sunday I suggested that the reason Gorbachev had ended the jamming was because he liked listening to the English football results on the BBC World Service on a Saturday night. I then had to decide which team he would support. Rather than the glamour clubs like Manchester United or Liverpool, I thought it would be fun to have the world's leading Communist supporting a really unfashionable "working class" team. Wigan Athletic fit the bill, a small Lancashire club and in those days in a low division. Also the town's industrial roots with textiles and coal mining associated with George Orwell's novel *The Road To Wigan Pier,* made it the sort of place that might just appeal to the leader of a socialist republic. Remember, this was written in a weekly humour column and was clearly not meant to be taken seriously.

Imagine my surprise when a couple of days later I received a telephone call from the BBC in England saying that in the English newspapers there was a story, citing "informed sources in Bangkok" that Gorbachev was Wigan's number one fan. The club was so pleased, they had reportedly sent a package to the Soviet leader containing a replica shirt, scarf and assorted souvenirs. Did I know where the story came from?

After recovering from the initial shock, I tried to explain that I had made it all up - it was just a piece of whimsy for a humour column. They sounded a little disappointed, but I was asked to "go along with it" as it was a fun story and gave a brief radio interview on the BBC on possible reasons why Gorbachev had chosen to support Wigan.

But the story had legs of its own. To this day, references pop up in assorted sporting encyclopedias and reference books that Wigan's most famous supporter is Mr. Gorbachev. The only consolation is that I could call it my own little contribution to *perestroika*.

I should have known better than to make jokes concerning a Communist leader. Back in 1981 I had written a rather silly item about North Korean President Kim Il Sung, extolling the virtues of "the great leader." To illustrate it there was a sketch of Kim, with a halo over his head - not a good idea. On the Monday morning I arrived at the office to find two men in suits sitting at my desk and they didn't look too pleased. They were from the North Korean Embassy and wanted to know if I intended to write any more articles on this topic. They were particularly puzzled by the halo. I explained it was just to emphasize how truly great the leader was. We talked at some length and I must say they were quite polite, but very serious. When they eventually took their leave, they asked whether I would be writing on that subject again. Probably not, I hastily replied.

One of my favourite stories that kept the column going for a while concerned a black panther called Ai Dum, which escaped from a household near Makkasan in June 1981. What a house in the city was doing with a panther in the first place I really don't know, as it is hardly your average pet.

It certainly captured the imagination of the Bangkok public and there were regular reported sightings of the panther in the old railway engine graveyard at Makkasan. Assorted panther traps only succeeded netting dozens of stray dogs attracted by the meaty bait. The creature remained on the run and the public were increasingly concerned… and just a little sceptical about the very existence of the panther. A breakthrough was desperately needed.

It came after 41 long days. Out of the blue, Ai Dum was dramatically captured by two wildlife officials. Their story and photographs were all over the front pages of every newspaper in Thailand the next morning. The two men explained how they

THE PERILS OF POSTSCRIPT

fearlessly captured the panther with tranquiliser darts and they were duly acclaimed the "Heroes of Makkasan". Shortly afterwards the panther, a fine specimen with a shiny black coat, was released at a wildlife sanctuary in Uthai Thani and it appeared on all the front pages. End of the tale. Well, not quite.

Proud panther: The saga of the escaped black panther Ai Dum captured the imagination of the public and the PostScript column. Here, Ai Dum is released into the Uthai Thani jungle in 1981. - Bangkok Post photo

A few days later an irate zoo owner from Bang Pa-in showed up in Bangkok demanding to know what had happened to the black panther two men had "borrowed" from him the week before. They had told him they needed the panther for "a show" in Bangkok. Of course, it was the two heroes, who later admitted they had rented the panther and had hoped to return it to the owner when all the fuss had died down. But they hadn't bargained on the authorities quickly releasing the creature into a wildlife sanctuary. The two fellows had to spend the next two years paying back the zoo owner.

The ongoing Ai Dum tale received a number of mentions in *PostScript* and for several years I regularly received postcards addressed to "Professor Crutch" and signed "Ai Dum", relating anecdotes about life in the Uthai Thani jungle. My belated thanks to whoever was responsible for that. Every time I pass the overgrown Makkasan railyard, I can't resist looking to see if there is a black panther running around, because they never actually caught the original escaped panther.

A distinguished American writer once said: "it is always fun when columnists screw up". Fun it may be, unless you happen to be the columnist in question. I earned the wrath of Yorkshire some years ago by mistakenly locating the resort town of Bridlington in the wrong county of Northumberland. I was deluged with emails from people in both counties. One lady even sent me a map of Northumberland, which was very thoughtful.

Then there was the time I observed that it was rather an odd coincidence that the chief prosecutor in what became known as the "Dingo Trial" went by the name of Mr. Barker. Dingo lovers quickly pointed out that dingos don't bark.

But none really matched the furore prompted by the less than complimentary comments in the column on that noble British dish, mushy peas. Fans of mushy peas rallied in defence of their favourite dish. One reader wrote that he was "shocked, nay horrified, at the derogatory comments about one of the world's greatest unheralded cuisines."

One Sunday, in 2007, the column failed to appear at all, although I'm not sure that anyone noticed. There were no hidden dramas or anything remotely sinister. The column simply disappeared into cyberspace, courtesy of my unmatched ineptitude with computers. It was a reminder that deep into the computer age, you don't have to get drunk to make a mistake - just press the wrong combination of keys and all sorts of strange things can happen - like columns disappearing.

Writing a column can be a humbling experience. One day I received a small package from a reader and opened it up to find it contained a used paper bag. An odd gift one might think, but it was not just any paper bag - it was made out of the *Bangkok Post*, and more specifically my *PostScript* column. The reader attached a note saying he bought some fried bananas at his local market and

THE PERILS OF POSTSCRIPT

was amused to find they were packed in the column, adding that he enjoyed the bananas more than the column. Not to worry. I was quite pleased to see that the column can occasionally serve a useful practical purpose.

One character that kept popping up in the column was my maid, known to the readers as Ms. Yasothon. That was not her real name. She was born Koon Chantha, but to myself and Tony Waltham with whom I shared a house for many years, she was known by her nickname, "Tong".

The following chapter is dedicated to Tong, who sadly died from cancer in 2003 at the age of 50. She contributed so much to making our time in Thailand enjoyable, providing three decades of happy memories.

21. A MAN NEEDS A MAID

Three decades with Ms. Yasothon and her minions

Over the years one of the first questions people have asked me is "How is Ms. Yasothon?" Many are curious as to whether she was aware that she had become something of a minor celebrity. Others were not even sure she was a real person, simply a figment of my imagination. But she was very real.

She had seen her photographs in my two earlier books and in the *PostScript* column, and was aware that I had on occasions written about her, but appeared unfazed. Back in January 1996, she was interviewed by the *Outlook* section (now *Life*) on how she had remained so loyal, being my maid for three long decades. She was refreshingly honest in her response. "When he's in a bad mood, I just keep quiet," she said. So I must have got a bit grumpy at times.

But she did add, "They (Tony and myself) are friendly and make me feel like I am living in my own home." Well, that was a rather nice thing to say, wasn't it?

She was slightly bemused why anyone would want to write about her. She would have been even more puzzled why so many people she had never met took so much interest in her activities.

One day in 1999, I spotted her peering at a copy of my second book, *PostScript: Forgotten But Not Gone*, which I had brazenly left lying around at home. It seemed an appropriate moment to break the news to her that I was the author. Her face then turned into a puzzled frown. "That's a sketch of me on the front," I said proudly. Yes, it looked like me, she agreed a little too readily, especially the giant red nose and the bulging stomach.

"There's even a picture of you in it," I said. She looked at me in horror. What on earth has the *nai* gone and done now? I turned to page 12 and there was the photo of Ms. Yasothon and her underlings in the garden, preparing some barbecued chicken for her cart. She giggled a bit and asked how much the book cost. I told her it was 210 baht. She frowned. *"Peng"* (expensive), she said, no doubt thinking how many plates of *somtam* she could buy with such a sum.

It's probably just as well she didn't review the book. She would have probably come up with the Thai version of: "This book is not to be tossed lightly aside, but thrown with full force." As I seemed to be getting deeper into the mire, it felt prudent to inform Ms. Yasothon that there was an entire chapter about her, all in the best possible taste, of course.

Home away from home: Tony Waltham relaxing on one of our regular trips to the maid's village in Yasothon.

Our first meeting was not entirely auspicious. It was 1973 and I was living on Sukhumvit Soi 8 with some other journalists. Our previous maid had sensibly given up city life and fled back to the farm. Word had got around that we needed a maid and one morning three nervous young ladies clad in sarongs appeared at our door - Ms. Yasothon and her sisters, fresh from their village in the northeast. They looked like they had just stepped out of the paddy field, which in fact they had. When I first asked her name, she jumped backwards in fright. It turned out that it was the first time she had ever been spoken to by a *farang* and my disheveled state in the morning was enough to scare anyone. Little did she, or I for that matter, know then that she would go on to work for me and be a good friend for the next 30 years.

Initially she was very shy and we hardly got a word out of her in the first few months. Looking back, it must have been a traumatic time for this farmer's daughter adjusting to life in the city, keeping house for an untidy and unconventional bunch of foreigners, who kept very strange hours and listened to even stranger music. Little did she know that one of the albums being constantly played in our house at the time was *Harvest* by Neil Young, which featured a track *A Man Needs a Maid*. Never was a song more appropriate as she cleared up the mess after us. However, working for us couldn't have been that bad, because six years later when we moved house, Tong was still with us. The only difference was now she was accompanied by her husband-to-be, Noi, who I am pleased to say turned out to be a very responsible fellow.

One thing she didn't have to worry about was job security. The reason was quite simple - she was the only person who could understand my Thai, or at least pretended to. By the same token, I was the only one who could understand her English, not that she knew more than a couple of words. So we established a certain feeling of mutual respect based upon our linguistic limitations. More often than not I didn't even have to say a word. When I tottered down the stairs in the morning, she knew I was desperate for a cup of tea. If I looked a bit rough, an aspirin would soon put in an appearance. Thankfully, when she did speak to me, she would switch from her natural *Isan* dialect to Central Thai.

Like most Northeastern people with a farming background, Tong was an authority on the weather and always seemed to know when it was going to rain. We would indulge in regular conversations about meteorological conditions. "*Rawn*" (it's hot) she would say. "*Rawn*", I would reply with sweat dripping off my face. "*Rawn mahk*" (very hot) she would venture if she was feeling talkative. I would concur, sagely nodding my head at the wisdom of our observations. In the cool season it was the same conversation except that *"naow"* (it's cold) had replaced *"rawn"*. Our sparkling conservations wisely steered clear of discussions about occluded fronts, isobars and the like. Oscar Wilde once commented: "Conversation about the weather is the last refuge of the unimaginative." He may have had a point.

During our many years on Sukhumvit Soi 49, Tong was always bringing creatures back to our residence after her periodic forays to Yasothon. On one occasion she turned up with a white rabbit, a cute but rather useless creature. She even got me feeling sorry for it, feeding it carrots and lettuce. I ended up rescuing it from near-drowning one stormy night during a major flood in 1986 (See Soi 8 Greens).

Then there was an owl which arrived after one excursion to the village. All the wretched creature did the whole time was stare, looking superior, occasionally hissing when it felt hungry. In the garden you could always feel its presence, watching your every movement. More importantly, it only ate live food, which meant Tong and her minions spent all day running around chasing toads and lizards instead of looking after me. But to its credit, it didn't resort to making loud hooting noises.

Her real triumph, however, was the parrot. While I am generally fond of our feathered friends, parrots are something else altogether. I visited a friend's house in Bangkok once and his parrot spent the entire time making ear-splitting screeching noises. The one Tong produced was marginally better in that it squawked rather than screeched. Much to my relief, after a month or so the parrot suddenly vanished. I did not enquire as to its whereabouts.

Tong was an easygoing person and I don't recall ever seeing her angry. Mind you, there might have been a trace of a frown when I once attempted a spot of gardening and dug up what I thought were weeds but turned out to be her new vegetable patch.

Over the years we got to know one another pretty well. Her natural shyness meant that she didn't like asking for anything directly. If she needed something, she developed a very natural way of what I would call "hovering", usually indicating there was something not quite right.

One morning I was sitting in the living room reading the newspaper and became aware that she was more attentive than usual - offering to make a cup of tea, insisting on giving me toast. Then she began cleaning and dusting everything in the room. Something was definitely afoot. When she started polishing our wooden stairs, I knew it was serious. Cleaning the stairs was a task that was always delegated to her husband or niece.

I looked at the date on the newspaper, February 5, I think it was. Five days after payday. Then it dawned on me, I had forgotten to pay her monthly wages. Old Scrooge had struck again. Yet she wouldn't actually come out and tell me. I nipped upstairs and returned with her salary, which prompted a big *wai* and the hint of a giggle. Then she scurried off, abandoning all the polishing, dusting and cleaning that had been so important only minutes before. Another successful "hover" accomplished.

Like many people from *Isan*, despite the lack of a proper education, Tong was quite a bright person. It wasn't long before she started selling *somtam* (spicy papaya salad) and *gai yang* (grilled chicken) from a cart at our house on Sukhumvit Soi 49. I regularly awoke to the distinctive aromas of barbecued chicken as the smoke wafted across the garden. Even before the cart left for its designated spot on Soi 49, opposite Samitivej Hospital, it attracted to the garden a gathering of neighbourhood maids, grannies, waifs and dogs - a microcosm of Thai village life. I even ended up taking orders on the phone from people in nearby offices for things like "three plates of sticky rice, two plates of *somtam* and half a chicken." Business was brisk and eventually, with the combined funds of assorted relatives, they graduated to a small shophouse opposite Samitivej. Although in later years, due to deteriorating health, she did not play a major role.

Periodically, Tony and I visited the village in Yasothon where Tong grew up, about 50 kms south of the provincial town. Ban Glang Nah - "village in the middle of a field"- is an accurate description of the place. Just about every house had its own resident buffalo, something you are unlikely to see these days. We were always made welcome. On our very first visit I recall waking up in the wooden school where we had slept overnight as "special guests", to be greeted by Tong and her nieces with a plate of toast, bacon and eggs, and a large mug of coffee. It was just like home.

A taste of Yasothon: The maid Tong (Ms Yasothon) and her husband Noi prepare barbecued chicken at our Sukhumvit Soi 49 house.

Over the years it seemed like most of the maid's village had passed through our residence, especially at Soi 49. There have been mothers, babies, uncles, aunts, sisters, close cousins, not-so-close cousins, extremely distant cousins, assorted waifs, and innumerable scrawny chickens. So it was always nice to turn the tables occasionally and visit them on their home turf.

Inevitably there were a lot of familiar faces in the village belonging to those who had graced our Soi 49 residence, including one girl who used to answer our old landline telephone holding it upside down. No wonder she could not hear anybody on the other end of the phone.

Most of our visits to Yasothon coincided with the annual *Bun Bang Fai* festival in early May, in which giant home-made rockets are fired, or quite often misfired, at heaven to entice the normally reluctant rains to water the parched land.

Ms. Yasothon's village had its own lower-key rocket festival. Sometimes it had already been raining heavily and the actual rocket-firing had lost some of its symbolism. But this did not stop the villagers from firing off lethal-looking contraptions. Every time you heard a "whoosh" as the rocket blasted off, it was prudent to duck as some had an unfortunate habit of taking off horizontally, sending spectators scattering. The missiles also have a tendency to blow up during launch, with spectacular results.

The main entertainment on these visits was the *molam*, a large singing and dancing group that performed in the local temple grounds from 9 p.m. until near dawn. The entire show was performed in a Lao dialect, so I couldn't understand much of it. The fact that all the songs seemed to sound the same didn't bother the villagers and just about everyone, including grannies, would get up and enjoy a little dance.

Night-time at the village was also a time to become acquainted with assorted bugs that came to inspect me as I lay on a mat trying to get some sleep. There were fat bugs, skinny bugs, small bugs, tall bugs, hairy bugs and bald bugs. One morning Ms. Yasothon appeared, holding a giant brown bug. "*Aroi mahk*," (delicious), she said as she walked off with the bug perched on her shoulder like a pet parrot. Well, her lunch had been sorted out anyway.

Much of the time in the village was spent trying to avoid consuming lethal concoctions of *lao khao* proffered by the village elders, not with much success judging from the wretched state I was in some nights. But most importantly, on our trips we experienced a typical uncomplicated *Isan* schedule mainly involving eating and drinking - with not a hint of a traffic jam.

Tong with her son Jak on a trip to her Yasothon village in the 1980s.

In 2001, the trip had more significance than usual as Ms. Yasothon's son, Jak, was being ordained into the monkhood in a ceremony known as *"buat nahk."* It was a proud moment for Tong and her husband Noi, as Jak was their only child. I was very pleased for them. However, it did make me feel a bit ancient as I remembered Jak when he was just a bun in the oven. At the ceremony he was already 22 and taller than me. Up to that time

Jak had lived almost entirely in our household. I watched him grow up from a polite young kid to an equally polite young man.

I always remember when Ms. Yasothon informed me she was going to have a baby, back in 1979. She knew I was a trifle sensitive about unnecessary noise and feared that a bawling baby would not go down too well - she was right in that assumption. However, as it turned out, Jak was of the non-bawling variety and for that I was ever thankful. I think the only serious altercation we had was when he was about five and left some marbles strategically placed on the stairs. I ended up on my backside after an involuntary flip.

When Jak grew older, he was the one who was always sent out to get the beers when we ran out, further cementing our relationship. However, I particularly enjoyed his younger years because at Christmas/New Year I could buy him toys. He became bored with them after a couple of days, enabling me to unashamedly play with them for the rest of the year.

For Jak's ordination there was great excitement in the village from the early morning - a bit too early for me - as we lined up to snip a lock of Jak's hair. There followed a parade around the village with the usual dancing, which I was dragged into by a couple of old crones. It was approaching noon and already stinking hot, and I was getting lobster-faced. So I was quite relieved to settle inside the temple for the remainder of the ceremonies. Mind you, after an hour of sitting in the *pap piap* position, - legs tucked to one side - it took me the rest of the day to get the creaking joints back in working order.

One of my fondest memories of Tong and her family was on my 50th birthday, a frightening number of years ago. I had kept very quiet about it with no party or anything like that. I was sitting at home when Tong, her husband, son and niece appeared, clutching a rather garish multi-coloured birthday cake with my first name written on it in Thai. It even looked to have 50 candles, an attention to detail I could have done without. The candles probably cost as much as the cake. Then, amidst a considerable amount of giggling, they launched into singing

A MAN NEEDS A MAID

Happy Birthday splendidly out of tune in their best English, while I nearly suffered a heart attack trying to blow out all those candles. I must admit to holding back the odd tear or two after that - it was just the simplicity of it all. Incidentally, Noi the husband, always presents me with a *phuang malai* flower garland on the late King Bhumibol's birthday.

It was very hard to observe Tong suffering so much during her final days and particularly difficult for her husband and Jak. Lying there in the hospital bed, so helpless and frail, was this lady who had once been so robust and full of life. Even so, she wanted to leave the hospital because she was worried that she was costing us too much in medical bills.

In February 2003, we had a birthday party for my wife Aon at the Vientiane restaurant, just off Sukhumvit Road. Tong came along, with her sisters and relations, but was looking very weak. There was a touching moment when one of the guests, an Englishman who had read about Ms. Yasothon in the column, went up to Tong and asked for her autograph, explaining that she was a famous lady. She didn't really understand, in fact she was totally bemused. But she knew it was all in good fun and it brought out a lovely smile and plenty of laughter. And she gave the autograph. Sadly, as her illness kicked in, that was to be her last outing. She passed away five months later in Chulalongkorn Hospital, 30 years after I had first employed her.

The memories remain. When I look at the old *PostScript* files, her name crops up everywhere. In the years immediately after she had passed away, I would find myself glancing out of the back door, half expecting to see her at her familiar perch munching away at her favourite dish, *somtam*. It was a privilege to have been a close friend for so many years. I still miss her.

22. SOI 8 GREENS

There's no place like home… as long as it has a garden

In all my years in Bangkok I have been fortunate enough to live in houses, as opposed to apartments or condos. All but the first two houses had a garden, something which I think has helped me avoid going completely nuts. An element of greenery has great therapeutic value in a big city. It has also meant I have had to move progressively further out of town - from Pratunam to Phra Khanong - as inner city houses were demolished to make way for development.

The first house at Makkasan is mentioned in "An Apple for the Teacher". It was a wonderful experience, and Clarence and I made lots of Thai friends. We were certainly never lonely there because people were always dropping by. But after a while we needed a bit more privacy. We were also only a minute's walk from the college where we were teaching, which meant we were easily summoned if another teacher called in sick. So after about six months we decided to move "upmarket", to a 1,200 baht-a-month residence on Sukhumvit Soi 1.

Just as the Beatles' *"White Album"* triggers memories of my overland trip, *Abbey Road* reminds me of that second house I shared with Clarence, and Steve Van Beek, who was working at the *Bangkok World* at the time. It was 1970 and I was a regular listener to Filipina dee jay, Bessie Casteneda on an FM English-language radio station. Bessie often played *Something* and *Come Together* from the album.

The old wooden house was right down the end of Sukhumvit Soi 1, adjacent to the malodorous Khlong Saen Saeb and its deafening long-tail boats. I regularly took the boat to Pratunam for the grand sum of one baht on my way to work both at the college and the newspaper. Apart from the smelly water, it was great fun. The boats used to belt along at an alarming speed - an excellent way of clearing the cobwebs out of your head in the morning.

SOI 8 GREENS

On one occasion I was waiting at the Soi 1 landing, when a boat pulled in and a corpulent American businessman got out... or tried to. As he attempted to step onto the landing, the boat went one way and he went the other, plunging into the murky waters with a theatrical splash. He was quickly hauled out and was actually laughing about it, but he looked a sorry mess, covered in the horrible black ooze masquerading as water. He had to laugh, primarily because everyone else was in hysterics - after all, there is nothing funnier than a fat *farang* falling into a *khlong*. It was just like a Thai movie. I don't think I would have laughed if it had been me.

On occasions I would hop on a boat going in the opposite direction, out of the city. I usually headed for Nong Chok, which at that time was still pleasantly rural, with orchards, rice fields and rickety old wooden bridges over the *khlongs* - a wonderful spot for a newly-arrived foreigner to walk around. The entire ride out there only cost five baht. I often took visitors on that route, where they would see more of Thai life in 45 minutes from the boat than a whole day on a tourist bus. Once the *khlong* made the left turn at Phra Khanong, the water was noticeably cleaner - more of a light brown colour. All along the banks people were still engaged in traditional *khlong* life with their fishing nets and bathing. Just about everybody waved and grinned. You really felt that you were in a special place ... which, of course, you were. It actually *was* the Land of Smiles.

On one of my first days at the Soi 1 house, it was just before dusk and I was sitting on the canal bank struggling to play the guitar. I only knew a smattering of chords, no doubt wrecking an old tune by Creedence Clearwater Revival, who were all the rage in Thailand at the time. I looked up as this small wooden boat silently drifted by, with an old lady paddling at the back and a younger sarong-clad woman perched at the front. At first I didn't take much notice, but then there was another boat... and another. In fact, there was a whole fleet of them, a virtual armada in a kind of procession, all with the same format - a girl up front and an older woman with a paddle in the rear. They were eerily silent, in stark contrast to the racket made by the regular long-tail boats. It was all rather weird.

I later discovered the fleet "docked" just below the Chalerm Loke bridge at Pratunam, where they stayed all evening, with the working girls "servicing" customers on the small boats. On occasions there were tales of couples tumbling into the murky waters when things got a bit too passionate on board. It became known in our house as the 'Pratunam Armada'.

After a year on Soi 1 and the *khlong* getting smellier and noisier by the day, it was time to move down the road a bit and share a modest, but very pleasant house halfway down Sukhumvit Soi 8 (Preeda). Best of all, it boasted a large garden, presided over by a marvelous flame tree that every cool season would carpet the whole residence in its rich red blossoms. The garden fence was entirely bougainvillea bushes and for most of the year the purple, pink and white blossoms were a wonderful sight. It was at this house the lady I was to call Ms. Yasothon in the *PostScript* column first took up her job (see A Man Needs A Maid). By this time Clarence had left Thailand, although he was to return a few years later and is now a Chiang Mai resident.

"Soi 8", as we and many friends called it, was a vibrant house in that there were people coming and going all day and night. In fact it was too vibrant at times as I would often return home from the late shift at the *Post* to find assorted people in various forms of repose, spread around the living room.

Over the eight years I was there, the personnel residing in the house changed quite regularly, but it was always a cast of characters. For a period, what was supposed to be the maid's quarters round the back acted as the office of a friend's nascent advertising company. Thus, Patrick Gauvain's Shrimp Studios was born, although he lived in another part of the city. His secretary at the house was a delightful Chulalongkorn graduate called Kwanchai, who was to later marry one of the house residents, Derek Enscoe, an amiable English journalist who was working at the *Post* at the time.

Apart from the journalists, at various times the house included teachers, Vietnam vets and professional people primarily from

Britain, the US, New Zealand and Thailand. We even had a Khmer refugee called Khek stay with us for quite some time. One thing we unfortunately had in common was very little money, so the weekly treat was to wander down to Bharni's restaurant between Sukhumvit Sois 21 and 23, and partake of the splendid three-course special for the grand sum of 20 baht. Now that was bliss… and a bargain. In fact there were no items above 100 baht, with the exception of a year-round turkey dinner.

Bharni's, named after the owner's daughter, was unique in many ways. The extensive menu was written on the wall and covered just about any type of food you could think of. It was also a hostel for female students and quite often the youngsters taking your orders would be clearly practicing their language skills and earning a few baht in the process. At the time there was a popular song by Arlo Guthrie entitled *Alice's Restaurant* and we adapted the first line to: "You can get anything you want at Bharni's restaurant." Whenever I passed Bharnis in the ensuing 30 years that song always sprung to mind.

Two of the people I first shared the Soi 8 house with - Julian Spindler and Mike Berry - had also travelled overland from England to Thailand. But unlike me they came in their own vehicle, a Land Rover nicknamed "Smo" after its registration SMO. The vehicle was a strong, deep orange colour, set off by jungle scenes and wildlife painted by one of the household's more creative members. "Smo" was active around town for a while, but the rigours of Bangkok eventually took its toll and it expired. However, it was not abandoned, but took a prime spot in the garden, parked underneath the flame tree. The vehicle had courageously battled its way thousands of kilometres from England across Europe and through the wildest deserts and mountains of Asia. But it couldn't handle Bangkok.

The vehicle remained in our garden for several years and became a kind of house mascot. "Smo" would crop up in conversation as if it were a member of the family, or pet, which I suppose in a way it was. At least we didn't have to feed it. The Land Rover became a familiar part of the scenery in our garden and blended in surprisingly well and was not an eyesore. Over the years it even began to produce its own plant life. There were all sorts of weird giant leafy things growing out of it, resembling *The Day of the Triffids*.

Something I associate with Soi 8 was the night watchman striking a bell every hour after midnight - once for 1 a.m., twice for 2 a.m. and so on - to alert residents to the time and make them feel more secure, knowing the good guys were patrolling the streets. I must admit the familiar sound of the bell as the night ticked away was quite comforting.

The guard on Soi 8 was a lovely old fellow who was known as *Loong*, or "uncle", but watching him totter down the *soi* with his bell, he hardly inspired confidence security-wise. Poor old *Loong* wouldn't have stood a chance against the bad guys. Also he didn't get much rest, because it took him the best part of an hour to waddle up and down the *soi*. Once he completed a lap, the old chap had to set off once again.

Loong wasn't about one night in October 1973, shortly after the student uprising, when there was absolutely no police presence on Bangkok's streets. It was about 10 p.m. and I was sitting at home chatting with New Zealand friend Dick Wood, who was living there at the time. We suddenly heard shouts of "*Kamoy! Kamoy!*" (thief!), followed by the sounds of people running. Although he was only wearing a *pakoma*, Dick dashed down our small drive out into the *soi* and set off in hot pursuit of the muggers. Then I heard two gunshots and thought "my God, they've shot Dick". Never was I more relieved when I saw Dick appear at the gate, *pakoma* still intact. "When they started shooting at me, I thought it was time to give up the chase," said Dick. A very wise decision.

Because of the sizeable garden we hosted a few Christmas parties. They were quite wonderful, sitting out on the grass in the afternoon embracing the relatively cool December weather. It was at one such party in 1973 that I found myself talking to a couple of attractive European women, one Dutch and the other a French blonde. They said they were actresses and had been filming in Chiang Mai. They did not seem too enthused by the film, but had an entertaining tale to tell. One scene required them to bathe *"au natural"* in Mae Klang waterfall. Not surprisingly this attracted a huge crowd of local villagers… and also the police. When the scene was finished, the boys in brown escorted the actresses off to Chom Thong police station. The starlets were fined the princely sum of 250 baht each for "creating a disturbance", which they could hardly dispute. Apparently the film crew had told police they were making an "educational film", which no doubt it was for some of the male villagers.

I didn't think any more about it until a few weeks later I saw a story concerning a new French film, primarily shot in Thailand. It was to be released later in the year and was said to be pushing the boundaries as regards sexually explicit scenes. The film was *Emmanuelle* and when I saw the photograph of the star, Sylvia Kristel, she looked suspiciously like one of the two who had attended our party. She was unknown at the time, but once the film was released that changed in a hurry - she was the hottest thing around. And *Emmanuelle* became one of the most successful French films ever.

About a year later I was in London and took the opportunity of watching *Emmanuelle* at a cinema on Oxford Street. I was intrigued how the film would portray Thailand, which was little-known in the West at that time. But it was more about Kristel in various stages of undress and making love at 30,000 feet. She also managed to do it in a Bangkok squash court and aboard a Lampang horse and cart, which was passed off as a typical Bangkok night scene.

Anyway, I hope Sylvia had fond memories of that 1973 Christmas in Bangkok. A heavy smoker, she sadly died in 2012 of throat cancer.

One regular visitor to the house, a young Englishman called Charles, practiced yoga and I would often come home to find him standing on his head meditating, sometimes in the middle of the night. He gave me hell of a fright one night when I opened our front door only to see in the gloom what appeared to be an apparition of a headless body. I briefly thought I had spotted my first ghost, until I realized it was simply an upside down Charles. He was a talented guitarist and singer. While staying at our house, he compiled a tape of his music, including one number dedicated to the house, entitled *Soi 8 Greens*.

Another interesting character who spent time at Soi 8, was Bill Schiller, a Vietnam Vet. I first met him when he used to pop round to the house in the afternoon after finishing his day's work with one of the big US electrical companies. He later moved in when there was a room available.

Bill had served in the US Army and was with the First Cavalry in Vietnam during the 1960s where he fought as a helicopter door gunner. He was also involved in backing up patrols at the time of one of the big clashes of the war, the Battle of Hamburger Hill.

I would listen spellbound to Bill's tales of his experiences in the war, although he didn't talk about it too much. He loved rock 'n' roll music and went on to run the successful Paradise Bar and Bungalows on Phuket's Patong Beach for 20 years.

Those were happy times at Soi 8, and I would have been content to live there for many more years. With the garden and blossoms it never felt like you were living in the centre of a city. But in 1978 the landlady - a charming professor from Chulalongkorn University - appeared at the doorstep to collect her 2,800 baht rent and apologetically announced her family was selling the land to developers, and we would have to move. By this time there were just two of us living there, Tony Waltham and myself.

The enforced move was a blow to the heart and to the pocket. A couple of months later, Tony and I found ourselves paying more than twice as much rent for a much less attractive house only two *sois* further down on Sukhumvit Soi 12. The view was no longer bougainvillea or a flame tree, but the Darling massage parlour. Somehow it wasn't quite the same. It was called Soi Sookjai (Soi Happy Heart), but in those days seemed to be permanently flooded and was definitely not a *soi* of happy hearts. However, just down the *soi* was the delightful Cabbages and Condoms restaurant, which more than made up for the occasional soggy socks.

Meanwhile, at our former residence a condominium was going up, the very first on Soi 8. I am pleased to say that several people who lived at that Soi 8 house all those years ago - and many more who frequently visited - still reside in Thailand, admittedly a bit more wrinkly than those early days. Now, that says something about the kingdom.

After the rent was significantly increased at Soi 12, Tony and I, along with the maid and her husband, moved down to a small *soi* off Soi Thonglor (Soi 55). Within a year we were off again to set up residence in the very peaceful Soi Torsak, just off Soi 49. We were to stay there for more than two decades. Twenty-six years is a long time to live in one place. We were in Soi 49 the entire 80s, 90s and half of the "noughties". To put it more simply, from 1979-2005, or in Thai terms, long enough to experience five coups.

The Soi 49 house was my sixth residence in Bangkok and like Soi 8, had a pleasant garden. The only downside was that the *soi* and its environs was very low-lying, which made it vulnerable to flooding in the monsoon season. There was a period late in 1983 when daily storms led to widespread flooding and made it look like the city was about to become another Atlantis. It was the worst flooding in Bangkok in four decades.

By coincidence, our next-door neighbour was the Bangkok governor, Admiral Tiam Makarananda. Day after day the media howled for his blood, demanding the governor stop the floods forthwith. But the poor man's own home, quite modest for a man of his stature, was itself badly flooded. I remember seeing him one morning at the height of the crisis, standing forlornly in his inundated garden, trousers rolled up and water up to his knees, a lost soul, looking a bit like King Canute. Despite being an admiral, he couldn't control the flooding at his own residence, let alone the entire city.

On one occasion following an almighty storm in 1986, I had to walk, or rather wade, from the house on Soi 49 to the office at the U-Chuliang opposite Lumpini Park. It took two-and-a-half hours. I battled through scenes of indescribable chaos, wading down *sois,* falling down submerged holes, rescuing marooned cats, pushing stranded cars and buses on Sukhumvit, which was totally awash. I had never experienced anything quite like it. When I eventually staggered into the office, soaked and exhausted, clutching soggy shoes and even soggier socks, a colleague asked: "Has it been raining?" He went on to smugly inform me that he lived in the Sathorn area, which was dry as a bone and untouched by the floods.

Soggy Socks Time: A rather damp greeting one morning in 1983 at Soi 49.

A couple of years later there had been a massive storm and I was stuck on Silom late at night trying to get home. At the very mention of Sukhumvit, taxi drivers shook their heads in sage-like fashion, muttering *"nahm too-um"* (floods). So I had to settle for a *samlor* - not a good idea.

After a tortuous journey in the driving rain, involving several wrong turns, it came as no surprise that the roads approaching my residence were deep under water. About one kilometre from the house, down a small *soi*, the samlor driver refused to go any further and I didn't blame him. The water was getting quite deep and I was growing concerned about the maid's pet rabbit, which lived at the back of the house. It would quickly become a drowned rabbit unless it had learned the breaststroke.

It was raining heavily, too. A limousine sloshed slowly past me and then ground to a halt. For some stupid reason I decided to be helpful and give the limo a push. So there I was at 2 a.m., in driving rain on a deserted dark *soi,* water up to my knees, waving my arms at the driver and making pushing gestures. By the look on his face and that of his lady friend sitting in the front seat, they thought I was a madman, mugger, ghost, or all three. They were terrified. So I left them to it and waded off to rescue the drowning rabbit. Fortunately the wretched thing had found a perch inches above the floodwater, otherwise it could have been rabbit pie the next day.

Meeting of the minds: Fellow authors (from left) Colin Piprell, Jim Eckardt and Bill Page with Crutch tasting beer and somtam in the garden at the Soi 49 residence.

When we first moved in at the Soi 49 residence, the large garden was a bit bare and uninviting, but the maid's husband Noi transformed it into a jungle retreat, with a strong *Isan* flavour. There was every shade of green supplied by every conceivable variety of foliage - trees, bamboo, ferns, potted plants and some unidentifiable specimens. It was a pleasure just to sit there and soak it all in. Quite a few *PostScript* columns began life while I was taking in that view, watching the squirrels at play.

I was fortunate to be able to stay there for so long, most of the time sharing the place with Tony. When I was finally booted out at the end of 2005, it was probably time to move anyway. The house was falling to pieces, just like its occupants.

I am happy to say Noi is still in charge of foliage activities at my current residence on Sukhumvit Soi 77 (Onnut). Once again he has done a splendid job, creating plenty of shady spots in which I can doze off while watching the dog chase the squirrels and run away from the frogs.

23. THE HARDEST-WORKING LEGS IN SHOW BUSINESS

When concerts in Bangkok were rare, Tina Turner and Eric Clapton came to the rescue

In recent times Bangkok has witnessed concerts by most of the world's pop music legends and it is no big deal when such stars as Elton John, Pink Floyd, Santana, Sting, Alicia Keys and Lady Gaga perform in the city. But when I first arrived, it was very different. Bangkok was something of a backwater when it came to promoting shows of any kind and there were very few famous names coming to perform. Those who did show up were usually well over the hill.

In the 1970s, any pop concert in Bangkok featuring international stars was such a rarity that you tended to go along whoever was performing. You may or may not have heard of them, but wanted to enjoy a live music experience with appreciative crowds.

That can only explain my attendance in 1976 to a performance by the Australian group Sherbert. They played at the unlikely setting of the Nimibutr Gymnasium near Suphachalasai Stadium. The group had enjoyed just one big hit internationally called *How's That?*, which was extremely popular in Thailand. They naturally left that song for the finale and I wondered just how they were going to fill the remainder of their concert. Sherbert turned out to be quite a solid rock n' roll band and sensibly played a lot of Beatles numbers and other familiar rock songs, which the Thai audience knew and enjoyed.

The next group I saw, in 1978, was the Doobie Brothers, who played at the old Phrakhanong theatre. As the Doobies were not particularly well-known in Thailand, I was a bit concerned about how big a turnout they would get. I needn't have worried because what seemed like half the International School of Bangkok showed up, replete with banners welcoming the Doobies to Bangkok. The mainly American kids were all down the front and contributed a lot to the atmosphere, including dancing in the

211

aisles, something Thai audiences never did. This appeared to inspire the band. Led by Michael McDonald, they were in good form as they pounded out *Takin It To The Streets*, *Minute-By-Minute* and all their early hits.

A couple of years later, at the same venue, I was dragged along by a Thai girlfriend to see Leo Sayer, who was responsible for what was a massive hit in Thailand, *Love You More Than I Can Say*, with that "Whoa Whoa Yeah Yeah" refrain that drove me mad. I hated that song, primarily because I heard it everywhere I went in Bangkok, with the ladies of the night cheekily corrupting the title to "Love You More Than You Can Pay". However, I quite enjoyed the concert as Leo was a talented guy. Most importantly, it was live.

It must have been in 1980 that Eric Clapton managed to fit in the City of Angels at the start of a long and successful Asian tour, that would include Japan. It was something of a comeback for Clapton, who had experienced a few erratic years with drugs and domestic problems.

The concert was held at the National Theatre, which with its dodgy acoustics and rather formal ambience was not the ideal location for a rock concert. Despite the staid atmosphere - it felt more like the National Museum - Eric was in good form and back to his best. To have any concert in Bangkok was great. To have Clapton playing was like having God turn up in your back garden.

One thing I will always remember from that concert was right at the beginning when Clapton strolled onto the stage and took a long drag on a roll-your-own cigarette. After the welcoming applause had died down, there was a brief silence when, with a great sense of timing, an American teenager in the audience shouted out: "Are you sure that's just a cigarette you're smoking, Eric?"

This drew a wry smile from Clapton and much laughter from the audience, before he launched into *Layla*, and the concert was off and running.

Gradually big names began to perform on a more regular basis in Bangkok. Most of the shows were well worth waiting for,

THE HARDEST-WORKING LEGS IN SHOW BUSINESS

including Blondie and the lovely Debbie Harry, who quickly became the most popular female singer amongst young Thais.

Rod Stewart made a big impact with a rousing performance, which ended with him kicking footballs all over the place at Hua Mark Stadium. Stevie Wonder also put on a wonderful show at the stadium. At one point Stevie was joined on stage for a duet with a young Thai girl and they performed his biggest hit, *I Just Called to Say I Love You*. The Thai singer was Tata Young, who went on to become one of Thailand's major singing stars.

The David Bowie concert, part of his Serious Moonlight Tour, was slightly different in that it was open-air, held at the Army Stadium in December 1983. Bowie had just released the *Let's Dance* album and I remember him performing a cracking version of *China Girl*. It wasn't a massive crowd, a few thousand perhaps, but it turned into a night to remember thanks to his extraordinary talent. Being December, the cool weather complemented a really cool show.

Bowie's performance was all the more remarkable considering the problem he had getting to the stadium. According to Amporn Chakkapak, one of his promotion team, the official limousine taking Bowie and the band to the stadium broke down. They all had to get out and squeeze into a passing taxi, not known for their comfort in those days. For many pop stars that might have been the cue to throw a tantrum. But Bowie took it all in his stride regarding it as part of the rich experience of Bangkok life.

Not all concerts went entirely according to plan. The Pointer Sisters performed at Thammasat Auditorium, where the sound system kept packing up. It was something of a stop/start show while engineers kept trying to fix the sound. Nevertheless, the girls kept going, God bless 'em, sometimes singing without any accompaniment. And they managed to pull it off, a truly great effort.

Then there was Tina Turner.

A little background is required. As a teenager I first became aware of Tina performing with her husband Ike and the Iquettes through black and white television in the mid 1960s. I had never seen such a dynamic stage show and was immediately hooked.

She was later dubbed the "Hardest-Working Legs in Show Business", which was no idle claim. After the stunning single *River Deep and Mountain High* came out in 1966, I was a fan for life, even if she never recorded one more song.

I was lucky enough to see Tina in concert twice in Bangkok. The second time was in about 1988 when she was a born-again superstar, putting on a tremendous show singing hits like *Private Dancer* and *Simply The Best* in front of about 10,000 screaming fans at Hua Mark stadium. People were fainting all over the place because of the heat, but those "hardest-working legs" kept going, not to mention the "hardest-working voice".

Simply the best: Anchalee Chongkhadikij on stage with Tina Turner. - Bangkok Post photo

But the first concert Tina gave in Bangkok was an entirely different experience. It was about 1977 and Tina had been out of action for several years as a result of traumatic domestic issues with her husband Ike. Her *Private Dancer* comeback was still some years away and she had been out of the entertainment news for years.

THE HARDEST-WORKING LEGS IN SHOW BUSINESS

Frankly, most people in Bangkok had never heard of her at that time and the concert, held at the Oriental ballroom, attracted only a few hundred faithful fans, mostly of my age. I must admit to feeling a little embarrassed for her at the modest turnout, although those in attendance were certainly enthusiastic enough. I felt like running outside and shouting in the street: "Hey don't you realize you've got one the greatest entertainers ever performing in here?" Tina actually tried to make the audience feel more comfortable, saying that she did not like huge crowds as it felt like performing to a "bag of beans". (She was to experience that in dramatic fashion in 1988, when she performed in front of 180,000 fans at Rio's Maracana Stadium in Brazil, a world record for a concert).

Tina's son was playing bass guitar that day at the Oriental. I think it was his 17th birthday, so Tina and the band had bit of a celebration on stage, which rubbed off on the audience. She was in superb singing form and in the end I felt exhilarated and at the same time exasperated that so few people had witnessed it. That was not to be the case next time she was in Bangkok.

While Tina produced the most energetic performance, the most beautiful voice I heard in concert was that of Randy Crawford. Her show was also at the Oriental, and the ballroom was an appropriate setting for exquisite renditions of such songs as *Almaz* and *You Bring the Sun Out*, which were enough to send shivers down the spine.

How can I explain attending a Boney M concert, of all things, at the Ambassador Hotel in the late 70s? It was not my sort of music, but my girlfriend was desperate to see them. So I reluctantly went along hoping that no one would spot me, only to find myself sitting next to Bernard Trink and family. I was almost rescued when a major power cut wiped everything out. However, to their credit Boney M carried on singing in pitch darkness and without any amplification, for which they earned my grudging respect. They could easily have walked off the stage and no one would have blamed them.

On one of my visits back to Reading a few years later in the mid-80s, my dad told me how a few weeks before when he was struggling back home up a steep hill with his shopping from Caversham village, a car pulled up next to him. What he called a "Jamaican" lady leaned out the window and offered him a lift home. He said she was very friendly and told him she was a singer in a pop group. I asked dad what the group was called, but all he could remember was "Bones something ". It wasn't until later I discovered that Boney M's lead singer Liz Mitchell lived nearby, so it was almost certainly her. Anyway, a somewhat belated thanks for helping out my dad, Liz - he really appreciated your kindness. Although he was probably the only person in Caversham who had never heard of Boney M.

Many years later, in August 1993, Michael Jackson came to town. There were two sold out concerts on his rather aptly named "Dangerous Tour". His arrival coincided with the surfacing of allegations of child molestation back in the US. Everyone knew that Michael's presence in Bangkok would liven things up a bit, but no-one could have forecast the magnificent soap opera than ensued that week.

His first concert on the Tuesday night went ahead at the Suphachalasai Stadium without any major problems in front of an enthusiastic 40,000 crowd. But as the accusations against him flashed around the world that night, there were obvious concerns that the singer would not be in the right frame of mind to perform his second show in Bangkok. Things were getting so bad that Elizabeth Taylor flew across the globe to comfort him. It wasn't looking good and must have been a nightmare for the local promoters.

Sure enough, word surfaced that the second scheduled Pepsi-sponsored concert had been cancelled. The official word was that Michael had come down with dehydration, much to the glee of a rival soft drink producer, who within hours had come out with a full page newspaper ad that read: "Dehydrated? There's Always Coke!" - one of the great moments in advertising.

For the next two days nobody had the faintest idea whether the second concert would take place. Michael even had an impact on the home front. My maid, Ms. Yasothon, and her son, who was 13 at the time, had expressed considerable interest in seeing the superstar perform. I passed on a couple of tickets to them, but after two abortive visits to the show on the Wednesday and Thursday, I think she had given up hope of a second concert.

By Friday afternoon, following two days of cancellations, the *Bangkok Post* was bombarded by phone calls from would-be concert-goers wondering whether it was worth battling the traffic on a third, and possibly futile expedition. A colleague called someone in the know whose secretary came out with the not entirely reassuring "It's definitely on... I think."

Thankfully she was right. By all accounts Michael was in pretty good form, too, which was quite amazing considering the mental pressure he must have been under. Most importantly, the maid and her son enjoyed it, which confirmed that Michael's visit was a roaring success. And the housework briefly improved as well.

24. TERROR OF THE TONES

Grappling with the Thai language can have its lighter moments

Having struggled with French at school - "tries hard without much success" was the teacher's comment on one report - I didn't rate my chances when coming face to face with Thai. After all, I experience enough problems with the English language.

Considering I have spent four decades in the kingdom, my command of the Thai language is quite woeful. But I know enough "to get by", well aware that a smattering of language helps immensely when travelling around Thailand. Even for someone of my limited linguistic skills, learning Thai has been a pleasurable experience, helped considerably by the fact that Thai people are not averse to flattery. They will quite brazenly tell you how good your Thai is, when they know it is utter rubbish. On one occasion, a Bangkok taxi driver praised my linguistic ability when the only words I uttered were "*bpy* Robinson".

Tones create the biggest problems for foreigners tackling the language. Often when trying to tell someone I was a journalist (*nak khao*), I was in fact announcing that I was a mountain man, or even worse, a knee man.

The word *ma* is probably the most abused by those grappling with the Thai language, as it can mean "horse", "dog" and "come" among other things, depending on the tone. It is not unknown for foreigners attempting the simple greeting "*bpy nai ma*" (meaning "where have you been?") to be politely told later that they had in fact said "where are you going, horse?" or, worse still, "where are you going, dog?".

I still have problems differentiating between near (*gly*) and far (*gly*). Although 'near' has a falling tone and 'far' an ordinary tone, the two words sound the same to my uncultured ear. Back in the days when you had to bargain with taxi drivers, I've agreed to pay outrageous sums when I was under the impression that somewhere was *gly*, when it was actually *gly*. You see the problem. Even to this day, when I ask people if somewhere is *gly* and they answer "yes", I still haven't a clue whether it's near or far.

TERROR OF THE TONES

Despite all the flattery from Thai people, you can quickly come down to earth. One of the most deflating experiences for long-term residents is to use basic Thai you thought you had mastered years ago, only to be greeted by blank looks. It is particularly embarrassing if you are accompanied by visitors you are trying to impress with your linguistic skills. It soon becomes obvious to your friends that the Thai people you are trying to communicate with haven't got a clue what you are talking about. The harder you try, the worse it gets.

The odd couple: Crutch and American author Jim Eckardt ready to sign our respective books during the Ploenchit Fair held in the British Embassy grounds.

A couple of years ago I took some visitors to dinner in Bangkok. Displaying my command of the local language, I reeled off a number of dishes in Thai, just like an old hand. But the waitress stood there, staring at me with a puzzled expression. It soon became clear she hadn't the foggiest idea what I was talking about. I subsequently suffered the ignominy of pointing to pictures of the dishes on the menu, just like the tourists.

Sometimes, knowing a little Thai can be a bit dangerous, as an Australian friend discovered. He lived in an apartment block and was approached by a tearful maid. As far as he could understand, her young daughter Maew had been knocked down by a car. Although she was okay, there was a considerable medical bill. Being a good-natured fellow, the Aussie persuaded everyone in the apartments which the maid served to contribute. The money was duly handed over to the appreciative maid.

The next day he received an irate call from one of his neighbours. The fellow had discovered that it was not the maid's daughter Maew who had been run over, but the apartment block's kitten *"luk maew"*. To make matters worse, the Aussie was told that it was *his* car that ran over the wretched kitten when he returned home the previous night. His neighbours were not impressed with donating to help stitch up the feline that he had squashed.

However, miscommunications usually provide a laugh in the end. Some years ago I was trying to get hold of a Thai businessman on the phone and his secretary explained in English that he was not available because he was "in the lift". Being told someone is unavailable is not uncommon, but "in the lift" seemed unusually specific. "Is he in the lift on his way to work or leaving work?" I asked. "Yes, in the lift," she said.

I tried a different approach. "When will he be in the office?" I asked. "Next week," she replied. Now we were getting somewhere. Obviously he wasn't in the lift. So what was she saying? Lift…live…leaf… leave! "He's on leave," I announced triumphantly down the phone. "Yes," she said, delighted we had finally sorted it out, "he's in the lift."

Visits to restaurants in Thailand are always going to be an adventure. A friend, who had only been in the country a few weeks, ordered a ham omelette for breakfast at one establishment. Ten minutes later the waitress returned with a radiant smile and a plate on which there was just a slice of ham, but no omelette or egg in any form. In her other hand was a bottle of Amarit beer - the "omelette", - not exactly what he had in mind at nine in the morning. As it was, the smile more than made up for the absent omelette.

Another breakfast disaster occurred in a hotel coffee-shop in Ubon Ratchathani. My colleague, who was a little under the weather after a heavy night, could only face poached eggs, which he made the mistake of ordering in English from the young waitress. She appeared to understand, saying something like "pocher" and trotted off.

The waitress returned triumphantly some time later with a large pork chop, which presumably to her ears sounded identical to "poached eggs". It was also swimming in a sea of spaghetti, not quite the light breakfast my friend's stomach had been hoping for.

The innocent pineapple (*sapparot*) has been the source of numerous entertaining misunderstandings over the years. An American visitor told me he was dining with friends, who at the end of the meal asked in English for "separate checks". The waitress duly departed and after a few minutes returned, not with the bill, but a large plate of pineapple. To her ears "separate" had sounded like "*sapparot*".

An English friend, who had not been in the country long, attempted to show off his command of the Thai language by ordering a plate of pineapple. The waitress simply stared at him as if he was some kind of madman, not without reason. It turned out he had mixed up his vocabulary and instead of asking for "*sapparot*", he had come out with "*sokaprok*". He had just ordered a dirty plate.

Adding to the joys of eating out in Thailand are some of the delightful menus, which, particularly in the old days, were really good entertainment value. Top of the list was the legendary Bansuan restaurant in the northeastern town of Nakhon Phanom. The restaurant probably expired long ago, but it is still memorable for its splendid menu, if not the actual food.

I should point out here that all the following menu items are genuine, either spotted by myself or *Bangkok Post* readers.

Most restaurants will do anything to disguise the fact that the food they serve up might have come from tins. Not the Bansuan, however. It seemed to be proud of the source of certain items. Under desserts, it featured a curiously named *Tin of Supper* section with such mouth-watering delights as *Pineapple of Tin, Rambutan of Tin* and *Truffle of Tin.* For true tin connoisseurs there was also *Longan of Tin* and *Lichi of Tin.* No fruit was spared - it all came proudly from tins. You certainly couldn't question the restaurant's honesty.

To round off the meal, you could wash it all down with a lively bottle of what the menu listed as *Spite.*

The Bansuan didn't only specialise in tin delicacies, however. Like all good restaurants it offered hors d'oeuvre, or as this establishment called it, *Auderp 5Taste.* If you didn't fancy the *Auderp,* you could get stuck into the *Bansuan Flesh Perfume*, with a choice of *Hen Perfume* and *Goose Perfume.* Whether one was supposed to eat or sniff these dishes was not entirely clear. Then there was the formidable sounding *Everything Curry.* My favourite was a tempting plate of *Morning Gory Salad.*

In the northeastern town of Khon Kaen, customers at one establishment were invited to try the *Seafoot Cocktail.* Amongst the "seafoot" delights were *Fried Squit* and the unforgettable *Boiled Crap.* In a Nong Khai restaurant overlooking the Mekong River, I enjoyed some tasty *Fride Ponk*, possibly related to the pig population, and the delightful *Fred Fish With Garlic.*

A Phitsanulok menu featured such treats as *Omdette With Minced Ports* and the house special, *Fried Beef And Ogster Sauce.* In fact, *Ogster* must be a local delicacy, as it was featured throughout the menu.

While the most appetising menus were found in the provinces, occasional gems would pop up in Bangkok. At one Surawong Road restaurant there was the particularly charming *Vegetables With Hushrooms*, presumably for people who like to eat in peace. The same place also offered *Pickled Plumps* and something called *Horning Gory With Snail Oil*, an exotic dish if ever there was one.

At a Siam Square restaurant, a colleague perused a menu of dishes allegedly "From the Sea" and came across *Striped Calms* and *Prawn Cocklait.*

One of the more bizarre offerings spotted on menus around the kingdom is *Crab Cooks Whore Dust*. Apparently in the old days "curry" was Thai slang for prostitute, so the dish is in fact crab with curry powder. But admittedly, the alternative version makes a better conversation piece.

Western-style dishes are not immune to language mangling. For some years a Bangkok restaurant was offering *Legg of Lamp*, not to be confused with a newspaper advertisement promoting *Lack of Lamb*. A colleague enjoyed a special promotion at a Silom restaurant offering *Brabecue*.

One restaurant in Phitsanulok also offered such western delights as *Sewed Spaghetti* and the particularly appealing *Cardonglue*. But the best of luck with the *Sliec Loin of Baf*.

One of my favourite breakfast dishes came from a Songkhla hotel, which offered *Horridge*, a dish which reportedly lived up to its name. Also available at the same establishment was *Beacon and Ebbs* and *Tost Marmalude*.

Then there was the Patpong café that came up with *Ham on Toes*, which could be washed down with a *Bloddy Marry*. And for the really brave, one restaurant in the northeast had a notice proudly announcing "Breakfast severed daily".

Something visitors have to get used to quickly in Thailand is the use of first names rather than family names. I find it a very pleasant custom and soon adapted to being called "Mr. Roger", or more frequently "Mr. Loger", and sometimes just "Ger". It seemed agreeably informal, especially when your name was called out at a government office or in an immigration queue, as opposed to the rather cold "Mr. Crutchley", as was the case back in the UK.

It was probably just as well to use first names. In those early days very few Thais could pronounce my surname anyway, and I definitely could not pronounce Thai surnames. Admittedly my name is bit of a mouthful, but I soon became used to being called "Crusherly" and even "Crotchety" and variations thereof. Westerners should be thankful that the Thais have done everyone a great favour by not calling people by their surnames.

The use of first names is of considerable help to editorial staff at the *Bangkok Post* and other English-language publications. For a start, we would never get Thai surnames to fit in the headlines. Thus we can write things like "Somchai gets top post" or "Veera says, no", instead of using the second name that could require more than a dozen characters.

This apparent informal usage of names can seem a bit strange to visitors, because there are tens of thousands of Somchais and Veeras in Thailand. So how do we know which one the newspapers are talking about? To visitors it is almost the equivalent of reading "Fred new president" or "Bert speaks out". However, after a while we get to know that there are only a handful of Somchais or Veeras influential enough to warrant mention in newspaper reports. You soon have a good idea which one is making the news.

It is nicknames which save the day in Thailand, as just about everybody seems to have one. Most Thai nicknames are acquired shortly after kids are born, so the names tend to reflect the smallness of size. That's why Lek, Noi, Nid and Toi, all meaning small or tiny, are very common. When these people grow up, sometimes it seems a bit incongruous that a large strapping man is called Lek or Noi. Other kids are named after what are regarded as cute things like *Gratai* (rabbit), *Tukatar* (doll) or even *Noo* (mouse). One fairly common nickname is G*op* (frog), although I am not sure why. A *Post* reader once told me that his wife, of Indian origin, was nicknamed *Gop* by her Thai friends. Their landlord even put up a sign outside their village which read *Baan Khun Gop* (Mrs. Frog's House).

The use of nicknames and first names certainly makes life easier. But this does not mean there are no misunderstandings and many foreigners will find their name pronounced in a unique way. But that's all part of the fun of living in Thailand.

Anyone by the name of Steve has to very quickly get used to being called S*a-teve*, but that's a minor problem. Other variations are *Sa-tiff* and *Sa-diff*. People called Mike will be referred to as *Mi*, while all the Bills become Mr. *Bin*. Most people called Paul are quite familiar with *Pon,* and if your name is Vince you will usually be greeted as *Wince*. Those called Hugh or with a surname Hughes, will find themselves being referred to as *Huge*. If your name is Julian, I am afraid you are condemned to hearing *Durian* for the rest of your time in Thailand, accompanied by assorted jokes concerning the smelly fruit.

If you are a Jerry or Gerry, you will have to put up with being called *Jellee*, while Chris will likely be known as *Kiss* by the local populace. A *Post* reader told me a friend called Cyril attended a dinner party in Bangkok where everyone's name was placed at the appropriate place on the table. He hunted around for Cyril, but couldn't find his name anywhere. He finally asked the Thai hostess, who pointed to the sole remaining seat. In Cyril's allotted place was the name…*Zero*.

The letter 'R' is a constant hurdle amongst Thai speakers. A well-known Thai actor told me years ago that his favourite Hollywood star was *Lobert Ledford*. Ladies are not spared. If your name is Ruth, be prepared for anything, including *Loof, Loot, Root, Roos* and *Loos*. One lady, whose surname is Holmes, informed me that she was always referred to as Mrs. *Homeless*, which was preferable to suffering interminable jokes about Sherlock.

Having said all this, we foreigners must thank the Thai people for being so tolerant. We pronounce Thai names horribly wrong every day of the week without hearing a word of complaint.

When I was first in Thailand, any expedition in Bangkok would almost certainly involve hearing the joyful greeting, "Hey you, *farang*, one baht" from the street kids. You would hear it every time you went out. I even wondered if the first English lesson they were taught at school was that "Hey you, *farang*" was the proper way to greet a foreigner.

Of course, a lot of the street kids had never been to school and were using the only words of English they knew. The "one baht" wasn't so much a monetary demand, but their way of saying "hello". Mind you, they didn't complain if you lobbed a few coins in their direction.

You soon got used to all the attention and the "hey you" cries became an accepted part of the Bangkok experience, up there with the rattling *samlors*. Although your reaction depended somewhat on what frame of mind you happened to be in. One thing for sure was that as a *farang* you were never lonely on the streets of Bangkok.

Inevitably inflation took hold and after a few years the greeting had been updated to "hey you, *farang*, five baht". And it wasn't long before it had progressed to 10 baht. These days you hardly hear this greeting at all in Bangkok.

During my very early days wandering around rural parts of Thailand, I was regularly subjected to the cry of "Django" from the kids. This was usually accompanied by lots of giggling as they scampered away through the paddy fields, fleeing this big-nosed, sweating stranger trudging through their territory.

I was a bit puzzled by the name. The only Django I was aware of was the French jazz guitarist Django Reinhardt, who had died back in 1953. It seemed most unlikely he would be familiar to kids sitting on a buffalo in a remote part of Thailand.

I later discovered that the previous year there had been a hugely popular movie in Thailand called *Django*. One of the early "spaghetti westerns", it starred Italian actor Franco Nero in the title role as a drifter-cum-gunslinger who for some reason dragged a coffin around with him. Incidentally, in Britain this film was regarded as too violent and was banned until 1993. However, unlike nudity, violence has never bothered the Thai censors and *Django* became a cult hit, even in Nakhon Nowhere. So, any foreigner who strayed off the beaten track in Thailand and looked a bit dishevelled, became an obvious target for the "Django" appellation. Anyway, it was preferable to being called *farang kee nok* (cheapskate foreigner), *hua lan* (baldy), or *puhm poey* (fatso).

25. THIS SPORTING LIFE

From interviewing legends to playing elephant polo

Two years after we moved to the present Bangkok Post building in Klong Toey in 1992, I became sports editor at the *Post* and was to remain in that position until retirement. I was only the third sports editor in three decades, following in the footsteps of Anton Perera and Edward Thangarajah, both Sri Lankans. Wanchai Rujawongsanti became the first Thai sports editor after my retirement and has done an excellent job.

Edward sadly passed away in 2016 at the age of 84. He was dedicated to his profession and one of the hardest-working journalists I have ever come across. He would regularly go out to cover stories during the day and then stay in the office until late at night, supervising the sports section.

Having an inbuilt appreciation of most sports, the job was perhaps a natural choice for me. It was also a good change as it required going out of the office a lot more than in my previous positions at the *Post*. It was also very hard work, especially in the early days when we were really short-staffed. I often found myself racing out of the office as dusk fell to cover local rugby, football, badminton and occasionally international snooker tournaments. Because of heavy traffic most evenings, this entailed many hair-raising journeys riding pillion on motorcycle taxis. This was followed by an equally terrifying journey back to the office to write up the match report and oversee the sports pages. With the deadline always looming, time raced by.

One of the benefits of being a sports editor in Thailand is that you are more likely to get access to visiting sports personalities and in a much more relaxed atmosphere than you would, say, in London or New York. Only a few days before writing this chapter, I found myself face-to-face with star golfers Bubba Watson, Sergio Garcia, Martin Kaymer and Lee Westwood with only a smattering of other journalists around and it was all so pleasantly informal.

Over the years I was fortunate enough to meet many famous sportsmen and women. Admittedly many of them had retired, but that made them no less interesting to interview.

My most cherished moments were spent with childhood hero Sir Bobby Charlton on several occasions in Bangkok. In particular, when he came out in 1998, I spent half the day with the great player as he gave a football clinic to children at Bangkok Patana School.

As a 19-year-old in 1966, I had been glued to the television set at home watching England's World Cup exploits. England had begun with a drab 0-0 draw against Uruguay and the second group match against Mexico appeared to be heading the same way. The Wembley crowd was getting restless.

On our way to Bangkok Patana School more than three decades later, Sir Bobby recalled what happened next: "I got the ball just inside our half and began running with it. The Mexican defence kept backing off and I thought, if they give me a few more yards, I might have a crack at goal." And what a crack! The ball sailing sweetly into the back of the net from 35 yards out, an absolute screamer.

Was it his best-ever goal? "It wasn't bad," Charlton said with his customary modesty, "but it was more a great sense of relief. We thought we would never score." That goal turned the tournament around for England and, as everyone knows, they went on to win the World Cup.

I could write a whole chapter on Charlton alone. Suffice to say he is how you would imagine, a down-to-earth person with no airs or graces - a gentleman on the football pitch and off it.

I met another star from the same England team a couple of times - Sir Geoff Hurst, the only player to score a hat-trick in a World Cup final. I first interviewed him at the Emporium on Sukhumvit Road when he was signing autographs. There were thousands of people milling around and the noise was so overwhelming that we had to shout at one another while he dealt with the autograph hunters.

He laughed about that Bangkok experience a couple of years later in London, where he was one of the ambassadors trying to help England's ultimately fruitless bid to host the World Cup.

Walking out of the tunnel at Sunderland's Stadium of Light with 1966 World Cup hero Sir Geoff Hurst on a trip to England in 2000.

Hurst was the scorer of one of the most controversial goals in World Cup history in that 1966 final against West Germany. For England's third goal (his second) Hurst swiveled to crash the ball against the underside of the bar. What happened after that is still debated to this day. The ball bounced down over the goal line say England fans, not so say the Germans. Sir Geoff said he was not bothered over the controversy, although he was sure the ball went over the line. "In fact, the more they talk about it, the better it is," he said.

Another England footballing legend I encountered in Bangkok was Sir Bobby Robson, when he came out to raise funds for tsunami victims in 2005. I had always nurtured a soft spot for him, because the very first time my dad took me to Wembley in April 1961, Bobby scored the opening goal in what turned out to be England's historic 9-3 rout of Scotland.

Robson almost fell off his chair when I told him I had witnessed that goal 44 years previously. "Even my wife didn't see it," he said. Apparently she was stuck in the traffic and missed his ninth-minute strike.

Robson, who became an astute manager, was a wonderful character and a striking figure with his silver hair, always eager to talk football. You could feel his passion for the game. When he was in Bangkok, he had just been sacked by Newcastle, yet even at the age of 71 he was keen to get another job and put the past behind him. "Never look back, always look forward," was his parting words to me.

Among other football managers whom I met in Bangkok were Sven-Goran Eriksson, then the immaculately tailored manager of Manchester City, and Gerard Houillier with his Liverpool team. I recall Houillier being baffled by the Thai crowds cheering for both teams. "That wouldn't happen in England," he said.

Another familiar face in Bangkok has been Liverpool legend Ian Rush, who played in a number of charity tournaments. He is a friendly fellow and always happy to have a chat even while standing on the touchline waiting to go on the pitch.

During the past two decades, three former England football players took up the challenging task of managing team Thailand. Unfortunately, for all their undoubted expertise, Peter Reid and former England captain Bryan Robson could not translate their experience and tactical knowledge into improving the underperforming Thai squads.

However former Aston Villa and England striker Peter Withe spent nearly five years at the helm. Withe suffered similar frustrations to Reid and Robson, but he also experienced a few highs and became a popular figure in Thailand.

When Withe arrived in October 1998 the Thai national team was in disarray. The team had been temporarily banned by the Asian Football Confederation after being involved in a farcical match in Vietnam against Indonesia, in which both sides tried to lose.

However, a few months later, at the Asian Games in Bangkok, Thai fans were ecstatic after Thailand pulled off a most unlikely 2-1 win in the quarter final over South Korea, a team they had never previously beaten. And they did it with just nine men, scoring a "golden goal" winner from a free-kick by Thavatchai Damrongongtrakul.

Withe recalled that moment with pleasure. "The crowd erupted and all of us jumped up and down like mad things." It got even better shortly after when Thai goalkeeper Chaiyong Kampium congratulated Withe and said: "You have now become a hero in Thailand."

Another proud moment for Withe came in May 1999 when Thailand beat Arsenal 4-3 in a thrilling friendly at Rajamangala Stadium. Kiatisak "Zico" Senamuang was outstanding, scoring two superb goals. "Arsenal got the shock of their lives," Withe said. "I don't think Arsene Wenger was too pleased." Withe was right. About a year later I was at a media dinner at Lancaster House in London where Wenger was guest speaker. I asked him if he recalled Thailand beating Arsenal the previous season. He gave a withering look, but then smiled: "You must have enjoyed that," he said. "Thailand played very well."

Thanks to the DHL Bangkok Lions and their annual rugby dinners I had the opportunity to meet a host of rugby union stars over the years, including All Blacks favourites Eric Rush and Jonah Lomu, Australians Tim Horan, John Eales and the legendary - and very talkative - David Campese. England's rugby notables included Steve Thompson, Brian Moore and Martin

Bayfield, whose physique was so large that he doubled as Hagrid in the early Harry Potter films.

One of the most uplifting interviews was with Lomu, arguably rugby union's biggest ever name during his outstanding days with the All Blacks. He was one of the few players to capture the imagination of people outside the sport.

It was his extraordinary skills that initially caught the eye, but when I met him in Bangkok in 2007 at the age of 32, it was his battle against a debilitating kidney disease and subsequent transplant that had made him an inspiration around the globe. Despite his superstar status, Lomu was a humble and accessible man and very honest about his beginnings and how rugby had steered him in the right direction.

"Rugby is a great game because it gives you discipline and self-respect," Lomu said. "I needed that as I was a bit wayward as a kid." Sadly, Jonah passes away in 2015.

A number of former Test cricketers came to Thailand, thanks primarily to the success of the Chiang Mai Sixes and later the Hua Hin Sixes. When Dennis Lillee played in Chiang Mai in 1994, he quickly became a crowd pleaser both on and off the field. He was "one of the lads", enjoying the banter and good humour that typifies Sixes cricket. When I was introduced to him, the first words he uttered were "G'day mate, fancy a beer?" Of course, he got a positive response.

Other colourful cricketers I encountered in Hua Hin were former England captains Allan Lamb and Mike Gatting. When asked what it was like going on tour with his mate Ian Botham, Lamb replied, "Bloody hard work." However, he didn't mind being Botham's roommate on tour because he hardly ever saw him. When I asked Gatting about "the ball of the century", when he was clean bowled by Australia's Shane Warne with the spinner's amazing first ball on English soil in the 1993 Ashes at Old Trafford, he said he had never seen a ball turn so much.

In the early days, the *Bangkok Post* fielded a cricket team in the local Bangkok league. Nearly all of the matches were played at the Royal Bangkok Sports Club (RBSC). One Saturday morning I rolled up at the ground just before the game started. We were batting first and I noticed two players already padded up. They weren't regulars, but one of the faces seemed quite familiar. At that point our captain, Edward Thangarajah, appeared and introduced me to our two new opening batsmen, snooker star Steve Davis and promoter Barry Hearn.

It was when Davis was in his prime and regularly playing in exhibition matches in Bangkok. Edward had met them and brought them along to the match. They were very sociable and chatted with everyone. Unfortunately their opening partnership didn't last long as Steve was definitely a better snooker player than cricketer. But Hearn knocked up a tidy score. Whenever the topic of snooker crops up in conversation, I usually manage to slip in about the time I played with Steve Davis. I very carefully do not specify which sport.

It was at the Oriental Hotel's Authors Lounge in 1996, I interviewed three-times Formula 1 champion Jackie Stewart. The amiable Scot was bursting with energy and praised the improvements in F1 racing since he was racing back in the 1970s. "In my day, if you raced for more than five years there was quite a chance you were going to die," he admitted.

The sport I covered most was golf. I am a hopeless player and the only golf prize I have ever won was for having the prettiest caddy. But I love the game and have been fortunate enough to report on the best in the world.

The best of the best was Tiger Woods. When Tiger came to Thailand in 1997 for the Asian Honda Classic aged 21, it was just after he had exploded on the scene. There was total chaos when he arrived at Don Mueang Airport. The local television cameras even got on the plane before he got off - so much for security. For a moment Tiger sat there on the plane helpless, looking like the proverbial rabbit in the headlights. He hadn't slept for 24 hours and being swamped under a sea of flower garlands amid unprecedented media frenzy, you couldn't blame him for looking a trifle bewildered. There was no harm done, however, and Tiger went on to stroll to victory at the Thai Country Club by a handy 10 strokes.

A year later he was back, this time playing in what turned out to be a memorable Johnnie Walker Classic at the Blue Canyon Country Club in Phuket. After three rather ordinary rounds, on the final day, Woods came from eight shots back with a 65 to catch leader Ernie Els and then beat the South African on the second play-off hole. It was a spectacular comeback, even by Tiger's standards, and the atmosphere was electric as the large galleries showed their appreciation of such sparkling golf.

There were similar scenes two years later as Tiger ran away with another Johnnie Walker title, this time at the Alpine Golf and Sports Club, north of Bangkok. Now 24, Tiger finished in an amazing 25-under par, his lowest score in a four-round tournament.

Tiger had been under fire for seeming indifferent to his Thai background but commented: "Coming to Thailand is great for me as it's part of my culture and heritage." Alas I only got to speak to him at press conferences and never managed an interview. I always got the impression that he found his visits to Thailand a bit overwhelming.

What has impressed me most on the golf scene, however, was the performance of Thai players. Golf is one sport in which Thais have truly emerged as world-class competitors, both men and women.

For the past 20 years I have been privileged to watch at close hand players like Thongchai Jaidee, Thaworn Wiratchant, Prayad Marksaeng, Kiradech Aphibarnrat and veteran Boonchu Ruangkit competing in Malaysia, Singapore, Macau, China and, in Thongchai's case, Valderrama, Spain.

The most successful player has been Thongchai and his name is known and respected around the world. With an affable personality, the former paratrooper has been a great ambassador, not just for Thai golf but for the kingdom as a whole. Whatever country you are in people know "Jaidee" as he is called abroad and speak of him in the highest terms.

In addition to his 13 victories on the Asian Tour, including three awards for topping the Order of Merit, Thongchai has notched an impressive eight European Tour titles, including the 2012 Wales Open, his first victory on European soil.

Thongchai could only speak a few words of English when I first met him, but now you can't stop him talking in English once he gets going. He has been well supported by his wife and manager, Namfon, who regularly follows Thongchai's progress around the course.

Thailand's lady golfers have also made their mark internationally, none more so than Ariya Jutanagarn who in June 2017 at the age of just 21 became Thailand's first-ever world number one golfer, topping the demanding LPGA Tour rankings.

It came after an amazing 12 months during which Ariya won six LPGA titles, including a major, the British Women's Open. Success didn't come easily and she had suffered a number of heartbreaks. But when the breakthrough came it was little short of spectacular. In May 2016 she won an amazing three LPGA tournaments back-to-back.

Ariya has received crucial moral support from her elder sister Moriya, an accomplished golfer herself, who in 2013 was LPGA Rookie of the Year. Few will forget the traumatic moment at the 2013 LPGA Honda Thailand Open at the Siam Country Club Course when 17-year-old Ariya had just blown a two-shot lead on the final hole. Moriya was on hand to console her distraught younger sister and the two hugged one another tearfully on the 18th green. It was one of the most poignant golfing moments I have ever witnessed.

Blazing the trail in the earlier years, and winning the US Women's Amateur in 2003, was Virada Nirapatpongporn, neatly nicknamed by her US colleagues who initially struggled with her name, as 'Virada Three Ps'. Pornanong Phatlum has also enjoyed several excellent seasons, although at the time of writing is still looking for that elusive first LPGA title.

Two other Thai stars who proved great ambassadors for the country are tennis players Paradorn Srichaphan and Tamarine Tanasugarn.

Tamarine, who was briefly ranked 19th in the world in 2002, has such a cheerful personality it is hard to imagine she was sometimes unhappy with her performances. She enjoyed a tremendous record at Wimbledon, making it to the quarter finals in 2008, where she was beaten by eventual winner, Venus Williams. She also reached the fourth round on an impressive six occasions. Tamarine, who partnered Russia's Maria Sharapova in many doubles matches, was hugely popular on the WTA circuit, which doesn't surprise anyone who has met her.

Paradorn reached No. 9 in the world in May 2003, the first-ever Asian player to make the top ten. It was a remarkable achievement and possibly one not fully appreciated by his compatriots. Even Paradorn finds it hard to believe just how well he has done. When I spoke to him a couple of years later, he commented with commendable frankness: "I sometimes look back to when I was in the top ten and think 'how did I do that?' I look at all the names below me and think - wow!"

One of his most notable scalps was Andrei Agassi, who Paradorn beat at Wimbledon in 2002. In the following year at the US Open, Agassi commented: "Paradorn is one of the nicest guys here. I'm a fan of his on and off the court."

During the 1970s, I played in the Farang Soccer League for a team called the Cosmopolitans (Cosmos), which lived up to its name, at times fielding 10 different nationalities. In addition to the Thai goalkeeper we had players from Vietnam, the Netherlands, Italy, Russia, Austria, Spain, the US, Israel and England. It was a wonderful experience and I made many friends.

I also became friends with the chief referee, Sukit Chitranukroh, a former Thai national team player and a real gentleman. He had represented Thailand in the 1956 Melbourne Olympics and later became an accomplished Fifa referee. There were very few problems in the matches that Sukit was in charge of, primarily because he was a good referee and respected by all the players. It always amazed me why Sukit would want to officiate in a league full of unfit expats playing a mediocre standard of football, but many thinking they were Pele.

Motley Crew: The Cosmopolitans football team in the early 1970s featured up to 10 different nationalities. The author is standing second from left. Far right is Farang League organiser Gunther Glomb, a former star with FC Nurnberg in Germany.

In the early 1970s I had the honour of playing against the Thai national women's football team. The girls were preparing for a major regional tournament and wanted to play against some "tough opposition". Obviously they couldn't find any and had to settle for a hastily assembled Farang All Stars XI, beer bellies and all. Several thousand spectators turned out at the newly-built Thai-Japanese stadium at Din Daeng to support the ladies - they certainly hadn't come to see our team. Our captain told us to "take it easy" and I envisaged a leisurely hour or so. There was also the promise of a free dinner and beer after the match, which made it even more enticing. Not a bad way to spend a Sunday afternoon.

It didn't quite work out as planned.

I was playing centre-half and anticipating a stroll in the park. My attitude took an abrupt change after about two minutes when Ms. Lek, a diminutive young woman, came thundering through and whacked me on the ankle. It hurt like hell, but I put on a brave face - it would have looked bad being stretchered off against the ladies. What made it worse was when she heard my howls of pain, she stopped, turned around and gave me an apologetic *wai*. Now, you don't get that at Wembley. For the rest of the game I limped around chasing shadows and kept well clear of Ms. Lek and her lethal left boot.

Newspaper derby: Exchanging pennants with the captain of the Straits Times Singapore, during a regional newspaper football tournament at the Port Authority ground in Klong Toey in November 1981.

The final score was a somewhat manufactured 4-3 win for the girls, while for me it was bruised ego to match my already bruised ankle. But the food afterwards was great, as was the beer. Never has a defeat been so grandly celebrated. My first and last "international".

Probably the daftest sporting event I ever got involved in was elephant polo. In 2003, the *Bangkok Post* and the *Nation* were persuaded to field teams as a humorous prelude to the King's Cup Elephant Polo Tournament in Hua Hin. A large crowd of spectators showed up, tipped off that a bunch of journalists from Bangkok were about to make total fools of themselves ... and they were not disappointed. None of us had been aboard elephants before and it definitely looked like it.

In the opening chukka, I spent the whole time trying not to fall off, while teammates Jim Hawker (now at the *Times* in London) and sports editor Wanchai were in much the same mode. The elephants quickly realized that the people aboard them hadn't a clue what they were doing and on occasions picked the ball up in their trunks as a kind of protest, prompting a splendid "elephant stopped play" ruling from the umpires.

Nothing to trumpet about: An uncomfortable Crutch (left) aboard a pachyderm while preparing for an Elephant Polo match in Hua Hin.

The *Nation's* team, led by Alan Parkhouse (who went on to edit the *Phnom Penh Post*) and author James Eckardt, seemed to adapt better to the conditions and sneaked into the lead when Eckardt managed to squirt the ball over the line. They hung on for a commendable victory, while we settled for an "honorable defeat". The *Post* team took consolation in the fact that no one actually fell off during the entire proceedings.

We went on to repeat these mighty gladiatorial contests for several years. I can safely say, we didn't improve any, although the *Post* did eventually sneak a win. There was relief all round when I announced my permanent retirement, citing a bruised backside.

Some have questioned whether this activity is cruel for the elephants, but the pachyderms appeared to enjoy it. According to the mahouts, the elephants love it and they certainly gave little trumpets of triumph when they made a clever move and were rewarded with some crunchy sugar cane. The only people who really suffered were those daft enough to sit on them.

I experienced 15 really enjoyable years in the sports section which also gave me the opportunity to write the Nobby Piles column. It originally began in 1994 just for the World Cup in the US, but refused to sit on the bench and has been appearing for more than two decades.

I would never have survived without the hard work and support of my colleagues on the sports desk, including current editor Wanchai and his deputy Ravipan Pavasuthipand. I am glad to say they have also become good friends, as too have other members of the sports team, past and present - Parani Pitakwong, Kittipong Thongsombat, Tor Chittinand and Kritini-U-dompol who became Sunday Design Editor. And not forgetting two great guys from England who went on to better things, Jim Hawker and Julian Turner.

26. THE MORE THINGS CHANGE...

Older and fatter, but not any wiser

I am frequently asked about what changes have occurred in Thailand in the past four decades. My answers are always hopelessly inadequate. So much has changed, but so much remains the same. For every suggestion of change there is an immediate contradiction. As I write this, I am completing my 48th year in Thailand. It is hard to believe time has flown so fast. It has been a journey from Young Crutch to Old Crutch, from Skinny Crutch to Tubby Crutch, from Penniless Crutch to Still Penniless Crutch.

Admittedly, arriving at the commencement of Songkran in 1969 was a bit like being thrown in at the deep end. My introduction to the festival was just a couple of days after Clarence and I had arrived in Bangkok. We were walking near the old Makkasan Circle, when a group of middle-aged ladies wearing colourful sarongs approached us dancing the *ramwong*. They proceeded to throw water at us in good natured fashion from their bowls and covered us with powder and paste. We had no idea what it was all about, but it was so hot that the cooling water didn't seem such a bad idea. I wasn't so keen on the paste.

As we continued our expedition through Pratunam, we were subjected to a real soaking, primarily from kids with buckets, and they were all grinning. Welcome to the Land of Smiles. It was in the days before those ghastly giant plastic water guns and we enjoyed the experience. There was a feeling we were in a country that was very different to any other we had been in - and that is one feeling which has not changed over the past four decades. But I don't like getting soaked anymore, absolutely loathe those plastic weapons and sadly have become a Songkran stay-at-home.

Was life better in Thailand in 1969 than it is now? It's hard to say, primarily because my circumstances and age were so different then to the present time. It was certainly more exciting for me in those days because just about every experience was new - the pungent aromas, the food, the ubiquitous stray dogs, the mysterious nightlife. You never knew what was going to happen next. In that respect nothing has changed. It is probably true to say that the longer you live here, the less you seem to know about Thailand.

Life goes on: Thankfully the Thai smile will always be with us as displayed by the author's wife Prapatsorn (Aon).

There have always been traffic problems in Bangkok, although the 1970s jams were arguably not quite as horrendous as some we have experienced in recent years. In the old days the jams were primarily caused by not enough roads, now it's far too many cars. Taxis in those days were not air-conditioned, which made the

THE MORE THINGS CHANGE...

gridlock far more uncomfortable. During Songkran, taxi passengers with their windows open were a prime target.

Certain aspects of transport in the city have improved considerably. The BTS Skytrain and MRT Underground have been a great benefit, although it took ages to actually get round to building them. It is a pity that it took so long to recognize how essential they are and they are now suffering from overcrowding. The plight of the State Railway of Thailand (SRT) is a real shame. After decades of neglect, what was a slow but sure system has deteriorated into a slow and unsure system.

Shopping was a quite different experience in those early days. There were no malls and the only big outlet was Central Department Store on Silom Road, with a much smaller branch at Ratchaprasong. Unlike the present day, nowhere had everything under one roof. Instead, you had to trudge around from shop to shop, many of them without air-conditioning. Sometimes you had to travel to a totally different part of town that specialized in a particular product.

While shopping might well have been a rich cultural experience, it was quite hard work. It was simply too bloody hot. I unashamedly prefer the comfort of the present-day malls, although I don't like the crowds and always avoid those places at the weekend. Maybe it's just the air-conditioning that attracts me. At least I don't return home totally exhausted, unless I've been shopping with the wife.

Fashion has evolved just as rapidly as anywhere in the world. But there has been quite a change in acceptable wear. In the old days all the maids - and there were plenty of them - wore sarongs in their households and out on the streets, although sometimes jeans might put in an appearance on their day off, if they had one. You never saw women wearing shorts, apart from the occasional lady of the night. These days shorts are quite acceptable for just about everyone, although maybe the *khunyings* beg to differ.

And then there is women's hair. It was always black and very beautiful. Now, it's all shades of the rainbow. A few highlights can actually look quite nice, but I still find blonde Thais a bit incongruous. To be fair, the vast majority are still proud of their wonderful black locks, the best-looking hair in the world.

In the provinces in the early 1970s, if you looked out of a bus, car or train at any given moment, you could almost guarantee seeing a buffalo, usually with a little kid perched atop. It was a scene which personified Thailand. Not any more. In a few years, spotting a buffalo will be a major sighting.

It is a sign of the times that there are now special buffalo villages promoted as tourist attractions, when little more than a decade ago nearly every village in the kingdom was a buffalo village. The buffalo has gone out of fashion in the farming world, replaced by the *E-tan*, the "iron buffalo". There used to be a saying that the buffalo would survive because it does not rust or need spare parts. Unfortunately it looks like the only survivors in a few years will be the buffaloes used in those annual races in Chonburi, or the animals tarted up for fancy dress contests to promote tourism.

Of course, the people are key to the enjoyment of any country. For me the Thais will never lose their appeal, with their inherent good nature and an inbuilt desire to have fun (*sanuk*). They have become more materialistic in last four decades, but what country or people hasn't? The smartphone revolution is admittedly bit of a worry. The preoccupation with these phones, particularly amongst the younger generation, is certainly having a negative impact on people enjoying normal conversations. But again, this is a problem every country in the world is facing.

Tourism has had a huge effect. There was a time when a popular expression was *"Poo dee Angrit",* which translates roughly as "polite English gentleman". People in Thailand genuinely believed all English people had good manners. Over the years as reality set in and Thais were exposed to a broader spectrum of English society, this expression began to fade away. But the same probably goes for all nationalities. Mass tourism comes at a price. I remember in the early 1970s, a lot of fuss was made when for the first time Thailand welcomed one million tourists in a year. The latest figures are more than 35 million.

THE MORE THINGS CHANGE...

One thing that has made living in the kingdom so enjoyable is that Thai people have a great sense of humour - and they need it with the politicians they have to put up with. Who can forget the MP who caused much mirth when he explained a few years ago that when politicians have their eyes shut in Parliament, despite the snoring noises, they are not asleep but are "deep in thought". So, if there is any hint of something to laugh at in Thailand, there will be laughter. If the joke is repeated, it gets even funnier. Slapstick humour of the banana-skin variety goes down particularly well.

I have a particularly fond memory of Bangkrachao, that unique oasis of greenery often referred to as the "lung of Bangkok", just across the river from Klong Toey. It was late 1979 when Tony Waltham and I were ambling through one orchard - trespassing is what it would be called in England - when we came across a family sitting outside their modest wooden house. Far from telling us to buzz off, which they had every right to do, they invited us to sit with them. Our enquiry as to what fruit a certain tree bore was met with one of the kids scurrying off to return with an armful of *chompoo* (rose apples) for us to eat. On learning we liked mangoes the father immediately began picking the ripe fruit off the trees and presenting them to us.

Granny then emerged and scolded her family for giving us plain water rather than coconut juice to quench our thirst. Quickly one of the youngster climbed up a palm tree and proceeded to lob down coconuts. There were even apologies that some fruits were not in season. We eventually staggered off with enough fruit to open our own stall and an invitation to return a fortnight later to celebrate one of the sons who was entering the monkhood.

Return we did and enjoyed a wonderful feast, followed by dancing in the orchard to the strains of an enthusiastic Thai band belting out the big hit of the time, *My Sharona*. Now that's what I call hospitality.

It is said that Thai people are not as happy as they once were and the Land of Smiles is becoming the Land of Frowns. From my observations, the population might not be as happy, but they have not quite reached the stage of *Les Miserables*. There are still plenty of smiles to savour.

While covering a golf tournament near Pattaya in 2013, I came across a caddy acting as a ball spotter in one of the more remote parts of the course. She was tucking into her lunch, which looked suspiciously like *somtam*. As I approached, she gave a wonderful smile. Nothing unusual in that, you might say. But after four decades I still get a kick out of an unsolicited Thai smile, which is a tribute to the quality of that smile. She wasn't trying to sell me anything. It was just a spontaneous smile upon seeing a total stranger, admittedly a rather funny-looking one. I was the recipient of similar smiles from caddies all over the course.

Admittedly not all smiles are as natural as those of the caddies. A Thai smile can mean a dozen different things and span a whole range of emotions. One very effective smile I see rather too often is from my long-suffering wife, Aon. I think it is called *yim tak tan*, or to put it bluntly, "sorry, but you are wrong again."

I recall an eye-catching photograph on the front page of the *Bangkok Post* of a group of Thai women all sporting big grins. It wouldn't have been out of place in a tourist promotion campaign. But the women had nothing to smile about at all. They had just lost their jobs as a result of an economic meltdown. All these smiling people were actually protesting the loss of their jobs. They were smiles of desperation - *yim soo*, simply hoping things could get better. It is hard to imagine Karl Marx would ever have envisaged downtrodden workers protesting with big grins.

Smiles of embarrassment are quite common. In flood situations I've observed Thai people accidentally plunging into flooded holes, picking themselves up and sporting a big grin. It is an affirmation that an embarrassed grin beats a scowl in Thailand.

Some people believe Thai smiles come a little too easily, but I don't subscribe to that view. There are plenty of superficial smiles, of course, and even some disguising ill intent. So it definitely pays to be a bit cautious. But you can overdo the analysis. Suffice to say, I would rather live in a country where people smile too much, than in a place where they don't smile at all. And I must admit to using a hasty smile on more than one occasion to get out of an awkward situation. I think they call that *yim yair-yair*.

So there's nothing wrong with a smile, whether you are protesting, ripping someone off, falling down holes, making a fool of yourself, or simply saying hello.

To round things off, in capsulated form, here are some of my favourite stories that have appeared in the *Bangkok Post* over the years. They are all 100% genuine and probably sum up why I have stayed in the kingdom for so long.

Whose side are you on?: In the late 1960s there was considerable confusion when a group of undercover Thai policemen in the guise of communist terrorists, including Mao hats and matching gear, surprised a band of communist terrorists, who just happened to be disguised as policemen, in the jungles of Surat Thani. A most interesting standoff ensued, with nobody quite sure whose side they were on and who they should be shooting at.

Frankest Excuse: The senior government official who was transferred to an inactive post because of lack of productivity. When asked why he had done nothing, he replied that nobody had asked him to do anything.

Craftiest Fortune Teller: There was a young lady down on her luck who saw a fortune teller at Sanam Luang. He explained that her luck would improve if she had sex with him. She obliged on a regular basis, but her luck didn't improve. He then suggested the obvious solution was to increase the frequency of their sex sessions. This they did, but still no good luck. So eventually she sued him, not for sexual harassment, but for being a lousy fortune-teller.

Daftest Crook: The fellow who went to a Bangkok police station asking them to help retrieve a large box that went missing on a bus journey from Korat to Mor Chit. Upon recovering the box, police opened it to discover it was stuffed with six kilos of opium. I think he did 10 years for that.

Most appropriately-worded explanation: After two Thai rock stars were involved in an extremely embarrassing punch-up on stage during a concert in New York, the organizer explained quite seriously that one of the fellows, a leading guitarist, was "highly strung".

Happy Families: Accused of illegally disguising his wealth, a senior politician claimed in his defence he was so badly henpecked that he let his wife handle all financial transactions, hence his complete innocence. He was actually backed up by his wife, who admitted controlling the purse strings because "mother told me never to trust men."

Almost the Great Escape: A buffalo which escaped on its way to the knacker's yard when the truck it was aboard broke down at the entrance to Don Mueang Airport. The buffalo trotted up the ramp and after taking a few bites out of some suitcases, it became excited at the sight of hundreds of passengers in the departure lounge. Pandemonium ensued as the buffalo, with airport officials in hot pursuit, charged around the lounge sending passengers fleeing. All it wanted to do was say 'hello'. Alas, the buffalo was eventually subdued to continue its journey to the Great Meatball in the Sky.

Best sharpshooter: A crucial witness in the trial of an "influential person" suddenly retracted his testimony, claiming his eyesight was so poor, he couldn't read the statement that he had earlier signed. When asked by the judge what his profession was, the fellow with the wretched eyesight confirmed he was a sharpshooter for the crack Special Warfare Unit.

Super Sleuth: The senior Northeastern policeman who told reporters in 1992 he suspected a Thai policeman was involved in a big Laotian bank robbery. He was absolutely right. One week

THE MORE THINGS CHANGE...

later he himself was arrested for being one of the masterminds of the robbery.

Welcome To Bangkok: The baby elephant on its first visit to Bangkok. It was walking past a school when a kindergarten band suddenly emerged playing an out of tune *Colonel Bogey March*. The poor elephant went nuts at the sound of the discordant trumpets and ran riot through the streets, before it was eventually sedated a couple of hours later.

Taking Off: A Don Mueang airport employee who found an empty room with some video equipment and proceeded to watch a pornographic movie for his private viewing. What he didn't realise was that the video machine was linked up to the terminal's television network. The naughty movie suddenly appeared on all televisions in the airport, causing a considerable stir amongst the passengers. However, most of them agreed it was more interesting than the list of flight departures.

It's been a lot of fun and the past four decades have simply raced by. But the most rewarding experience at the *Post* has been working with people from so many different ethnic and cultural backgrounds - a veritable United Nations. And I have learned so much from my Thai colleagues.

Although we are the same age, the *Post* will keep going for much longer than me. I wouldn't mind betting there will be some good tales to tell in the coming years.

EPILOGUE

Life in Thailand has not been quite the same since His Majesty King Bhumibol Adulyadej passed away on October 13, 2016. Although the monarch had been seriously ill, the news of his death came as a shock to most Thai citizens. The King's longevity on the throne meant he had ruled the country since before most Thais were born and few of his subjects had known anything different. He had always been there and in times of trouble was such a reassuring figure. Suddenly he was gone. It was hard to accept and it left the nation in a communal state of sorrow.

There follows a personal appreciation of the late King which first appeared in the PostScript column on October 16, 2016.

An appreciation of a remarkable monarch
Not being Thai, whatever I say concerning His Majesty the late King will be inadequate. But having lived in Thailand for the past 47 years, I feel that he has also become my King and I would like to at least attempt to express my admiration for what he has achieved.

Upon arrival in Thailand I knew very little about the country. But within a few hours it soon became clear how much His Majesty was revered in the Kingdom. On that first day wandering around the streets of Yaowaraj, it was noticeable that every shop carried portraits of Their Majesties. I had been brought up in England, a country with strong royal traditions, but had never seen anything like that - royal portraits in the UK were generally limited to government offices and institutions.

It was not just the portraits, which have also been in evidence in virtually every Thai home I have visited in the past four decades. In any conversation with Thai people concerning His Majesty, it became clear just how much they revered and admired him.

EPILOGUE

When the streets near the *Bangkok Post* office at Ratchadamnoen Avenue and Sanam Luang lit up in December 1969 to celebrate His Majesty's birthday, it was a truly uplifting experience. I had never witnessed a display quite like it before.

Rural rides
Working at the *Bangkok Post* proved to be a great insight into just how much His Majesty loved his people. It struck me how frequently the King travelled to the provinces, not for a well-earned holiday or relaxation, but to organize development projects for the rural poor in every part of the country. And he visited the remotest places, where government officials were seldom seen. The adoring looks on the villagers' faces said it all. His Majesty became a familiar figure in newspapers and on television, striding through fields on assorted irrigation and agricultural projects, consulting detailed maps and with a camera always slung over his neck. He truly was a working monarch, slogging around in the tropical heat and rain.

The Vietnam War was still raging in the early 1970s and there were fears that Thailand would become a victim of what was known as the "domino effect", with the country succumbing to Communism. I am convinced that it was the people's love for His Majesty throughout the country, but particularly in the vulnerable Northeast, that held the kingdom together at that time.

When 100,000 marched
While His Majesty was a constitutional monarch with limited powers, his influence on the daily lives of people was indisputable. The respect with which Their Majesties were held came to the fore during the student demonstrations in 1973, which led to the October 14 uprising against the Thanom Kittikachorn government.

It was 43 years ago, when an estimated 100,000 university students, immaculately dressed in uniforms of white shirts and dark trousers or skirts, filled up every inch of Ratchadamnoen Avenue as they marched peacefully. What caught my eye was that many were holding portraits of Their Majesties the King and Queen. It was an eloquent protest and an unforgettable sight.

Many years later, in 1992 there came an astonishing moment. The country was in turmoil following protests against the government and many people had been killed on Bangkok's streets in what became known as "Black May". The situation was critical when on May 20, His Majesty summoned the two main protagonists in the conflict to the palace.

I recall the concerned *Post* editorial staff gathering around the television that night as His Majesty admonished the warring parties. His brief speech began: "The nation belongs to everyone, not one or two specific people." The *Post* newsroom applauded. His Majesty had brought the country back from the brink.

Soulful songs
It is well-known His Majesty enjoyed music, especially jazz and he was an accomplished saxophonist. He really believed music played a role in the well-being of the country. In the *Post's* picture library many years ago, I came across an iconic photo of the King jamming with Benny Goodman in Bangkok in 1960. Four years earlier he played at Goodman's house in New York. His Majesty also performed with Stan Getz and Benny Carter.

In 1946 His Majesty composed three memorable jazz numbers - *Falling Rain*, *Candlelight Blues* and *Love at Sundown*. They all have bluesy feel to them and His Majesty was said to be "overjoyed" when he heard that the people really enjoyed his compositions.

A love supreme
His Majesty always had a love for animals and in his later years worked hard to improve the life of stray dogs. He famously

EPILOGUE

adopted a stray in 1998 and named her *Tong Daeng* (Copper). The King loved the dog and it touched the hearts of the Thai public. More importantly it changed people's attitudes to dogs and their welfare. His Majesty praised the dog for its respectfulness and loyalty, despite its humble beginnings. It came as no surprise that when the King published, *The Story of Tong Daeng*, it was a bestseller. A parable for everyday life, it inspired people to believe in themselves, no matter what their backgrounds.

Observing the grief of the Thai people from all walks of life it is clear Thailand was very blessed to have such an inspirational figure at the helm for such a long time. Everyone will miss him so much.

Printed in Great Britain
by Amazon